Pierrepoint:
A Family of
Executioners

Pierrepoint: A Family of Executioners

THE STORY OF BRITAIN'S INFAMOUS HANGMEN

STEVE FIELDING

JOHN BLAKE

Published by John Blake Publishing Ltd,
3, Bramber Court, 2 Bramber Road,
London W14 9PB, England

www.blake.co.uk

First published in hardback in 2006

ISBN 1 84454 192 4

British Library Cataloguing-in-Publication Data:

A catalogue record for this book is available from the British Library.

Design by www.envydesign.co.uk

Printed in Great Britain by Creative Print & Design, Wales.

3 5 7 9 10 8 6 4 2

Pictures reproduced with kind permission of Stewart McLaughlin,
Frank Mackue, Tom Leech, Robert Maxfield, Tony Homewood
and the author's collection.

Papers used by John Blake Publishing are natural, recyclable products
made from wood grown in sustainable forests. The manufacturing processes
conform to the environmental regulations of the country of origin.

Every attempt has been made to contact the relevant copyright-holders,
but some were unobtainable. We would be grateful if the appropriate
people could contact us.

ACKNOWLEDGEMENTS

For help in compiling this book I would like to thank the following people: Firstly, Lisa Moore for editing the manuscript and typing up the final drafts; Matthew Spicer for information covering the whole of the book, but in particular data and photographs relating to the work Albert carried out in Germany, for reconciling information on all cases, and for supplying other pictures from his own collection; Tim Leech for a variety of information on all three members of the Pierrepoint family, and the main photographs of Tom; David Martin for tracking down vintage television recordings of Albert Pierrepoint; Stewart McLaughlin for help with photographs from his own collection and information on cases from Wandsworth Prison; Frank Mckue for permission to use his personal photographs of Albert Pierrepoint; Robert H. Maxfield for permission to use his photograph of Albert and pony 'Trio'; Russell Stoddart for obtaining the missing copies of Henry's memoirs; Tony Homewood and Wilf Gregg for help with a variety of information. The late Syd Dernley (former assistant executioner) supplied me with a wealth of information during the research for earlier projects that led to this book. For help with data-inputting and proof reading I would like to thank Janet Buckingham. Finally, thanks also to the numerous people who contacted me with information on Albert Pierrepoint following appeals in various newspapers over recent years, but in particular to J. Fred Wright for allowing me to view rare papers in his collection.

CONTENTS

THE SENTENCE OF DEATH

'The sentence of the Court upon you is, that you be taken from this place to a lawful prison and thence to a place of execution and that you be hanged by the neck until you be dead; and that your body be afterwards buried within the precincts of the prison in which you shall have been confined before your execution. And may the Lord have mercy upon your soul. Amen.'

INTRODUCTION

This book mainly covers the period of 1901 to 1956, and deals with the lives and times of a unique family: a father, Henry Pierrepoint; a son, Albert, and an uncle, Thomas, who each, at one time, held the position of Hangman of England.

Henry Pierrepoint applied to become a hangman just three weeks after the death of Queen Victoria, whose reign of sixty-four years had seen numerous changes in the way law and order was applied and carried out. During her reign, a sentence of death was passed for a variety of crimes, including burglary, rape and attempted murder. Gradually sentence of death ceased for all crimes apart from wilful murder, although the sentence was still carried out in public. It is remarkable to think that in the late nineteenth century, one could travel by underground train in London to watch an execution carried out in front of the prison gates at places. Public executions ended in 1868, although members of the press were still present to report in macabre detail what they had witnessed.

All the people executed during the period covered by this book were convicted of murder, except during the period when Thomas Pierrepoint officiated; during the First World War one person was convicted of treason and hanged, and fifteen men were hanged as a result of the 1940 Treachery Act. Added to this are a number of American servicemen convicted of offences that were not deemed worthy of the death penalty in twentieth century Great Britain.

Furthermore, during Albert Pierrepoint's time as Chief Executioner, over two hundred people were hanged for offences punishable by the death penalty under the rules of the War Crimes Commission. Albert also hanged the last men convicted of treason during the Second World War.

The Pierrepoints' stock in trade was being skilled at conducting the final act in the penal life of a condemned man – the physical process of hanging him by his neck. The process changed little over the three generations involved, and the cold, unemotional tones of the 1953 Royal Commission Report description would have rung true to all three Pierrepoints.

PROCEDURE

Immediately a prisoner sentenced to death returns from court, he is placed in a cell for condemned prisoners and is watched day and night by two officers. Amenities such as cards, chess and dominoes are provided in the cell and the officers are encouraged to join the prisoner in these games. Newspapers and books are also provided. Food is supplied from the main prison kitchen, the prisoner being placed on hospital diet.

In most of the English prisons equipped for execution the execution chamber adjoins the condemned cell. The chamber itself is a small room and the trap occupies a large part of the floor. The trap is formed of two hinged leaves held in position from below by bolts, which are withdrawn when the lever is pulled, allowing the leaves to drop on their hinges. Above the trap a rope of a standard length is attached to a strong chain, which is fitted to the overhead beam in such a way that it can be raised and lowered and secured at any desired height by means of a cotter slipped into one of the links and a bracket fixed on the beam. This enables the length of chain to be adjusted to make the drop accord with the height and weight of the prisoner.

The executioner and his assistant arrive at the prison on the afternoon before the execution. They are told the height and weight of the prisoner and are given an opportunity to see him from a position where they themselves cannot be seen. While the prisoner is out of the cell they test the apparatus to ensure that is working satisfactorily. For this purpose they use a sack of approximately the same weight as the prisoner, having ascertained the proper drop from a table which gives the length appropriate to a prisoner's weight. Some adjustments in the length given in the table may be necessary to allow for other physical characteristics of the prisoner, such as age and build.

On the morning of the execution a final check of the equipment is carried out. The rope is coiled, fitted to the chain, and secured in position by a piece of pack thread which will be broken by the weight of the prisoner when he drops. Just before the time of the execution the executioner and his assistant join the Under Sheriff and the prison officials outside the door of the condemned cell. The Under Sheriff gives the signal: the executioner enters the cell and pinions the prisoner's arms behind his back, and two officers lead him to the scaffold and place him directly across the division of the trap on a spot previously marked with chalk. The assistant executioner pinions the legs, while the executioner puts a white cap over his head and fits the noose round his neck with the knot drawn tight on the left lower jaw, where it is held in position by a sliding ring. The executioner then pulls the lever. The medical officer carries out an immediate inspection to assure that life is extinct and the body is then left to hang for an hour before being taken down.

CHAPTER 1:
BEGINNINGS

February 11th 1901
Dear Sir,
I wish to inform you that I should be very
thankfull if you would accept me as one of the
public executioner's should at any time Mr
Billington's term expires as I have always had a
desire for that appointment. I am 24 years of age,
height 5ft 8½ inches. Should you require
particulars of my character I shall be very glad
to give you all the information you require.
Hoping the application will be off no offence.

I am yours
Respectfully
Henry Albert Pierrepoint
No 53 Fielden St.
Off Oldham Road
Manchester

It was this short note, sent to Home Secretary Sir Matthew Ridley in the early part of 1901, which set in motion a chain of events that resulted in the Pierrepoint family name becoming one of the most famous in modern British criminology, and being connected with capital punishment for the next half century.

Henry 'Harry' Albert Pierrepoint was born in 1878 at Sutton Bonington, Nottinghamshire. He was the fourth child, and second son, to Thomas and Ann Pierrepoint, who ran the King's Head on 14 Main Street, at East Leake. Soon after Harry's birth, Thomas found work looking after the horses at a Yorkshire quarry and the family uprooted from Nottinghamshire. The 1891 census shows they lived on Wolsley Street, Clayton, near Bradford; Thomas Pierrepoint and his eldest son, also named Thomas, were listed as being employed as quarrymen.

Harry was working at a worsted mill in Clayton, aged 13, when he read about the exploits of the well-known Bradford hangman James Berry, whose career as the country's chief executioner had come to an end following a series of botched executions and run-ins with prison authorities. After reading about James Billington's appointment to succeed Berry, Harry quickly decided it was what he wanted to do too – an ambition that stayed with him night and day, never leaving him. Other boys dreamt of becoming soldiers or engine drivers; Harry's dream was to become an executioner. Over the next few years he hungrily lapped up newspaper accounts of Billington's thrilling adventures across the country as he dashed by railway from one prison to another carrying out his official duties, executing the criminals whose exploits had been splashed across the weekly scandal sheets – names such as the notorious Dr Cream (the Lambeth poisoner) and baby farmer Amelia Dyer.

Harry harboured a desire to travel, one more than likely stimulated by reading the hangman's newspaper accounts. When his father found out he was unhappy working in the local mill, he arranged an apprenticeship for his son at one of Bradford's largest butchers. Harry lasted three years as a butcher until, on reaching his 18th birthday, he decided to leave the business. He travelled across the Pennines to Manchester where his sister Mary was one of the managers of Robert Boyle and Sons, cabinet makers, at 316 Oldham Road, Manchester.

In 1898, while he was living briefly in Prestwich, Manchester, Harry met a local girl named Mary Buxton; after a brief courtship they married, and within a year they had their first child, a daughter. Then, in February 1901, Harry Pierrepoint composed his brief letter to the Home Secretary, offering his services as an executioner. He was a month short of his 23rd birthday when he applied for the post – not 24, as he himself claimed when applying for the job and when later he penned his memoirs in *Thomson Weekly News* and *Reynolds News*. All census records from 1881, 1891 and 1901 confirm that Henry Albert Pierrepoint was born in March 1878; it's more than likely that he had added a couple of years to his age to support his application and then kept up the pretence throughout the rest of his life.

Many years later, when he wrote his memoirs, Harry admitted that at the time of applying he felt the post of executioner was morally reprehensible, but this didn't deter him in his quest. (Although the occupation would have been regarded as 'unsavoury' by many, it provided a working-class man with a relatively easy way of earning a considerable amount of extra money.) He was at a loss as to whom to address his letter, until after some consideration he decided to post it to no less than the Home Secretary himself. To his great joy he received a letter almost by return, stating his request was being considered and that he would hear again in the near future. On 18 February 1901, the Home Secretary wrote to Governor Cruickshank at Manchester's Strangeways Gaol:

> Prison Commission
> Home Office
> Whitehall S.W.
> Please send for H. A. Pierrepoint, whose letter is enclosed, and say whether he would make a satisfactory Assistant Executioner. If you think that he is, you might ascertain confidentially from the local police whether he bears a good character.

That his application was being taken seriously was soon proved when detectives called at the Manchester furniture store to make discreet enquiries about Harry. He received a positive reference from his employer and soon after another letter was received at his new home. This time it was marked confidential and came from the governor of Manchester's Strangeways Gaol, inviting Harry to attend for interview at the prison.

Although Harry had long desired to become an executioner, it was an ambition that he had not shared with anyone. When he arrived at the prison gates, having told no one of his appointment, he was overcome with feelings of embarrassment and a sense of shame at what he was doing. 'I dare not tell you my particular business,' he told the guard, 'but I shall show you this letter.'

His reticence in revealing the purpose of his visit caused an embarrassing episode for the young hangman-to-be. Approached by a principal warder, Harry was asked if he had come for a job in the prison service. Answering in the affirmative, he was taken to a nearby doctor's room and put through a rigorous medical only to be told he had failed on account of his height. Downcast and disconsolate he trudged home. A day or so later the misunderstanding was cleared up and he received another letter inviting him to see the governor.

Governor Cruickshank was to be the key to Harry achieving his ambition. Tall, and in his mid-fifties at the time, he wore a bushy beard and had the appearance and bearing of a country squire. Cruickshank had recently taken over at the Manchester Gaol after a successful governorship at Durham Gaol. He spoke sternly and in a dignified tone to the aspiring hangman, and following the brief interview, in which searching questions were asked for the reason for the application, Harry was told before he was accepted he would have to undertake six days' training at London's Holloway Prison.

While Harry waited to hear if his application had been successful, Cruickshank wrote to the Home Office at the beginning of March 1901:

I have seen this man and I am of the opinion that he will make a satisfactory Assistant Executioner. He tells me that he can get away at any time either to attend a week's training at Newgate or to assist at an execution.

Harry duly received the letter informing him he had passed the interview. There was just one small snag: the training had been arranged to start on the following Monday, meaning that Harry would now have to inform his wife of his new career choice.

Mary Pierrepoint was at first convinced it was a joke, but when Harry told her of his life-long ambition, and then produced the letter and testimonial from governor Cruickshank, she realised he was serious. She made several vain attempts to get him not to go through with the quest, but by now the train tickets had been purchased, and Harry had arranged leave of absence at the furniture store.

Buoyed up with the excitement of travel and ambition, Harry boarded the stuffy express train on the cold morning of Monday, 11 March 1901. Upon arrival in London his shyness and reticence to reveal the purpose of his first visit caused him a certain amount of worry. How was he going to reach his destination if he was afraid to ask directions? He eventually summoned up the courage to ask a policeman and soon presented himself at the gate of Holloway Gaol. After a brief interview with the governor, Harry was informed that there had been a change of plan and that his training was to be carried out instead at Newgate Gaol. Within the hour he was entering, for the first time, the forebodingly grim walls of the soon-to-be-demolished gaol.

By this time, Newgate was no longer a holding prison for convicts serving sentences of imprisonment; rather, it was now a remand prison for those awaiting trial at the adjoining old Central Criminal Court. The site had been a prison for several centuries, but it had been earmarked for demolition and was to be the site of the new criminal court, the Old Bailey. It was still the principal centre of execution for persons condemned for crimes committed to the north of the River Thames, though. When Harry's training was being arranged, the authorities had intended to use a wing of the prison that was empty, as prisoners were being redistributed in readiness for the closure of Newgate. When it became clear that the wing would still be occupied, the officials were left with the dilemma of either postponing Harry's training for two or three months, or arranging for it to be carried out at Holloway. Letters were sent out to this effect, but then it was decided to move Newgate prisoners to another part of the prison and for the training to go ahead as originally planned, at Newgate.

Harry was introduced to Governor Millman, a white-haired, kindly man, who explained a little about the prison and his duties and then had one of the wardens escort Harry to his quarters for the duration of the stay. He was assigned to a dismal attic room up a flight of narrow steep stairs known as the 'Hangman's Room', conveniently situated so that it overlooked the execution chamber. The woodwork was pitted with carvings of a generation of former executioners who had occupied the room through the ages. Harry found it glum and depressing.

After depositing his bag in the room, he was allowed to walk around the grounds of the prison. He was later introduced to the man who was to be his instructor on the following day, who during their chat to the warder invited him to cross the city and accompany him that evening to Holloway Gaol, where he was delivering an important message. Glad of the company, and of another chance to see some of the city, Harry agreed.

He slept badly that first night inside the prison. The atmosphere of the room and the apprehension of the role he had taken on caused him to toss and turn fitfully, until daybreak allowed him to rise, take breakfast and then finally get the chance to get stuck into his duties.

In the company of his newfound friend and instructor, Harry was taken around the execution chamber, before being left to his own devices to work out how the traps opened and were reset. The duties of an executioner were carefully and patiently explained, and he spent most of the first day familiarising himself with the ropes and chains, how the noose was rigged up, and most importantly how to measure the drops. It was a long day with just a short time for a lunch break.

Day two began with a dummy execution. Harry was led to the condemned cell, where the 'victim' was pointed out to him, seated at a table in a dark corner. With little training so far under his belt, he approached what he expected to be a warder with a thumping heart, and his nerve was shaken further when, upon reaching the table, he saw the man he was to hang was a stuffed dummy with a grotesque painted face and its right hand making a salute. Wisely keeping any show of emotion in check, Harry pinioned the dummy's arms as he had been shown, and as two warders picked up the dummy, he followed them onto the trap, where he slipped the noose around the pseudo-victim's neck and pulled the lever for the first time.

Repetition was the key during the intensive course, which had been set up for would-be hangmen following the Aberdare Report in the mid-1880s. The report had been commissioned to address the issues regarding the appointment, conduct and all other aspects of being an executioner. This came as a direct result of a series of botched executions by a number of hangmen, in particular Bartholomew Binns, and Bradford's James Berry, who had finally hung up his ropes after a turbulent eight-year reign as the chief executioner in 1892. Berry had applied to carry out the double execution of two poachers at Edinburgh in 1884, and following the successful completion of the task he was given testimonials from the officials there, which was enough to secure him the title of Chief Executioner for

England and the rest of the United Kingdom. After a promising start, however, Berry had a run of messy executions, unsavoury incidents and run-ins with officials that led to him eventually leaving the post. The Home Office learnt its lessons from the affair, however: all subsequent hangmen would be thoroughly vetted and trained by their own officials before being allowed to undertake their duties.

Harry was among the first of the applicants to undertake this instruction and every day during the week's training he learned all aspects of the ritual required to dispense instant death. On the final day he had to carry out a repeat dummy execution as he had done on the second day of his training. This time the watchful eyes of Governor Millman and other officials were on him; Harry carried out the mock execution competently and efficiently. Prison medical officer Doctor Scott then gave him a short written and oral test before he was sent home to await the outcome. Detectives had already visited the furniture store managed by his sister, for a character reference; his conduct had been reported back as satisfactory, so all Henry had to do now was wait. His wife's original objections to Harry's new career diminished after she realised the extra wage would make a huge difference to their growing family.Soon enough, a letter was sent from Holloway to the Home Office, confirming Harry had passed the test:

HMP Holloway
March 19th 1901
For the Commissioner of Prisons

H. A. Pierrepoint.
Applicant from Manchester for the post of
Assistant Executioner at 24. I saw the candidate
at the commencement of his instruction, he there

appeared to me an apt and promising pupil, handy
and active and taking great excitement in his
early lessons at Newgate. As his instruction was
near completion I again saw him go through with
the pinioning and all the other steps necessary at
an execution with a dummy figure, he performed
all the duties satisfactorily and will I think
become a useful assistant at an execution. I agree
with the M.O. that the man should if possible be
employed as a second assistant at first.

* * * * *

Spring took over from winter and Harry went about his duties
selling furniture. What he didn't know was that in official
circles it was being proposed that he attend a double execution
scheduled to take place at Stafford Prison on 2 April 1901. On
22 March, the Home Office wrote to the governor at Stafford
to inform him that Henry Pierrepoint had recently undergone
a course of instruction to their satisfaction and it was
suggested that he should, if possible, be employed as a second
assistant in order to test his nerve and make him familiar with
the full details of execution procedure. They asked if the
governor would contact the under-sheriff to see if he would
agree to this. The governor concurred with this thought but
soon wrote back to the Home Office that this idea had been
rejected by the high sheriff:

The High Sheriff of Staffordshire objects to the
appointment of the new Executioner even as a
Second Assistant. The commissioners have
unfortunately no power to force any man on the
High Sheriff.

The gist of the letter was that Staffordshire didn't want to pay any fees for the extra assistant, for which they would have been liable, and concluded with the suggestion that the executioner should be employed at a London prison, where governor Millman could confirm that the assistant was suitable. On 23 March, Harry received a letter informing him that he had successfully completed the instruction and that his name had been added to the list for the post of executioner and assistant.

With his keen interest in murder cases, Harry had already read about an horrific murder that had taken place ten miles or so away, in Bury, carried by 59-year-old millwright William Goacher. Goacher lived with his wife of 30 years, although of late they had been on bad terms. He was seen drinking in a Bury public house one morning in March 1901; later that night after he returned home, screams alerted neighbours to a disturbance at the Goacher household. Upon investigation, they found Mrs Goacher had been beaten and was suffering from terrible burns, caused by her husband holding her head into the fire. She died from her injuries on the following day.

Goacher was sentenced to death at Manchester Assizes; an official letter requesting Harry Pierrepoint's attendance at Strangeways Prison arrived at his small terrace house at the end of April. Opening the slim brown envelope he read that he was requested to assist James Billington at the execution to be carried out on 18 May 1901. His euphoria at the news was soon dashed by a second letter, received a week later. Tearing it open he read that the Home Secretary had ordered a reprieve, and that his services would therefore not be required. Although evidently disappointed, Henry recorded that he satisfied himself that he had been prevented from helping to hang a man who may have been innocent. He waited patiently for the next call; his patience was rewarded when, on the last day of October, he received a letter from Governor Millman inviting him to assist at the execution of a French anarchist, whose crime had shocked the country only a few weeks earlier. Harry wrote back accepting the engagement, and on the morning of Monday, 18 November 1901, he boarded the train at Manchester's London Road station, aware that in 20 hours' time he would no longer just be a Manchester furniture salesman. At 8 a.m. on the following morning, provided he kept his nerve and there was no last-minute hitch, he would join a select group of men on the list of the hangmen of England.

Marcel Faugeron was a 23-year-old French deserter who had arrived in London in the spring of 1901. He had become friendly with Vincent Durant, a fellow Frenchman, whom he had asked to help find him lodgings and a job in his trade as a barber. He was taken to a boarding house near Tottenham Court Road, where he lodged with a number of other French immigrants.

Around this time Faugeron was introduced to Hermann Francis Jung, a 64-year-old Swiss watchmaker who carried out his business from a shop in Clerkenwell. Jung lived in the basement of the same premises, with his wife and two children. The young Frenchman had by this time discovered that a number of his fellow lodgers and new friends were anarchists, plotting to carry out activities in Belgium, and also planning to assassinate the Tsar, who was in France at the time.

On 3 September, Matilda Jung heard a disturbance upstairs in the shop and as she rushed from the kitchen she saw Faugeron, whom she recognised from previous visits, fleeing through the door. Her husband was lying on the shop floor; he had been stabbed to death. She shouted for help and Faugeron was arrested as he fled down the street.

At his trial before Mr Justice Bingham, Faugeron's defence claimed that he had stabbed Jung in self-defence after the old man had threatened violence against him if he didn't carry out an assault on Joseph Chamberlain, a prominent cabinet minister whom some factions held partly responsible for the war in the Transvaal. The prosecution claimed that Faugeron had gone to the shop in order to obtain either money or goods to fund anarchistic activities he and his comrades were planning to carry out.

When the judge concluded the passing of sentence of death on the accused in the usual manner (but in French), with the words, 'May the Lord have mercy on your soul,' Faugeron replied: 'I hope so. If that is what justice is in this country I hope I shall have better justice in the next world!' There had been almost no hope of a reprieve and, arriving in London, Harry confidently made his way across the city, where he finally got to meet James Billington in the entrance to Newgate Gaol. Billington had been the Chief Executioner for over a decade. In his early fifties at the time, he had been a mill worker, singer and wrestler before opening a barber's shop in Farnworth, Lancashire. In 1884, he became the executioner for Yorkshire, carrying out one or two executions a year before superseding James Berry in August 1891. Now, a decade later, he ran a public house in Bolton and was often assisted by his two eldest sons, Thomas and William Billington, who had both graduated from the executioner's training school.

After a brief greeting, Billington led the way as they set off to the execution shed to test the apparatus. Billington allowed Henry to attach the sandbag – filled to match the weight, age and general condition of the prisoner – to the noose; this was done before every execution, to take the stretch out of the rope. Billington rigged the drop and once he was satisfied all was in order he carried out a test drop in front of the governor and prison engineer. The rope was left stretching overnight and a prison officer was posted outside the execution chamber, which stood in the prison grounds, to make sure no one tampered with the apparatus.

After evening tea, Harry was shown his quarters and discovered that instead of sharing the attic room he had stayed in during training, he was assigned to the second condemned cell, utilised when a double execution was scheduled but otherwise empty. They retired after supper and, finding sleep hard to come by, Harry prowled around the room, taking in the grim atmosphere of the prison, knowing that the last occupant of this room was now lying below the neatly cut lawn across from the execution shed; at 8 a.m. on the following morning, the man in the cell next door would occupy an adjacent grave.

As he nosed around the cell he noticed a small peephole allowing him to spy into the condemned cell and he was greeted with a remarkable sight. The young Frenchman was walking up and down in the cell, smoking continuously. Harry watched, unnoticed, for almost an hour and was just about to retire to bed when the chimes from the church across the road caused the condemned man to point up to the sky and count off using his fingers until he reached eight, indicating that he was to die at 8 a.m.. Several times Harry watched as the hour loomed and each time as the chimes rang out, Faugeron repeated the ritual.

At seven the next morning the hangmen returned to the execution chamber. Billington pulled up the rope from the trap and adjusted his drop to account for the stretch while Pierrepoint went into the drop and pushed the heavy oak doors up; they were secured and the lever set. As the hangmen finished their preparations, the condemned man ate a hearty breakfast and was granted a last walk in the open air. Once he had taken the allowed ten-minute stroll in the exercise yard he was returned to the cell, where he sat in the company of two guards and a priest and waited.

At two minutes to eight, Harry stood beside Billington outside the condemned cell door. Beside them stood Millman, the governor; the Under-Sheriff of London, Mr Kymaston Metcalfe; Dr Scott, the prison medical officer; and a number of wardens. On the stroke of eight the door opened. Faugeron showed little sign of fear as his arms were pinioned behind his back and with a warder either side he walked slowly out of the cell, into the corridor and out into the yard towards the execution chamber. When the party came into view, the guard outside the chamber flung open the door and the procession entered. As Billington placed the noose around the Frenchman's neck, Harry swiftly slipped a leather strap around the prisoner's ankles and leapt off the trap door as Billington darted to his left and pushed the lever. The drop opened and the prisoner plunged to his death. Harry looked down into the pit and was relieved that he felt both calm and free from nerves. The body was left to hang for the obligatory hour, and they retired for breakfast. No sooner had they sat down to eat than they were approached by Dr Scott. He grasped Harry's wrist and felt for his pulse. Smiling, he told the hangman, 'You will do.'

The two executioners completed their duties, which included removing the body from the rope and placing it, wrapped in a shirt, into a thin wooden coffin. They then dismantled the ropes and chains and replaced everything into a padlocked trunk. By 10 a.m. they were at Euston Station, from where they travelled back to Manchester together. A week or so later, Harry received a letter to say that his name was now added to the list of approved executioners and reminded him that he must not discuss the appointment with any members of the press or public.

The year 1901 had been average for executions, with approximately one taking place every five or six weeks. Up until Harry's first engagement there had been eight executions in England and three in Ireland. Billington had carried out each of those, with the exception of one in Belfast and one in Dublin, which had been officiated by Huddersfield-born Thomas Henry Scott, a former assistant of Berry's who carried out one or two executions a year, usually across the water in Ireland. So far this year Billington had performed his duties as far afield as Bodmin, Maidstone, Stafford and Norwich. The latter was probably the most famous case he officiated at that year: Herbert Bennett was hanged for the murder of his sweetheart on a beach at Yarmouth. There was much disquiet at the verdict, and when the flagpole used to hoist the black flag snapped as the signal of execution was being hoisted, it was taken by many as a sign of a miscarriage of justice.

When Harry returned to Manchester he was pleased to find another letter waiting for him. This time the job was much closer to home and was scheduled to take place at Manchester's Strangeways Gaol on 3 December. Again, he was to act as assistant to James Billington.

Patrick McKenna had been sentenced to death on 13 November for the murder of his wife in Bolton. The crime had been made all the more remarkable by the fact that the victim was attended as she lay dying by William Billington, son of the chief executioner, who was passing the street when the incident took place. William's father was also acquainted with the killer. McKenna, who was a regular drinker in the Derby Arms – of which James Billington was the landlord – was immediately taken into custody, and although his guilt was never in doubt, there was a good deal of sympathy for him locally. His defence at the trial had been insanity, and once sentence had been passed great effort went into obtaining a reprieve for the condemned man. A local petition gathered over 22,000 signatures and the story filled the local press as the hangmen arrived at the prison on the Monday afternoon.

Although it had only been a fortnight since the two men had last met, there had been a sharp decline in the health of the chief hangman during the interim. For the last few days Billington had been confined to bed with a fever and sickness, and was also suffering badly from bronchitis. As they rigged the gallows in readiness for the morning it was clear to Harry that Billington was a sick man. Billington made a brief observation of the prisoner through the spy hole and easily recognised the tall man with the bushy beard as one of his regulars. The eight weeks' imprisonment had taken its toll on him and he looked thoroughly miserable and dejected.

After rigging the drop they returned to their quarters, where Billington collapsed on the bed crying, 'Oh Harry, I wish I'd never have come.' Harry offered to carry out the execution by himself on the following morning, but Billington was adamant he would be able to carry out his duties. In the company of a number of warders the hangmen played cards and drank a small quantity of beer in the gas-lit cell.

All was in readiness by 7.30 the following morning. Harry noted that the silence in the gaol was almost overwhelming as the chaplain entered the cell to give the prisoner some last grains of comfort before the dreaded hour arrived. On the stroke of eight the execution party entered the cell and, realising his last moments had come, McKenna broke out into loud sobs.

It was only a few short steps across the corridor to the gallows but the silence was broken by the condemned man's pitiful cries for the Lord to help him. Billington stopped him on the drop and noticed tears were rolling down his cheek; as the hood was placed over his head, McKenna cried out aloud:

'Lord have mercy on my soul!' Realising that not a moment was to be wasted, Harry strapped the ankles with great speed and no sooner had Harry cleared the trap than the lever was pushed and McKenna was dead.

The large crowd that had been gathering in the streets outside since dawn were still loitering in the hope of seeing the hangmen depart the prison. Having disposed of the body, and with the crowd still boasting a healthy total, the hangmen chose to leave the prison by crossing an underground passage linking the prison to the assize court where they were able to mingle, unnoticed, into the crowd.

They said their farewells at the railway station and Harry helped the sick man into the carriage. Less than a fortnight later, as a result of his illness, Billington passed away. The Bolton newspapers linked the death to his duties at the execution of McKenna and claimed he had caught a chill on the trip to Manchester that had hastened his demise. It may have been partly true, but Billington was dying anyway and his dedication to his duties would not have prevented him carrying out the execution of his former friend.

There were a number of engagements already in James Billington's diary and these were carried out by his second son William – although younger in years than Thomas, he had been an assistant for three years longer, had much more experience as an assistant in recent times, and had even pulled the lever once at an execution.

There were no further calls to Harry Pierrepoint that December, and it was to be March 1902 before the next official correspondence arrived. Opening it, he read that Richard Wigley was to hang at Shrewsbury Prison on 18 March. The letter asked if he was available to act as chief executioner. Harry replied that he was.

CHAPTER 2:
RECOLLECTIONS

Considering that the execution of the 54-year-old slaughterman for the murder of his wife was to be the first time that Harry Pierrepoint was solely responsible for an execution, he made little reference to it in both serialisations of his memoirs. Richard Wigley was convicted of the murder of 28-year-old Mary Eliza Bower at Westbury, Shropshire. They had been going out together for a number of years, since he had parted from his wife, and when they had met she was working as a barmaid. Mary soon left her job and found work at another public house, near Berrington, so they could spend more time together.

Mary suddenly ended the relationship and returned to her old job. Wigley took the split badly and began making frequent visits to her place of work. She told him there was no hope they would get back together and wrote asking him to stay away from her. She also told the other members of staff at the pub that if he called for her again, they were to say she was unavailable.

On the morning of Saturday, 30 November 1901, Wigley arrived in Westbury, some time before 10 a.m. He was wearing his butcher's apron and carrying two knives in a leather pouch. Inside the pub he ordered a drink, drank it quietly, but on asking for another was told by Mary he had drunk enough and that she refused to serve him any more. He asked again but Mary would not change her mind, merely turning her back on him and walking away briskly. Wigley followed her behind the bar, put his left arm around her neck and with his right, pulled a knife from his apron pouch and drew the blade across her throat, causing an enormous gash. She died almost immediately.

At his trial, Wigley said that he had killed Mary because if he could not have her, no one else would. He had written a letter before setting out to Westbury stating his intention to kill and said he would be ready to die for what he had to do. His only defence was insanity – evidence was presented to show that his mother had been admitted to the Salop County Lunatic Asylum.

When the Sheriff of Shropshire received notification to employ an executioner to carry out the sentence passed on Wigley he wrote to William Billington offering him the engagement. Following James Billington's death, all engagements in his diary were carried out by his middle son, William, assisted by the eldest son, Thomas. The latter had not been in good health himself and less than a month after his father's death he too passed away. William, however, was unavailable on that date, having accepted the offer to hang a young lorry driver at Maidstone. The only persons still active on the list of executioners were Harry Pierrepoint and Rochdale barber John Ellis, who so far between them had assisted at just three executions. Nevertheless, both had been fully trained to carry out an execution, and with Harry claiming seniority, by just a fortnight, it was he who was asked to officiate.

Arriving at the prison on the afternoon before the execution, Harry was introduced to Ellis, the man who was to be his assistant. He received the details of the prisoner: height 5 feet 10½ inches, weight 160 pounds. Discreetly observing Wigley at exercise, he noted he had a strong neck and accordingly worked out a drop of 7 feet 6 inches. Richard Wigley was duly dispatched without incident.

On 29 April 1902, Harry assisted William Billington for the first time: together, they dispatched 56-year-old Charles Earl, a retired baker from Mortlake, who had shot dead a woman out of jealousy. Earl was hanged at Wandsworth Prison, having told the governor on the day before his execution, on hearing that a reprieve had been refused, that it was, 'a good job too!'

The year 1902 was becoming a busy and profitable one for the young hangman. At the end of July he was at Derby to assist William Billington again. This time the condemned man was a labourer from Chesterfield who had used a poker to beat to death the woman he had been having an affair with after she refused to leave her husband for him. Two weeks later, again assisting William Billington, Pierrepoint was engaged in the execution of George Hibbs, a 40-year-old skilled mechanic from Battersea, who had killed his landlady, and sometime sweetheart, Miriam Tye. They had been out drinking and when they returned to their lodgings Hibbs tried to get her to pawn some items so they could buy more drink. When she refused he stabbed her to death. At the Old Bailey trial Hibbs said he blamed it all on the drink and hoped that his execution would serve as a lesson to others.

At the end of September Billington and Pierrepoint carried out the first execution at Pentonville Prison, using the giant wooden beams that had previously been in place at Newgate. Twenty-three-year-old John McDonald was hanged on 30 September for the murder of John Groves, whom he stabbed to death after a quarrel over money.

Six weeks later Harry was back at Pentonville, again assisting Billington, to hang Henry Williams, a 32-year-old former soldier, whom Pierrepoint later described as the bravest man he had ever hanged. Williams had slit the throat of his five-year-old daughter, Margaret, at their home in Fulham, in September. Having recently returned from serving in the Boer War to find his wife had been unfaithful, he had covered the body of his daughter with a union flag, then given himself up, telling police he had killed her so she wouldn't grow up to be like her mother.

He was sentenced to death at the Old Bailey and was hanged two months and a day after committing the murder. Recording the execution in his memoirs, Harry noted that Williams had walked bravely to the scaffold and stood erect on the drop while his executioners prepared him for execution. The memoirs then erroneously state that Harry placed the noose around the neck of the condemned man – an act *always* carried out by the chief and never delegated to the assistant. This was probably journalistic licence adding spice to the memoirs years after the event.

In December, Harry was back at Strangeways Gaol for the hanging of another Bolton-born criminal, when he assisted William Billington at the execution of Henry McWiggins (aka Harry Mack), who had committed an horrific murder in nearby Oldham. The 29-year-old Mack, a foreman fireman and petty criminal, had been living with Esther Bedford since June 1902. Initially they had a happy relationship, but subsequently he had started to act violently towards her. On 2 August, their landlady heard noises from the front bedroom;

on investigating, she found Mack dragging Esther around the room by her hair. He then struck her in the face and kicked her as she lay on the floor. A week later, as Esther slept, he woke her up by savagely kicking her, then hit her in the face with a shovel. Advised to call the police, Esther refused, saying that she didn't want to cause trouble for Mack. In truth, she was terrified of him. On 13 August screams were heard coming from Mack's room and Esther was found lying face-down on the bed in agony. Mack had thrown a kettle of boiling water at her before fleeing the house. Having spent the rest of the night drinking heavily, he returned at midnight and kicked Esther several times in the stomach.

On the following morning, a doctor was called, quickly followed by the police. Esther was taken to hospital, where it was found that the brutal kicking had caused her bladder to rupture. The police were advised that Esther was unlikely to last the day, and statements were taken at her bedside. Again she was too terrified to testify against Mack: she denied the landlady's claims that he had kicked her, and added that the scalding was an accident. She died the following day, and Mack, who had been held in custody following her admission to hospital, was then charged with murder. Tried before Mr Justice Jelf, the defence claimed that accounts of the attacks had been greatly exaggerated by the witnesses and offered a plea of guilty of manslaughter. It took the jury just 20 minutes to return a verdict of guilty of murder.

Mack weighed 168 pounds and stood just under 5 feet 9 inches tall. The drop was calculated at 6 feet 9 inches, and the execution was timed at 75 seconds. At the inquest the coroner recorded that death had been due to dislocation of the second and fourth vertebrae.

The next entry in Harry's diary notes that he assisted at the execution of Thomas Fairclough-Barrow at Pentonville on 9

December. He records that the condemned man was 49 years old, weighed 137 ½ pounds, stood 5 feet 8 ½ inches tall and was given a drop of 6 feet 6 inches. Barrow was a partially disabled man who lived with his stepdaughter Emily Coates (aged 32), as man and wife, at Wapping. In October 1902, Fairclough-Barrow saw Emily drinking with another man and became violent towards her, to the extent that she feared for her life. As a result, she left him and took out a summons for assault. On 18 October, Fairclough-Barrow approached her as she walked to work and stabbed her several times in the heart; she died instantly. At his Old Bailey trial, a weak defence was put forward based on a claim of insanity; it proved unsuccessful. Prison records list the hangmen as William Billington assisted by his brother John – no mention of Harry – and the details of the prisoner's height, weight and drop differ slightly from those recorded by Harry. It's difficult to see why he should record the details in his diary if he wasn't present. However, it is recorded in the diary and contributes towards the overall total of 105 executions credited to Harry Pierrepoint.

There is no confusion surrounding the next entry in the diary. William and Elizabeth Brown had been married for 22 years. On 2 November they were heard to quarrel in a public house at Mortlake and on the following morning 42-year-old Brown, a labourer, went to a neighbour's house and announced that his wife was dead. The police were called and found Elizabeth's body at the foot of the stairs. Arrested and charged with murder, William claimed Elizabeth had fallen down the stairs, but later he was alleged to have made a statement admitting that he had killed her. At his Old Bailey trial, held just three weeks after the death of his wife, Brown denied ever making such a statement. The key witness for the prosecution was a young neighbour, who claimed that through a window he had seen Brown beating his wife.

As sentence of death was passed, the father of the victim stood up in court and shouted to the judge: 'Give him mercy, my Lord. I know her faults and he was a good husband to her for twenty years.' But even as petitions for clemency were being forwarded to the Home Secretary, the Governor of Wandsworth wrote to Harry asking him to carry out the execution as the chief. As on his previous engagement as number one, he was assisted by John Ellis. Brown was given a drop of 6 feet and the execution passed off without incident.

The last execution of the year took place at Warwick on 30 December and again Harry was asked to act as chief, after Billington had to turn down the offer, being engaged for a job in Ireland at the time. George Place had taken lodgings with Eliza Chetwynd at Baddersley Ensor, Warwickshire. Shortly thereafter, the 28-year-old miner began a relationship with her 30-year-old daughter, also named Eliza. Within a year George and the younger Eliza were living together as man and wife and she became pregnant. A son was born and Eliza took out a bastardy naming George as the father of the child. When he heard about this, George became enraged, stormed out of the house and did not return for two days. On 23 August, he was seen brandishing a revolver in a public house, claiming he was going to make the Chetwynds pay. In the early hours of the following morning, an armed and angry George Place returned to the house. Shots were fired and Eliza senior and the still unnamed child died instantly; her daughter died later from her injuries. Eliza's brother heard three shots and saw Place come out of the bedroom holding the revolver.

At his trial Place said that it had been his intention to commit suicide after he had killed the Chetwynds, but that he had changed his mind afterwards. His defence was insanity; it was unsuccessful. Pierrepoint and Ellis went to work, and

Ellis noted that Harry worked with assured confidence, as though he had been doing it for years. Place stood just an inch over 5 feet tall and was given a drop of 7 feet. A total of 25 executions were carried out in 1902, with Harry being involved in nine of them – bringing in a healthy income to supplement his salary from the furniture shop.

1903 was also to be a busy year for Harry Pierrepoint. The first executions that took place were in Ireland, and were carried out by William Billington. The first date in Harry's diary was to help at the double execution at Holloway of two nurses who had been convicted at the Old Bailey for the murder of a young child.

Twenty-nine-year-old Amelia Sach ran a nursing home in East Finchley, London, where – for a hefty fee – unmarried mothers would be looked after until they had given birth and helped to find a suitable foster home for their newborn infants. Sach had a business partner, 54-year-old Annie Walters, to whom she would pass on the children for re-housing. On the occasions when she couldn't place children with suitable parents, however, Walters would resort to administering a few drops of morphine-based drugs, which caused the babies to die from asphyxia, or to smothering them with a pillow.

In August 1902, a Miss Galley gave birth to a boy at Amelia Sach's nursing home. By now the police had become suspicious about the activities of the two women, however, and on 18 November, when Walters left her lodgings carrying a small bundle, she was followed to South Kensington railway station, where detectives stopped her. The bundle contained the dead body of Miss Galley's child. Cause of death was found to be asphyxia; it appeared that the baby had been smothered. Walters claimed she had been taking the child to Kensington to meet a potential foster mother, and that when the child began to cry loudly she had administered two drops of chlorodyne in milk. She claimed that she hadn't realised the child was dead until she was stopped by the police.

Amelia Sach denied giving children to Walters, but when her home was searched more than three hundred articles of baby clothing were found. Detectives deduced that this suggested more victims – there had been a spate of small bodies found in the River Thames, or uncovered on rubbish dumps, in recent years. The pair may have been responsible for around twenty deaths, and were now finally to face justice.

Harry met up with both William and John Billington and travelled across to Holloway Gaol on the afternoon of 2 February 1903. The case had filled the newspapers since Mr Justice Darling had presided over the trial in December and as the date of execution became imminent crowds were already hovering around the gates of the prison, hoping to catch sight of the executioners.

The three men managed to slip inside unnoticed and made their way along the long, narrow corridors and up two flights of cast-iron stairs until they reached the cells of the condemned. Each woman sat with two wardresses watching over her. A matron entered the cell at the request of the hangmen and got the prisoners to move to the other side of the table so that they could assess their build and general physique.

Once William Billington had sized up the first of the condemned women, Harry followed and realised he was looking into the cell of Mrs Sach. He saw that she was a tall, gaunt woman who seemed to realise her position most keenly. Through the small eye-hole he saw she presented a pitiful appearance: 'A poorer wreck of humanity as I have ever seen,' he later noted. Weariness clouded her face and stray tears rolled down her cheek. Silently moving aside so the younger Billington could observe, he followed William down the corridor and waited his turn to observe Mrs Walters. The latter's demeanour presented the hangmen with something of a shock – her features showed no trace of emotion. Describing her as stout and stocky, Harry recorded that she was cheerful and talkative, as if unaware her last hours were ebbing away.

Details of the prisoners' weight and height were passed to the hangmen and as they rigged the gallows, it was decided that in case of emergency two male warders should be brought in from Pentonville. It was feared that Mrs Sach's distress may cause upset to the female warders if, as anticipated, she should be overcome with terror in the morning.

The morning broke cold and frosty as the hangmen went across to the execution shed to finish their preparations. At a few minutes to eight they were in position outside the condemned cells. As they waited for the signal from the governor, Harry silently raised the peep-hole into Mrs Sach's cell. She was, in his words, 'broken up', her appearance grotesque – her hair had been scraped up in a 'peculiar fashion' to prevent it fouling with the noose.

The chimes of the hour rang out from the adjacent church clock, and the party entered the cell. As Harry pinioned her arms, Sach swooned as if in a faint. A warder whispered words of comfort to her as she was led out into the corridor. In contrast, Mrs Walters submitted bravely to the pinioning, and followed Billington senior as he walked out of the cell.

At this point, the two women came face to face for the first time since sentence of death had been passed on them. Harry took a grip of Mrs Sach and steadied her on the short walk to the gallows. She was crying bitterly and barely conscious. Mrs Walters followed behind, quite bravely and calm. In a flash both women were placed on the trap and as Harry dropped to his knees to fasten the leg strap on Mrs Sach, John Billington did the same to Mrs Walters.

William Billington then placed the noose and caps over the culprits' heads and as he moved across to the lever, Mrs Walters cried out in a firm voice: 'Goodbye, Sach.' The younger woman was about to fall in a faint, and Harry was forced to leap to his feet and support her arm. Seconds later the doors crashed open; the Finchley baby farmers had paid the ultimate penalty. They had made no confession.

One month later, Harry was back in London, this time at Wandsworth Gaol, where he was engaged to execute 44-year-old Edgar Edwards, an habitual criminal with a long string of convictions for theft and burglary. (Newspaper reports of the trial had used the name Edgar Edwards, although his real surname was Owen.) Released in 1902, after serving five years at Northampton Gaol, he moved back to London, telling his wife he was taking over a shop in Camberwell. John Darby had put a grocery store in Camberwell up for sale; Edwards said he was interested in purchasing and asked to see the accounts. While Darby prepared the books, his wife, carrying their infant daughter in her arms, invited Edwards upstairs to view the living quarters. Alone with the young woman, he took a large sash weight he had concealed inside a rolled-up newspaper and battered her to death. He then went back downstairs, bludgeoned Darby to death, then callously strangled the crying child. Edwards began pawning Darby's belongings and, using the name William Darby, took the lease on a house in Leyton. Now believing he had got away with committing the murders, Edwards decided to repeat the venture. On 23 December, another grocer with a business for sale was invited to Leyton to discuss terms, and as he turned to leave was struck from behind. Despite a fearful beating the man managed to escape and raise the alarm.

Edwards was arrested for assault. The police searched the house and, finding pawn tickets in the name of Darby, soon directed their attention to Camberwell, where the bodies of the Darby family were uncovered. After being found guilty, Edwards burst into laughter; asked if he had anything to say, he replied, 'No, get on with it, as quick as you like!'

When Harry and William Billington went to observe Edwards on the night before his execution they found a big strapping fellow who had borne his fate bravely, asking his brother who had visited him earlier that afternoon to keep news of his execution secret from his aged mother.

Entering the cell at nine o'clock Harry recorded that Edwards stood between two warders with staring eyes that saw nothing. The grim procession made its way along the corridor then out of a side door and down a flight of steps into the prison yard, where the scaffold was awaiting him. Edwards began to recite the hymn 'Jesus, Lover of my Soul' as he neared the scaffold. His self-possession began to desert him a little as he reached the drop, but the executioners went to work quickly and seconds later he had paid the price for his triple crime.

There was still a healthy crowd milling around the prison gates when the hangmen departed the prison. Harry recalled that there was one woman dressed in deepest black, seemingly waiting for them to pass her. As they walked by, she asked Billington if Edwards had really been hanged all right. Exchanging glances, Harry spoke for him, replying, 'yes he was.' Without waiting for a response they walked on to catch their train. Afterwards, Harry often thought about the woman, claiming that he was never quite able to get the sight of her pale, tearstained face out of his mind.

Instead of returning home that morning, the two decided to spend the day at the Crystal Palace Exhibition Hall. Harry later told a story to his son about an incident that happened as they made their way home later that evening. Apparently, they decided to call into a public house before catching their train home from Euston. Leaning leisurely against the saloon bar on the Euston Road, they were enjoying a quiet drink when a group of young men – 'hooligans' as they were named in the press of the day – entered the bar and approached. One placed a clay pipe on the bar close to the arm of Billington, who had his back to the door. Harry noticed what had happened and whispered for Billington to take care. Turning to see what was afoot, he sent the clay pipe crashing to the floor. An altercation then took place, during which the young gang pulled out knives and picked up chairs as weapons. The hangmen were made of stern stuff, however, and in the ensuing struggle they were able to drive the men out of the bar. Harry told his son they were escorted to their train by a group of elderly local men who said it was the best sport they had seen in a long while. He also said that they were left without a scratch but this doesn't seem to be the case, as Billington arrived home sporting a badly bruised face and a damaged arm. He explained his injuries by saying he had been attacked in his train carriage and had fallen onto the track!

On 13 May, shortly before the birth of his daughter, Ivy, Harry made the short trip across Manchester to assist in the execution of William Hudson, a 26-year-old Birmingham soldier who had shot dead a fellow soldier at Fulwood Barracks in Preston.

The next letter engaging Harry's services was again from Wandsworth, and for only the fourth time in his short career he was to carry out the execution as the chief hangman; it also marked the first time that he was entrusted with a double execution. He was to hang a young London motor mechanic named William Tuffen, along with his lover and former housemaid, Mary Stone. They had been living in a house in south London, where the battered body of Tuffen's wife had been concealed. Acting on a tip-off from concerned relatives, police called at a house in Thames Ditton, where the body of one Caroline Tuffen was discovered; she had been battered to death. Tuffen and Mary Stone had vanished, but were soon located at Norbiton railway station and arrested. Mary claimed to know nothing about the death of Caroline Tuffen, William having told her that his wife had simply gone away. Both were charged with murder. Tuffen was found guilty of the crime, and Stone guilty of being an accessory before the fact. Sentence of death was then passed on both prisoners. Mary Stone was reprieved on 6 August and Tuffen alone went to the gallows a few days later.

A rare execution took place at Devizes on 17 November, when William Billington and Harry carried out the execution of Edward Palmer, who had shot dead his former girlfriend at Swindon. Palmer and Esther Swinford had been engaged, and she had given him money to buy furniture for their home, which he spent on drink. As a result, the wedding was cancelled. He became sullen and later moved away from Swindon. Several months later he heard that Esther was working as a barmaid in Swindon; Palmer found work on the Great Western Railway and moved. Carrying a gun, he called at the pub and, after a quarrel, shot her dead. In his pocket was a photograph of Esther, and on the back Palmer had written, 'The curse of my life.' He claimed that the gun had gone off accidentally, but the jury gave this short thrift. Harry noted in his diary Palmer was 25 years old, weighed 152 pounds and stood a little under 5 feet 8 inches. He was given a drop of 6 feet 6 inches; death was instantaneous.

December 1903 was a busy month for the executioners, with ten persons hanged and three others reprieved at the eleventh hour. On 15 December, Harry carried out the last execution at Hereford Gaol when, with assistant John Ellis, he was engaged to execute a 61-year-old quarry labourer named William Haywood, who had been convicted of the murder of his wife at Lucton. He had battered her to death while drunk and was then seen moving her body in a wheelbarrow. At his trial his defence council claimed Heywood was '… an imbecile of the higher grade'. Summing up, Mr Justice Bigham told the jury that lunatics should not escape punishment simply because they were lunatics.

On 29 December an execution was scheduled at Liverpool's Walton Gaol. Harry received a letter requesting his services as assistant, but instead of assisting the usual chief executioner William Billington, the letter was engaging him to assist William's younger brother John, who had himself only become an executioner following the death of his father, and had first witnessed an execution on the same day that Harry carried out his first job as chief in March 1902. It was to be John's second job as chief executioner, his first being earlier that month at Manchester, and as before, he had only received the offer because William Billington was already engaged to carry out a double execution at Leeds.

Henry Bertram Starr had married in the spring of 1903 and the newlyweds had moved in with his wife's mother. He soon took to drinking, however, and left his wife, only to return when she gave birth in August of the same year. The couple moved into their own home but she soon left and moved back to her mother's. A separation and custody order for the child were obtained. Then, on 24 November, Starr called at his mother-in-law's house and stabbed his estranged wife to death. It was Starr's second murder trial:

in 1896 he had been acquitted, but this time the jury returned a verdict of guilty without even leaving the courtroom to ponder the outcome.

1904 got off to a slow start for the hangman. Harry Pierrepoint's first job came on Tuesday, 29 March, when he travelled to Leeds to assist John Billington in the execution of a young tailor from Guisborough who had savagely murdered a 12-year-old girl. Elizabeth Mary Lynas had been to a Christmas service at her local church with some friends. They parted at the end of her street, but when she failed to arrive home her parents contacted the police. A search soon located her body in nearby woods: she had been brutally murdered, her hands and feet were tied and her throat had been cut.

Bloodstains were found in a neighbour's backyard and when the house was searched a bloodstained razor was found on a kitchen shelf. James Henry Clarkson lived at the house with his sister and his father, and while they both had alibis for the night of the murder James was unable to account for his movements. When bloodstains were found on his clothes too, he was formally charged with murder.

Throughout his trial he maintained his innocence, but the jury took just half an hour to find him guilty. On the night prior to his execution he repeatedly cried out: 'What made me do it?' He was hanged two days before his twentieth birthday. He weighed just 126 pounds and was given a long drop of 8 feet.

Harry's next job was to assist in the execution of two men at Liverpool's Walton Gaol on 31 May. William Kirwan, a 39-year-old sailor, had shot his sister-in-law dead during a quarrel; he believed she and his wife were using his house for immoral purposes and sleeping with other men while he was at sea. Kirwan had been under arrest and was taken outside the house after he had shot at, and slightly injured, his wife. When his sister-in-law came outside to berate him as he was being led away, he struggled from the policeman's grip, pulled out his gun and fatally wounded her. Sharing the gallows was Pong Lun, a 43-year-old Chinaman, who had shot dead his friend John Go Hing, following a quarrel over a bet on a game of dominoes. Harry and William Billington travelled to Liverpool together and as they made the short walk to the prison from Preston Road station they were recognised by the small crowd milling around outside the prison gates. Harry felt that in the glorious sunshine the prison looked like an old castle, and though he had been there before he still marvelled at the beautifully tended flowerbeds that flanked the path from the gatehouse to the governor's office.

They were billeted in the old hospital wing – no longer used, but conveniently close to the scaffold. After rigging the drops – 6 feet 3 inches for Kirwan, 6 feet 2 inches for the Chinaman – they took the opportunity to view the condemned men at exercise. Kirwan was sullen and morose, trundling around the exercise yard with his head bowed, while Lun was the opposite, smiling and content as he spent his last hour in the sunshine.

The two hangmen retired to bed that night, but Harry was soon woken by a noise and, striking a match, he saw the room was overrun with mice. Looking across at Billington he saw eight or nine of the rodents scurrying across the bedclothes and climbing up the bed frame. 'Get up Billy, you're being worried by mice,' he called out, startling the sleeping hangman. Despite the lack of sleep the hangman were up and ready for the duties on the following morning. It was decided to bring the two prisoners to holding cells in the old hospital wing directly below where the hangmen had slept. Kirwan was the first to be pinioned; he seemed resigned to his fate and more cheerful than he had been on the previous afternoon. Pong Lun was then taken from his cell and strapped in the corridor behind where Kirwan waited. 'Come on Ping Pong,' Billington called as the procession to the scaffold began. The prisoner bristled at this and replied tersely: 'My name not Ping Pong, my name Pong Lun.' As they took their place on the scaffold, the Chinaman looked up at the noose hanging down and began to laugh. Moments later the white cap was placed on his head and as the chaplain recited the litany the floor opened and both men dropped to an instant death.

Around this time Harry left the job with his sister at her Manchester furniture store and moved back to Bradford, settling at 14 Cowgill, Clayton, where he set up a carrier's business. Working for himself, transporting goods from the local railway station, gave him the freedom to be his own boss and the liberty to go away on official business when required.

William Billington and Harry carried out two executions in two days in July. On Tuesday, 12 July, they were at Pentonville Gaol, where they executed John Sullivan, a Durham seaman who had battered a young deck hand to death with an axe on the merchant ship *Waiwera* while at sea. After completing the execution without any incident they travelled together to Northampton, where they prepared the drop for Samuel Rowledge, a carpenter who had shot dead his fiancée on the day of their engagement, following a domestic argument.

Whether Harry resented the fact that he hadn't received the offer to carry out an execution as the chief hangman since the turn of the year isn't recorded, but he must have been dismayed to find that any work that William Billington was unable to carry out was seemingly now being offered to the younger Billington instead of to him. The lack of work would also have had financial implications: Harry's wife was pregnant again with their third child; he was now self-employed, and the difference between a chief executioner's pay and that of his assistant was substantial.

In August, Harry helped John Billington to dispatch John Thomas Kay, a 52-year-old Rotherham labourer who had killed the woman he lived with, then stopped a policeman in the street and confessed abruptly: 'I did it with a hatchet.' Kay's defence had been that he was under the influence of drink at the time of the attack, and therefore, as he was not aware of what he was doing, he was only guilty of manslaughter. The jury had disagreed.

On 13 December, Harry assisted William Billington in another double execution, this time at Pentonville Gaol. A paperboy had arrived at a newsagent's shop in Stepney, but was surprised to find the shop open and no sign of his employer, 65-year-old spinster Miss Matilda Farmer. The police were later contacted and, searching the shop, found the deceased old lady lying face-down on her bed, her hands tied behind her back and a towel fastened around her mouth. It was clear that the motive for the crime had been robbery: the bedroom had been ransacked and jewellery was missing. A witness told the police he had seen two men standing near to the shop: one he had never seen before, but the other he recognised as Charles Wade. Another witness described two men he had seen coming out of the shop on the morning of the murder. The descriptions fitted Charles Wade and his half-brother, Conrad Donovan (aka Joseph Potter). Both men had long criminal records for robbery and were picked out from identity parades by the two witnesses.

At their trial the defence discredited one of the witness's

testimonies by proving he had been shown pictures of the suspects prior to picking them out from the identity parade. Other witnesses who had claimed to see the two men on the morning of the murder had failed to pick them out when they attended the same line-up. Police had also failed to locate any of the missing jewellery, despite thoroughly searching both men's houses.

Although there was some doubt as to the guilt of the two men, the jury took just ten minutes to decide that the evidence was strong enough to convict them; as sentence of death was passed, both Donovan and Wade loudly protested their innocence. A few days before they were to hang, workmen at the Stepney newsagents found the missing jewellery under the floorboards in one of the rooms, indicating the thieves had not escaped with as much as police had originally assumed. As the hangmen arrived in London, and with protestations going on outside the prison that a miscarriage of justice was about to take place, Conrad Donovan made a statement to the prison chaplain: 'No murder was intended.' Four words that confirmed the sentence was a just one.

As Christmas approached, Harry accepted an engagement closer to home when he assisted John Billington in the execution of Edmund Hall at Armley Gaol, Leeds. John Dalby, Hall's father-in-law, lived alone at York. Hall had travelled over from Leeds to see him, and was seen being let into the house. Neighbours subsequently heard sounds of a struggle from next door and went to investigate. Dalby opened the door and collapsed. Hall appeared from inside the house, and – saying he would go for a doctor – leapt over the wall and vanished into the street. Dalby died in hospital later that same day, and Hall, who was known to one of the neighbours, was arrested at York station as he sat waiting for his train to pull out. He was sporting a gold watch and chain identified as one Dalby had been wearing earlier that day.

The year had almost come to a close without Harry carrying out a single job as chief hangman, or 'number one' as they were known. But then he travelled across to Ireland in what was to be one of the strangest experiences of his career.

John Flanagan had been missing from his home near Clones, Monaghan, since April 1903, and despite numerous searches there was no sign of his whereabouts. He had travelled into Clones carrying a large sum of money, to purchase items at the market. While in town he met up with Joseph Fee, a local butcher, who owed Flanagan £2 from a previous loan. Witnesses overheard Fee promise to repay the debt if Flanagan called at his house later that afternoon. When Flanagan's disappearance was reported to the police, Fee was questioned but gave them no cause for suspicion.

It was to be almost eight months later before the body of John Flanagan was discovered. Adjacent to Fee's slaughterhouse was a large pile of manure, which police had decided was a public nuisance, and Fee was ordered to remove it. He instructed some colleagues to dispose of it but asked them to leave the last few barrow loads, as he wanted to use it on his garden. While they were removing the manure, the men noticed an old boot protruding from the pile and, digging further, unearthed the missing Flanagan. He had been battered to death with an axe.

Fee was arrested and although there was only what could be termed circumstantial evidence against him he was sent for trial at Monaghan Spring Assizes in March 1904. The jury failed to reach a verdict and Fee was sent for a retrial at the summer assizes. Again no verdict was reached, and in November he was tried at the winter assizes at Belfast. This time the jury believed the prosecution's version of events –

that Fee murdered Flanagan for money and after stealing the £80 he had on him had buried Flanagan beneath the manure pile. The judge was clearly upset by the harrowing story, and was in tears as the black cap was draped on his wig.

When asked why judgement of death should not be passed upon him, Fee said: 'Well my Lord, the evidence is all lies... I am not afraid to meet my death... I am innocent.' Fee was to maintain his innocence throughout his time in the condemned cell.

Harry was engaged to carry out the execution and copies of the appropriate paperwork were dispatched to him. The identity of the executioner was usually kept secret in Ireland, as it was often a perilous position, with crowds often having little regard for Englishmen who crossed the water to hang one of their own.

Shortly after signing and sending the papers back to Armagh, Harry received a telegram on 14 December from the sheriff of Monaghan:

Pierrepoint, 14 Cowgill, Clayton, nr Bradford – No reply; wire immediately. Sheriff Monaghan

Harry replied immediately, assuring the sheriff all was in order when two days later, on the 16th, he received a letter dated the 13th.

Joseph Fee is to be executed at Armagh Prison on Thursday 22d inst, at eight o'clock a.m. You will be required to cross on Tuesday night 20th, and report yourself to the governor of the Prison, Armagh, not later than four o'clock on Wednesday evening, the 21st inst. I think your best and surest route is by Fleetwood and Belfast. You

40

would then arrive in Armagh on Wednesday about
9.30, and could go direct to the prison, where you
will be supplied with everything necessary. Let
me hear from you as to that arrangement.

Harry confirmed the details and was then surprised to receive
another letter a day later endorsed with a capital 'S' in the top
left corner and marked 'Strictly Private'. The letter warned
the hangman that the authorities suspected something was
afoot to delay or prevent him carrying out the execution and
that he was to only respond to any correspondence on this
affair from the under-sheriff himself and to stick rigidly to the
agenda contained in the previous letter.

Having carried out the execution of Edmund Hall at Leeds
on the Tuesday morning, Harry accompanied Billington back
to Manchester and caught the boat train to Fleetwood, from
where he was sailing later that evening. As Harry was
crossing the Irish Sea, over in Armagh a man approached the
gate at the prison and told the gatekeeper he had come over
from England to carry out the execution. His plan was
doomed to failure from the start. The name Pierrepoint had
never appeared in the press over in Ireland at this point and
the would-be impostor was soon rumbled and taken down to
the cells until the execution was over.

The journey across the sea was accomplished without
incident, but Harry had taken heed of advice given to him by
William Billington and made his way to the prison in a
discreet and unobtrusive way. Reaching the town he decided
to ask at the local police station as to the location of the gaol
and, after satisfying them with his credentials, he was
escorted to the nearby building.

Unlike in England and Wales, for executions scheduled in
Ireland and in Scotland – and a few years later in Jersey – an

41

assistant was thought to be an expensive luxury and the authorities refused to sanction payment. For the first time, therefore, Harry was to carry out the execution alone.

Having made the usual arrangements and tested the apparatus, he was then given a chance to view the prisoner. Fee was housed in a cell reached by a flight of stone stairs from the prison yard. Spying him in the cell, Harry saw he was a strapping, well-built fellow and with his details to hand decided on a drop of 6 feet. As he studied the man, Harry heard him repeat to the guards that he was innocent. A strange feeling ran through Harry as he studied the prisoner. Was he looking at an innocent man? But he reasoned that the decision to convict the man was not his and if he refused the task then someone else would do it and collect the fee.

At a few seconds to eight, Harry stood outside the cell to which Fee had been transferred earlier that morning and which stood a short walk from the scaffold. On the stroke of eight he entered and Fee, whose face had turned a ghastly white, submitted to the pinioning without a word. The procession began and moments later it reached the scaffold. Fee didn't flinch as his ankles were strapped; he was then noosed and the white cap placed over his head.

Realising finally that there was not going to be any last-minute reprieve, Fee called out loudly: 'Executioner! Guilty!' Harry darted to the side and yanked the lever. News that Fee had confessed on the scaffold made headlines across the country and Harry felt a little safer as he prepared to travel home knowing he hadn't been responsible for sending an innocent man to his doom.

The year 1904 ended as it had begun for Harry, with a trip to Leeds, this time to help John Billington hang 44-year-old Arthur Jeffries. Jeffries was part of a gang of poachers who operated in and around Rotherham. Another of the gang was

Samuel Barker, a close friend of Jeffries. In October, a row had broken out when others in the gang had gone poaching without Jeffries. The latter was enraged and issued threats adding he would 'do' for one of them. On 12 November, four of the poachers were walking home when Jeffries passed them. As they reached the alleyway close to Jeffries' home they found him standing with his wife. As they passed, Barker said, 'Good night, Arthur', but instead of returning the greeting, his friend swore at him and then a fight broke out. They stumbled into the alley, where Barker fell to the ground, a stab wound in his side. He was carried to a friend's house, but died within minutes.

Unfortunately for the accused, the trial judge was Mr Justice Grantham, a country squire with a hatred of poachers. His summing up sided heavily with the prosecution and the jury needed just a few minutes to find Jeffries guilty of murder. On the morning of his execution, he walked firmly to the gallows. His last words were, 'Lord, receive my spirit.'

1905 to be a pivotal year for Harry Pierrepoint. On 28 February 1905, a week before the birth of his son Albert, he travelled down to Wandsworth to assist John Billington in the execution of Edward Harrison, a brutal bully who had slit the throat of his married daughter when she refused to reveal the whereabouts of his wife after she had left him. Hanged barely a month after committing the crime, Harrison's last words on the drop were, 'I did it!'

Two months later it was back to London again, this time to Pentonville, where again he assisted John Billington. John was now the only member of the Billington family officially on the list, with William having had to retire following personal problems and trouble with the courts. However, he did carry out one last job: he travelled to Cork to hang a former policeman for the murder of an American soldier. John Billington was offered the engagement but he had already accepted the Pentonville job, as had Harry Pierrepoint. The only other man on the list at the time was John Ellis and he had yet to carry out an execution as a number one. The authorities therefore decided to ask William to come out of his retirement for one last execution and, accompanied by Ellis, he carried out the execution on the same morning that Harry and John Billington travelled down by train to Pentonville.

The man they were to execute in London was Alfred Bridgeman, a former soldier who had been convicted of the murder of his fiancée's mother. Bridgeman and his fiancée had broken off their engagement at Christmas 1904, but they remained friends. He was not, however, on good terms with her mother and while very drunk he called at her house, battered her with a poker then cut her throat. Bridgeman was executed less than eight weeks after committing the crime he had been condemned to die for.

When Harry travelled again down to London in May, he was about to come face to face with a pair of criminals whose names would pass into infamy as the first men convicted on fingerprint evidence in an English court.

William Jones arrived for work at a Deptford hardware store one morning in March, and was surprised to find the door locked. Gaining entry through a window he discovered the battered bodies of the proprietors Thomas Farrow and his wife Ann. Thomas lay dead in the parlour of the shop, while his wife Ann lay upstairs in bed. She had also been badly beaten but was still alive at the time, though she was to die four days later. Both had been battered with a piece of rope with a lead ball attached to it.

A cash box had been forced open and its contents, over £10 in coins, had been taken. Importantly, a clear, bloody fingerprint was found on one side of the box. Although fingerprint technology was still in the early stages of development, police knew if they could match the print, they would find their killer. Witnesses came forward to say they had seen a pair of local thieves, the Stratton brothers, on the morning of the murder; Alfred, the older of the brothers, had seemed to be hiding something under his coat. He was picked up in a public house on 3 April, and his younger brother Albert was arrested in Stepney on the following day. Both were taken to Tower Bridge police station and fingerprinted. The print on the cash box clearly matched that of the right thumb of Alfred Stratton and it was enough for both to be charged with murder.

Fingerprint evidence at the trial was to prove crucial. One member of the jury was even fingerprinted to demonstrate how effective the system was. The results were enough to satisfy the jury of the brothers' guilt, although there was other evidence linking them to the murder scene.

Possibly as a result of gaining no engagements as chief executioner in the previous year, Harry wrote to both the Under-Sheriff of London and the Governor of Wandsworth offering his services for the position of executioner. He soon received word back from the sheriff's office that John Billington had been appointed but that he would like Harry to act as assistant. This was contrary to the way things normally worked – it was usually the under-sheriff who engaged the hangman, whilst the governor of the prison was responsible for selecting the assistant.

Harry received a letter from the prison a day or so later stating that they had selected John Ellis as the assistant on this job. This left Harry in a tricky situation, so he wrote to the governor explaining that he had already been engaged by the under-sheriff to act as assistant. The governor replied that he would respect that decision but that he would still be employing Ellis as a second assistant.

Arriving at the gaol, the hangmen were furnished with the usual particulars of the two men and went to observe them in their cells. Albert, at 20, was three years younger than his brother, and had obviously been led astray by his influence. There was a certain amount of sympathy for him but little in the way of effort to secure a reprieve. Albert occupied the large condemned cell in the centre of the prison. He had just finished writing a last letter to friends when the hangman spied on him and they were able to get a good view of him as he walked nervously backwards and forwards across the cell. There was no bravado about him, rather just a calm, sorrowful look on his face.

Alfred Stratton occupied a cell directly above his brother. The hangmen climbed the cast-iron staircase and peered into his cell; Alfred didn't awaken any of the same emotions they had felt for the younger brother. With their calculations they went down to the scaffold and prepared the ropes. Albert, a stocky 172 pounds, was given a drop of 7 feet 6 inches; Alfred, some 25 pounds lighter, was given a drop of 1 foot less. With the sandbags loaded ready for the practice drop, Harry knelt down on the large oak doors and in chalk scribbled 'Albert' and 'Alfred' under the appropriate nooses.

On the following morning the prison was silent; even the warders walked across the landings as if on tiptoes. On a signal from the governor they entered Albert's cell and led him into the corridor. Harry noted he was placid and tractable and in seconds they led him into the corridor, leaving him for a moment in the care of the prison escort. Alfred, who had been removed to an adjacent cell after breakfast, had a surly look on his face but put up no resistance. Not a word had been spoken as the procession was formed and headed for the scaffold, only the quiet voice of the priest reciting the burial service breaking the heavy silence.

The hangmen followed a pace behind the brothers, both with necks bared for the rope, with an officer either side, as they walked steadily down the staircase and along the path that headed to the execution shed. As the procession came into view the doors were flung open. Albert was escorted across to the rope nearest the lever, while Albert stood to his right. As the hangmen busied themselves, Albert broke the silence: 'Alfred,' he said in a loud voice, his pale face half-turning to where his white-capped brother stood. 'Have you given your heart to God?'

For a moment there was no response, then in a muffled whisper his brother replied: 'Yes.'

As the drop fell Harry thought of how, at the very jaws of death, the younger brother's thoughts were more for his brother than for himself.

Harry paid his first visit to Maidstone Gaol on 1 August, when he was engaged as number one for the execution of an Algerian who had killed a fellow countryman in a Kent field. It was to be his first engagement as a chief on the mainland for 20 months.

In the spring of 1905, five Algerians had taken lodgings at a house in a village in Kent. They had earned a living as travellers, selling various goods and items. Some of the group had moved on to the village of Robertsbridge; the rest had travelled on to Tenterden, where on the morning of 17 June, the body of Hadjou Idder was discovered. He had been beaten about the head with a large stick and his throat had been cut. Nineteen-year-old Ferat Mohamed Benali was arrested and confessed to the crime. He said they had travelled from Ashford and had looked for somewhere to sleep. Idder had suggested the field and though Benali preferred to make other arrangements, money was tight and he went along with the plan. In the early hours he awoke to find Idder was sexually molesting him. In a rage, he drew his knife and slashed out. He then picked up a branch and battered Idder until he lay dead. As on all his previous jobs as chief in England, Harry had John Ellis as his assistant. They worked as an efficient team and Benali was dispatched without incident in a brisk and professional manner.

On 9 August 1905, Harry worked as an assistant for the last time when he helped John Billington at the execution of William Hancocks at Knutsford. Hancocks lived with his wife and young children in Birkenhead. The eldest daughter, 15-year-old Mary, was in service elsewhere in Birkenhead and, although she no longer lived at home she often returned to spend some time with her family. On one such visit she was attacked by her father and stabbed several times in the head. She died a few days later. No motive was ever clearly established for the killing and at his trial Hancocks' defence was manslaughter – that the wounds had been caused accidentally, during a struggle with his daughter. The jury disagreed, finding him guilty of murder, but adding a recommendation for mercy on account of him being drunk at the time of the attack.

William Hancocks had lost an arm many years previously in an accident on the railways and this caused a problem for the executioners when it came to pinioning his arms behind his back. In the days of James Berry, the condemned men's arms were often secured to a body belt. Nowadays, with speed an important part of the executioner's duties, clumsy body belts were no longer used, but the resourceful Harry modelled a strap on the principle of the body belt and was able to secure the man's arm on the following morning. Hancocks spent his final hours writing and left two letters in cell. He was a bigamist, and left a letter for each of his wives.

When two executions were scheduled for the same day in August 1905, prison officials found they had a shortage of assistants, as William Billington was serving a short prison sentence for failing to pay maintenance monies to his wife and family after a separation. Of the eight names on the official list of hangmen and assistants when Harry had joined the list in 1901, there now remained just three. Both James Billington and his son Thomas had passed away; Robert Wade hadn't assisted at an execution since the previous century; William Warbrick had only assisted at the first of the new century before his career had seemingly come to an end; and Thomas Scott hadn't carried out any work since March 1901.

This presented a problem when the governor at Leeds prison needed an assistant to help John Billington execute Thomas Tattersall. Both Harry Pierrepoint and John Ellis, the only active assistants on the list, were engaged elsewhere and so a letter was sent to Warbrick asking him to come out of retirement to assist.

On the afternoon before the execution, as the rope was being prepared on the scaffold, John Billington stepped back and tumbled down the open trapdoor that led to the pit below. He suffered cracked ribs and mild concussion in the fall, but was able to carry out his duties satisfactorily. After his return home, however, he was taken ill. He died a short time later at his home in Coppull, from pleurisy – attributable, the doctors believed, to his fall.

Unaware of the drama taking place at Leeds, Harry and Ellis were preparing the gallows for one of the most sensational murderers of the early part of the century. Arthur Deveraux was a 45-year-old chemist who had been convicted of the murder of his wife and twin sons in what the papers dubbed the Kensal Rise Trunk Mystery. In January 1905, Deveraux had been made redundant from the chemist shop he managed in Kilburn. With a wife and three young sons to support, he was desperate to open his own pharmacy but the only person he knew with the means to help was his mother-in-law, who refused his request for a loan.

Early in spring, Deveraux found work in Coventry and moved to the new job with his eldest son. He vacated the house and put the property into storage at a warehouse in Kensal Rise. After a time, his mother-in-law became concerned as to the whereabouts of her daughter and the young twin boys, but Deveraux was vague in revealing their whereabouts – thereby arousing suspicion. Enquiries among the neighbours gave his mother-in-law the name of the removal firm and she was able to convince the police to act. A tin trunk they found in storage aroused their interest, as it was extremely well secured – padlocked, strapped and sealed with wax. Forcing open the lock, and lifting the lid, the police discovered a layer of wooden planks, tightly butted together and screwed into place. They had also been sealed with glue and Boric acid, making the trunk totally airtight. Finally, the contents of the trunk were exposed: the bodies of Mrs Deveraux and two boys.

Deveraux was traced and arrested. He confessed that he had concealed the bodies, but denied killing the victims, claiming he had come home one day in January after spending the day trying to find work when he found the bodies of his wife and young sons. They had died of an overdose of morphine, apparently in desperation at their struggle to find work. He said he had put Stanley, the older son, to bed telling him his mother was asleep, and then put the bodies into the trunk.

At his trial, it was shown that when he had applied for the Coventry job he had written in his application form that he was a widower with one young son. Penned on 13 January, it was dated two weeks before his wife and son had disappeared. This was a damning piece of evidence and was held to show that the killings were premeditated. The jury took just ten minutes to decide his fate.

When Harry received the request to hang George William Butler at Pentonville on 7 November, he was the undisputed number one hangman. (For a time, just he and assistant John Ellis were on the list of the country's executioners.) Fifty-year-old Butler was convicted of the murder of Mary Allen, whom he lived with at Marylebone. Trouble had come to a head when a son from Mary's first marriage came to stay with them. The two men did not get on and following one fight Butler needed hospital treatment for a broken jaw. On 24 September, Butler was visited by his own son. They drank a great quantity of beer, but as Butler's jaw was still causing discomfort he was forced to drink through a straw. He told his son what had happened and threatened to kill both Mary and her son, saying he was going to buy a revolver and blow out their brains. Five days later Mary was heard calling for help. When her son entered the bedroom he saw that Butler had stabbed her four times. Placed under arrest, Butler claimed he had committed the crime because her son had broken his jaw. Mary Allen died two days later.

At his trial, Butler's defence was that he was unaware of his actions due to the effects of the large amount of alcohol he had consumed. Standing just 5 feet 2 inches and weighing 171 pounds, the hangmen gave him a drop of just 6 feet. Death was instantaneous. A week after Butler's execution, Harry made his first trip to Scotland when he was engaged to hang a young Basuto boxer named Pasha Liffey who had committed a murder on a road near Larkhall, Lanarkshire.

Liffey was well known in the Glasgow area, where he was a frequent visitor as part of a travelling circus. One night in August he savagely attacked an old woman as she walked home, cutting her throat with a razor. Her screams alerted passers-by, who recognised the fleeing Liffey. Police arrested him on the following day while an angry lynch mob combed the area looking for revenge.

Although he gave his age as 24, Harry thought Liffey looked no more than a boy as he observed him in exercise at Glasgow's Duke Street Gaol on the afternoon of Monday, 13 November. He was carrying out the execution alone, as his request for an assistant had been refused.

Harry admitted he had been apprehensive as he set out from Clayton on the Sunday evening. He knew from his conversations with William Billington that executions were a rarity in Scotland – as a result, a scaffold was usually borrowed from the English authorities and assembled prior to the day before. In this instance it was borrowed from London's Holloway Gaol and Harry accepted the governor's invitation to travel up on the Sunday so he could supervise the construction of the scaffold and check that it met with his satisfaction.

It was a bitterly cold night as he arrived at St Enoch's station, where after some hot refreshments he made his way to Duke Street Prison. The scaffold was erected in the engineer's workshop. Harry didn't much care for it – it had too many mechanical contrivances about it – but there was no real alternative. The chief concern was that the scaffold floor stood a good 8 inches above the concrete ground so that the trapdoor mechanism could fit underneath. The doors opened into a pit that had been dug below to receive the body. There was always the worry that a terrified condemned man would struggle and there was a chance he would fall or trip on the raised platform. Despite this, after a careful inspection, Harry decided it would suit the purposes.

Standing in the exercise yard as Liffey walked around in the chilly afternoon air, Harry donned a warden's tunic and cap so that the condemned man would be unaware his executioner was observing him at close quarters.

Liffey was only 5 feet 2 inches tall and weighed 9 stone 9 pounds. Harry worked out a drop of 7 feet 1 inch and completed a test drop with a sandbag filled to the same weight. Satisfied all was in order, he retired to his quarters, where he spent much of the evening in the company of warders, playing cards and talking.

At a few minutes to eight that Tuesday morning, Harry stood in the corridor waiting for the governor, with watch in hand, to give him the signal. When it came he went unaccompanied to the condemned cell. A surprise awaited him on arrival in the cell. The door was slightly open and as he entered the cell Liffey stood erect behind the door. Not a flicker of emotion showed on his face as Harry approached. Once he realised who the visitor to the cell was, Liffey gave him a broad smile.

'Come on lad,' Harry said in as kindly and considerate tone as possible, 'it is time to go.'

Liffey stood like a statue as his arms were secured.

'Buck up my boy,' Harry said, even though the condemned man showed no sign of failing courage.

'I will that,' Liffey responded, as they left the cell and walked towards to the scaffold. As they entered the workshop Harry noticed a large table had been set up facing the drop. Behind it sat a row of dignitaries.

They halted at the table and one of them spoke to the prisoner.

'Are you Pasha Liffey?'

Liffey murmured a reply, and at a signal from the City Chamberlain, who headed the table, Harry turned and led the prisoner across to the drop. He placed the noose and white cap over his head, and as Liffey had offered no resistance he did not strap his feet before reaching across and pulling the lever.

The execution had caused great excitement in Glasgow and as a result thousands of people crowded outside the gates of the prison as the black flag fluttered in the breeze to show that Mrs Welsh had been avenged.

Later that morning, Harry left the prison without attracting any attention and with a little time to wait for his train back south he stopped off into a hotel close to the station. He ordered a drink and stood at the bar. A short time later a man entered and spoke loudly to some friends sat in the corner.

'Do you know, I have just been talking to Pierrepoint the executioner who hanged the nigger this morning!'

Immediately the company became all attentive.

'What was he like?' one asked.

'A big strapping fellow, just the man for the job.' He described what Harry had been wearing and ended by saying, 'And he was carrying a leather bag in which he keeps the rope for hanging people!'

Harry listened in amusement as the man continued with what he described as wonderful romancing, and wondered at the temptation to reveal his identity and call the man's bluff. But he let him carry on with his tale, slipped out of the bar and went to catch his train home.

December was to be a busy month for Harry, and so brought a welcome boost to the family income. There were 11 appointments in the diary, but a number of these ended in reprieves for those condemned. The first execution was on 5 December, when he was at Worcester to execute William

Yarnold, a 50-year-old army veteran with 28 years' service. While Yarnold had been serving in the Boer War, his wife had left him and had gone to live with another man. When Yarnold returned to England his wife came back to him, but soon left him again for her lover. He discovered where she was living, called at the house, drew out his army knife and plunged it into her back. She died a few days after the attack.

Despite a petition that attracted 6,000 signatures, Yarnold became the first man to die on the gallows at Worcester for over a hundred years.

Both Harry and assistant Ellis were also engaged for a job in Newcastle on the following morning, and once the formalities had been completed at Worcester they hurried to the station to catch the train north. Henry Perkins and Patrick Durkin were tenants at a house in Newcastle upon Tyne. On the evening of 13 July, while drunk, Perkins stabbed Durkin in the neck. He told detectives he thought the other man was going to attack him first, so it was a form of self-defence. Durkin died from blood poisoning six days later.

When Harry made his second visit of the year to Maidstone on Wednesday, 20 December, he found himself accompanied by a new assistant – William Fry. They were there to execute a 60-year-old rag-and-bone man who had followed his estranged young wife and her new lover from Kent to Bedford, where, finding her alone, he had cut her throat and left her to bleed to death in the gutter. Fry carried out his duties by all accounts without any problems but it appears that once was enough and he was never called upon again.

Harry rounded off the busiest month in his career with three executions in three days. Ellis was his assistant for all three jobs; they met up in Manchester on the afternoon of Boxing Day and travelled together to Stafford Gaol for the first execution. The people of Stafford took great interest in the hangman, particularly as the execution he was about to carry out was on a man whose crimes had horrified the county. William Frederick Edge had been lodging at a house in Newcastle-under-Lyme, Staffordshire. His landlords had been Frank and Rose Evans and they had three children, the youngest a five-month-old baby, Francis. Although he had only been a tenant for five weeks, Edge was well in arrears and was told he would have to find somewhere else to live. He had packed his belongings but asked if he could cook the fish he had bought for lunch before he left. Mrs Evans agreed to his request and left Edge in the kitchen while she went upstairs to clean. Francis was asleep on a settee and when Mrs Evans heard a noise, followed by the door being slammed shut, she went downstairs to find the baby lying dead. Edge had cut its throat so deeply that the head had almost been severed. Edge had then walked into the police station, handed over a bloodstained razor and announced that he murdered the child out of spite at being evicted.

As Harry and Ellis made their way down the narrow path that led from the railway station to the prison, the large crowd of people eagerly scanned passers-by in the hope of spotting the hangman. Harry noted they eyed him suspiciously, although no one challenged him, and it was only when he reached the heavy gate at the prison that they realised who he was.

On the way to the scaffold Harry passed a board that had been set up to punish criminals who had been sentenced to the birch or floggings. The escort told the hangmen that it had been used on the previous day and was being left in place as another prisoner was due to be flogged shortly after the execution.

Edge was wearing gold-rimmed glasses and tearfully writing a letter when the hangmen sneaked a look at him that afternoon. On the following morning he had tears rolling down his cheeks again as Harry placed the hood over his head and then pulled the lever. The hangmen made their way through the crowds outside the prison again later, but managed to avoid recognition as they caught the train to Leeds and another execution.

George Smith was a former bricklayer but he hadn't worked for several years, preferring to live off the income his wife brought in from her work as a chambermaid. One day, Smith turned up at her place of work and, during a quarrel, stabbed her over forty times. He was arrested in Wakefield two days later and said he had done it because she had told him she had found herself another man and their marriage was over. Loud cheers rang out from the public gallery at Leeds Assizes when the jury found him guilty. Smith was hanged at 8 o'clock as snow fell gently over the prison yard. He was given a drop of 6 feet 9 inches.

From Leeds, the executioners travelled on together to Derby, arriving in good time in the afternoon to catch the condemned man at exercise as the daylight faded. John Silk had been discharged from the army in 1903, having served in India and South Africa. Returning to England, he went to live with his crippled mother at Chesterfield. He treated her well and helped with her mobility problems, but he was often drunk and on these occasions, Silk frequently became violent.

On 5 August 1905, Silk was drunk and was heard in a public house to say there would be a murder done that night. He went home and got into an argument with his mother after he refused to go and get her a half-bottle of whisky. Silk went back out and returned at 11.15pm. They got into another row, this time about a lamp in the room being in the wrong place. When his mother went to move it, Silk slapped her, knocking her into the lamp, which overturned and went out, leaving the room into darkness.

Her body was discovered on the following morning: she had been battered to death with one of her crutches and a chair leg. Silk, asleep upstairs in bed, was arrested and charged with his mother's murder. He had vowed to meet his death like a soldier and walked steadily to the gallows when the execution party arrived for him on the following morning.

CHAPTER 3:
KEEPING IT IN
THE FAMILY

A shortage of assistant executioners following the death of John Billington, the retirement of his brother William, and the fleeting appearance of William Fry, caused Harry to persuade his brother Tom to apply for the post. Some seven years older than his hangman brother, Thomas William Pierrepoint was working as a quarryman and helping out with Harry's carrier business when the suggestion was first put to him.

In the barn at the back of the shop that Tom's wife ran at Town End, Harry showed his brother everything he had learned, both on the training course at the now demolished Newgate Gaol and the practical experience he had picked up from working with the Billingtons over the last four years. Tom wrote out a letter of application and following an interview with a prison governor, presumably at nearby Leeds or Wakefield, he was invited to Pentonville for a one-week training course.

The staff at Pentonville realised quickly that Tom had received expert tutelage that even they could not possibly compete with, and it was no surprise that he sailed through the examination and practical test.

While Tom was waiting to hear if he had passed the course, Harry crossed the Pennines to execute a young soldier who had killed his sweetheart in Shaw, near Oldham a week before Christmas 1905. Katie Garrity had gone on an errand for her mother and when she failed to return home a search was organised. Her father discovered the body of his missing daughter; she had been strangled. Witnesses reported seeing 19-year-old Jack Griffiths, her former boyfriend, close to where the body was discovered. It was subsequently learned that a week or so earlier they had argued and he had struck her. She had taken him to court, where he was bound over to keep the peace. Clog marks in the waste ground close to where the body was found matched those belonging to Griffiths.

He behaved callously at his trial, accepting his fate resolutely, smiling at the judge and remarking, 'Well I've nobbut to dee once, I reckon.' The young strangler met his end bravely, asking his parents on their last visit to make sure his younger brothers and sisters went to Sunday school so they wouldn't end up like he had. Heavy rain failed to deter a large crowd forming outside the walls of Strangeways Gaol on the following morning, as inside Jack Griffiths walked firmly to meet his fate.

The next five engagements in Harry's diary ended in reprieves, one just as Harry was preparing to leave the house to travel to the prison, and in the meantime Tom received word he had been accepted as an assistant executioner. Although Harry had no influence to help him gain work in England, on the next execution Harry was engaged on, he was delighted to learn that Tom was to be his assistant.

Sarah Ann McConnell had left her husband James in September 1905, and went to live with 38-year-old Harry

Walters in Sheffield. A few months later, following a drunken quarrel, she was horrifically battered and sexually assaulted with a broken bottle and broom handle. She died soon after; her body was discovered lying naked on the floor of her apartment. Walters denied any knowledge of the dreadful murder and even at his trial he continued to deny any involvement, although he was unable to explain the bloodstains found on his clothing. Walters had the dubious honour of being the first occupant of the new condemned cell at Wakefield. The Victorian gaol had recently been modernised and was one of the first to have a purpose-built execution chamber with adjacent condemned cells all on the same level. This had many benefits for the whole execution process. It was now just a few steps to the gallows rather than a lengthy procession across corridors and down flights of steep stairs, which were often a great ordeal for a terrified man on the very brink of death.

Harry and Tom arrived at the gaol on the afternoon of Monday, 9 April 1906, and were shown the new execution suite situated at the end of 'C' wing. The cells occupied a second-floor landing in the five-storey-high wing, and the condemned cell was two old cells knocked into one to allow exercise in the cell rather than outside in the common yard, which was deemed not advisable.

The two brothers were furnished with the man's details and took a discreet look at him in his cell before heading over to the scaffold to rig the drop. Protruding from one side of the wing the gallows room was a high, green, glass-topped, purpose-made building with trap doors that filled most of the floor and which opened into the cell below. A large beam ran across the room with a chain hanging down and onto this they attached the noose. Together they rigged a drop of 6 feet 6 inches and left the rope to stretch overnight.

Wakefield was to be hanged at 9.30 a.m. Having reset the traps, coiled the noose to the correct height and secured it with pack-thread, Tom realigned the chalk mark to indicate where the man's feet would be positioned. After breakfast they took their position outside the condemned cell and waited for the signal to move.

Walters had enjoyed a hearty breakfast and was finishing his final smoke when the hangmen entered the cell. He offered no resistance as they secured his arms and led him the few short paces across to the scaffold. Harry had his man on the drop in seconds; Tom strapped his ankles and on a signal from the Deputy Sheriff, Harry pulled the lever. The doors crashed against the padded walls and held firm.

It was the sunniest day of the year so far and a large crowd waited outside in a hope of seeing the hangman depart, but as the local paper recorded later that evening, the hangman slipped away from the gaol as silently and rapidly as the bolts in the trap door floor slipped from their sockets.

When Harry travelled down to Nottingham in August to hang a sailor who had murdered his former girlfriend, he met up with another new assistant. William Willis was an Accrington-born man who had graduated from the executioner's training course a few weeks earlier. Edward Glynn and Jane Gamble had been living together as man and wife for some time, but in February she left him for another man. He made threats that he would kill her if he saw them together and on the night of 3 March, as they left a Nottingham public house, he stabbed her repeatedly before fleeing.

Before his execution, Glynn made a full confession to the murder, in front of his solicitor and three prison warders. The entrance to the gallows room at Nottingham was such that once the condemned man entered he had to be turned around on the drop so that the lever was to the left of the executioner after he noosed the prisoner. Glynn thought he was being walked off when he was suddenly moved after he had taken his place on the scaffold. A warder who had spent the last few weeks as his constant escort in the condemned cell, and had accompanied him on his final walk, burst into tears as the drop crashed open.

Tom was again Harry's assistant when he went back to Wakefield on 9 August to execute Thomas Mouncer, a Middlesbrough butcher who had strangled his paramour after a drunken night out.

There were two dates in Harry's diary for November: on the 13th he was at Wandsworth to hang Frederick Reynolds, who had cut his girlfriend's throat after she broke off their engagement. A fortnight later he was at Knutsford Gaol in Cheshire, where he dispatched Edward Hartigan, a Stockport builder who had battered his wife to death with a hammer.

Willis had again been the assistant at Knutsford, but when Harry travelled down to Chelmsford in early December, he discovered that no assistant had been engaged, and for the only time in an English prison he carried out the execution alone.

He had travelled to the Essex gaol to execute Richard Buckham a 20-year-old farm hand, who, along with his younger brother, had been charged with the murder of Albert and Emma Watson, the owners of a small farm near Basildon.

There had been a quarrel over access to a well and when the brothers felt hard done by, after losing the argument, they called at the Watson's farm, where they shot them both dead and stole money and jewellery. The younger brother was acquitted at the trial and Richard Buckman alone faced the hangman.

The final execution of the year took Harry and John Ellis back to Derby Gaol, almost a year to the day since they were last there. The culprit this time was a distinguished former soldier and Harry later commented that the execution was one of the most affecting of the hundred or so that he had carried out.

Walter Marsh had served 17 years in the army and had fought in several notable battles in the Boer War, before leaving the army in 1903. Along with his wife, he took over the running of a public house in Sheffield, but when this failed they moved to another in Chesterfield. When this too failed Marsh began work as a rent collector. By this time his marriage was in trouble and in June his wife attempted to take out a summons against him for cruelty. After a series of quarrels and separations he snapped, and savagely cut her throat as she slept.

Found guilty after a deliberation of just 20 minutes, Marsh refused to allow a petition for his reprieve, claiming he feared imprisonment more than he feared death. The scaffold had been erected in the coach house at the gaol and in the past this had necessitated a long walk across the prison yard to reach it. It was decided this time to move the prisoner on the morning of the execution to a cell next door to the scaffold so the last walk along the snow-covered ground would not be a long one.

Harry noted a very penitent and restless prisoner when he observed him shortly after his arrival at the gaol. Next morning he was brought down from his cell in the hospital wing and placed in the newly prepared cell. As the hangmen made their way from their quarters to the scaffold, Harry peered out of the small gatekeeper's window they passed en route. He noticed a crowd of people stretching back from the prison gates as far as he could see.

Marsh was crying softly as they entered the cell and he got to his feet slowly and feebly as they secured his wrists behind his back. His crying, which had gone on all through the night, continued as he stepped onto the drop. Harry believed it was shame at his position and not fear that caused the tears to fall.

Christmas festivities in the Pierrepoint household had, as in previous years, been put on hold when work called, but having left Derby promptly, Harry arrived home shortly after lunchtime. The experience of hanging the distressed and shamed soldier had played heavily on his mind and he was looking forward to a cup of tea and a relaxing hour by the warmth of the fire and the company of his young children. No sooner had he entered the house, however, than he heard shouts coming from outside. His wife, who was standing by the window, shouted, 'Harry, come look at this' as a partially naked man went tearing down the street. Harry went out into the street and found a gang of nine or ten young men laughing and pointing as the man, naked except for a shirt, ran past again.

'Why the Dickens don't you stop him?' Harry asked, only to be met with howls of laughter and pointing fingers as the man made his way back down the other side of the street. Harry set off after him and got within thirty yards when the man doubled back and headed straight for him. Preparing himself, Harry stood in his path and, seeing his route blocked, the man turned and jumped a wall. Harry was able to grab him and save him a long fall over the other side to an almost certain death or severe injury.

Moments later attendants from a nearby asylum came into view and gathered up the escapee whom Harry had brought under control. He was annoyed when the attendants simply collected the man and, without a word of thanks, set off back to the asylum.

On New Year's Day 1907, Harry's long-time assistant John Ellis finally got to act as a chief executioner when he performed an execution at Warwick. It had been a long time coming for Ellis, whose only previous offer as a number one, when Harry was engaged elsewhere, had come to nothing after the condemned man was reprieved.

One warm summer's afternoon in July 1906, three holiday-makers walking at St Saviour's on the island of Jersey had stumbled across the body of a partly dressed man in a field. He was identified as a young married man who lived close by and investigations led police to arrest his wife and her brother, 29-year-old Thomas Connan, for the crime. At Connan's trial it was alleged that his sister had persuaded him to murder her bullying husband, from whom he then stole items of jewellery. She was sentenced to 20 years' imprisonment while her brother was sentenced to death.

It was to be the first execution in Jersey for over thirty years, and the first to be held in private. Harry received the offer to hang the condemned man, with the execution date being set for Tuesday, 19 February, one month to the day from sentence being passed. Over five thousand people signed the petition for a reprieve, which, although Harry had received a wire to say the execution was to go ahead as scheduled, was still being considered when he boarded a boat from Southampton and set sail for Jersey.

A large crowd had gathered on the quayside as the boat docked, but any hopes they had of seeing the executioner were dashed when the chief warder from the gaol pulled up at the foot of the disembarkation ramp and herded Harry into a closed carriage and away to the prison. Several more daring men raced alongside on bicycles trying to peep through the windows, but the execution party reached the safety of the prison without an incident.

Following a breakfast and a chance to relax, Harry was shown the newly constructed gallows, and at once expressed concern at the flight of steps the condemned man was expected to climb to reach the drop. The chief engineer, who had constructed the gallows, had also made an exact replica model, a foot high, which Harry throughout his stay at the gaol tried in vain to get him to part with.

Connan spent his last night on earth praying and singing hymns, and met his fate bravely on the following morning. Harry had been surprised when he went in to pinion the prisoner to find that over half a dozen other dignitaries entered the cell at the same time, one of whom read out the death warrant to the stunned prisoner. It was less than fifty paces to the scaffold and in no time Connan was on the drop, noosed and hooded. He muttered, 'Lord have mercy on my soul,' as Harry pulled the lever.

Later that night Harry was entertained at a civic reception where his health was toasted, and after spending a further night in the prison he caught the 8 a.m. boat to sail back to Southampton. The ship was tossed around on gale-force seas, and Harry found himself reflecting that this was the kind of travel and adventure he had longed for when he left home as a teenager.

On 26 March, with Willis as his assistant, Harry executed Joseph Jones at Stafford for the murder of his son-in-law. He had three offers of work in London that spring, all of which came to nothing, and it wasn't until mid-July that he travelled down to Derby where he met up with Ellis. Together they rigged a drop of 7 foot 6 inches for William Slack, a Chesterfield painter who had attacked a barmaid with an axe as she pushed a pram down the street. (He was thought to have been the father of the child she was pushing and was wheeling the pram away when arrested.) He was abusive to the judge when sentence of death was passed, but showed no fear on the morning of his execution and almost ran to the drop.

Harry was engaged on three executions in seven days in August. The first was at Liverpool's Walton Gaol on 7 August, when Harry and Tom hanged Charles Paterson, a half-caste sailor from Moss Side, Manchester, who had pleaded guilty to the murder of his landlady. Paterson cut her throat after she had served notice evicting him.

Six days later, assisted by Ellis he hanged Richard Brinkley a Fulham carpenter who had mistakenly murdered two people in Croydon. After swindling an old lady out of her savings and forging her signatures on a will, Brinkley found his scheme thwarted when the granddaughter of his victim contested the will following the old lady's death. Fearful that his forgery would be exposed, Brinkley made up a poisonous mixture that he added to a bottle of stout that his intended victim, the granddaughter, would drink. Unfortunately for Brinkley, his landlord found the bottle in a cupboard and poured out the contents, which he then shared with his wife and daughter. The landlord and his wife died almost at once. The bottle was examined and found to contain prussic acid.

Harry travelled across to Cardiff later that day to execute Sunderland-born Mrs Leslie James, who preferred to use the name Rhoda Willis. Willis was a baby farmer who lived in lodgings in the Welsh capital. Short of money, and unable to find work, she placed an advertisement offering her services in finding places for unwanted babies. One of the replies came from a lady whose unmarried sister was expecting a child in May. They agreed a fee of £6 with a further £2 to follow. She had also arranged to take in another child but, finding herself unable to cope, suffocated one of them while travelling home on a train. Her landlady discovered the dead child in her room and called the police.

Harry had arranged to meet up with Tom at the railway

station, where a large crowd had gathered in the hope of seeing the hangman. They hailed a cab to the gaol where they found another large gathering. A policeman on duty helped them to get inside safely. A telegram had recently arrived stating there would be no reprieve, and the woman had collapsed and was still in a state of nervous prostration when they looked into the cell. Both were concerned she would give them trouble in the morning, such was her apparent terror. They were given her age as 39; she stood 5 feet 2 inches tall and weighed 145 pounds. The hangmen worked out a drop of 5 feet 9 inches.

At her request she was visited by her solicitor at 6 a.m. on the morning of her execution and, crying bitterly, she thanked him for coming, before making a full confession. At a few minutes to eight Harry was given his orders and, with his brother following close behind, entered the cell, where they found an attractive, smartly built, well-dressed woman with glorious auburn hair. She didn't rise to her feet as they entered, so Harry gently tapped her on the shoulder. She looked up with a pitiful smile.

'It is time,' he said gently as they helped her to her feet, 'be brave.' They swiftly fastened her arms and she was able to walk unaided as the procession made its way to the scaffold. Her eyes were fixed straight ahead but as they entered the small prison yard where the shed was situated, she looked up to the glorious blue sky and muttered something inaudible. As the sun glistened in her hair, Harry reflected that he had rarely seen a more beautiful woman. Seconds later she was stone dead.

The Pierrepoint brothers were to be in action on all subsequent executions that year. On 5 November they travelled together to Reading, where they executed William Austin who had murdered the daughter of the family he lodged with at Windsor. Three weeks later they were at Lincoln Gaol, where 47-year-old agricultural labourer William Duddles paid the ultimate penalty for murdering his wife with a hammer at their home in Lutton Marsh.

The final execution of 1907 involved a trip back to Cardiff, but instead of the flaming-haired beauty he had escorted on her final walk the last time he was in the principality, this time Harry was to hang George Stills – a Glamorgan colliery worker who had battered his aged mother to death while drunk.

After a barren two months with no work, on 5 March 1908 Harry carried out an execution on his own when he dispatched 25-year-old Joseph Hume, a deserter from the Highland Light Infantry, who had robbed and battered to death a kindly old man who had given him food and shelter.

Harry described the journey from his home in Bradford to Inverness's Porterfield Prison as one of the most memorable he had made in his career. He had been asked to report to the gaol on the evening of Tuesday, 3 March, as the weather was making travelling hazardous, and the authorities were anxious there should be no hiccup in arrangements, this being the first execution in the town since 1835. As it turned out, heavy snow north of Perth delayed his journey and it was well into the early hours of Wednesday before he reached his destination. Hume protested his innocence to his mother in a touching farewell interview and although he bore up well when Harry went for him on the following morning, he began to falter as they reached the drop. His final words were 'Don't blindfold me', but Harry did everything by the book, and after placing the noose he put on the white cap; in a move he often carried out when working alone, he chose not to secure the legs with the ankle strap. Sensing that Hume was about to faint he darted to his left and pulled the lever.

Arriving home from Inverness, Harry found a telegram from the Under-Sheriff of Durham asking him if he was free to officiate at a double execution scheduled for 24 March. Two Gateshead men had been convicted of separate offences, but as they were tried within days of each other before Mr Justice Channell at Durham Assizes, it was decided they would hang together.

Robert William Lawman had been the first to be convicted. A miner, he had cut the throat of his paramour at Gateshead before making a botched attempt to cut his own throat. When interviewed by the police, Lawman stated: 'I have killed her; I loved her, and I will swing for her,' claiming he had committed the crime after his lover had suggested they split up. The judge had tears in his eyes as he passed the death sentence. But there were no tears for the second man sentenced to hang beside Lawman.

There had been a number of burglaries at the Windy Nook Co-Operative Society, Gateshead, and staff took turns to keep a watch in case the thieves returned. On the night of 31 October, four employees concealed themselves in the butchery department; at around 4 a.m. a noise was heard, the door opened and a man entered. A violent scuffle ensued before two shots rang out, leaving one man dead and another with leg wounds. Although he had received a severe beating from the staff the killer escaped, but left vital clues at the scene. With police on the alert for a man who may have been showing the effects of his injuries, railway blacksmith Joseph William Noble was arrested on the following day. He was covered in bruises, which he claimed were the result of a fall at work. His footprints matched those found at the scene and a search of his home turned up jemmies and other burglar's tools. No gun was found, but cartridges in the house matched those recovered from the body of dead man. Asked if he had anything to say before being condemned, Noble replied, 'You can break my neck but you cannot break my heart.'

Arriving at the gaol with his brother, Harry saw that a fair-sized crowd had assembled and later claimed that he was instantly recognised by a group of men who had served on the coroner's jury after a previous execution there. He may have been mistaken on this point, however, as this was to be his first appearance at Durham Gaol.

Settling into their quarters, the hangmen found they were directly opposite the two condemned cells, which were situated side by side. This afforded them several opportunities throughout the afternoon and evening to check on the condition of the men to see how there were coping with the strain of their impending doom. Both at that time were showing no signs of distress.

Receiving the details from the medical officials, Harry found that Noble weighed in at 178 pounds, and only once before in his career had he executed a man that heavy. He was to be given a drop of just 6 feet, his companion on the drop – again a big strapping fellow but weighing slightly less – was given a drop of 10 inches longer.

Lawman was the first to be pinioned. He showed no fear as he was led into the corridor, but as his shirt was opened to bare his neck for the rope he spoke gruffly – 'Don't hurt my neck', a reference to the freshly healed scar from his failed suicide bid.

Noble joined him in the corridor and the two men covered the 35 yards to the scaffold without any sign of fear. A group of pressmen took notes as the condemned men took their places on the trapdoor and within seconds

Amelia Wood had been avenged and the Windy Nook burglaries finished forever.

Harry was paired up again with John Ellis for the first time in almost a year when they travelled to Manchester to hang John Ramsbottom, who had shot dead his brother-in-law in a public house. Although the two hangmen had got on well on previous occasions, a little bit of tension began to appear now, probably a combination of jealousy on the part of Pierrepoint that Ellis was now being offered roles as an executioner and taking fees that he, as the country's number one, should be receiving, and possibly from Ellis's side that his brother seemed to be being paired with Harry on a more regular basis, thus depriving him of potential income. It was an undercurrent that was about to build into something much bigger.

On 19 May, Harry travelled north of the border for what turned out to one of the strangest experiences of his career. The execution was to be at Ayr Gaol and the condemned man was Thomas Bone, who had pleaded guilty to the murder of his wife in April.

Harry made his way via Kilmarnock to Ayr railway station, where he was met by the town clerk and escorted to the gaol. There had been petitions in Bone's home village of Glenbuck, but as the prisoner had pleaded guilty there was no chance that the verdict would be overturned. The clerk, however, told Harry that as he had set out to meet the hangman's train a King's Messenger had arrived at the gaol carrying a telegram.

Sure enough on reaching the prison it was found that a reprieve had indeed been granted and Harry's duties were therefore no longer required. Bone had not yet learned of his fate and the official party, which included the governor and provost, were preparing to tell the man he had been spared the ignominious death on the hangman's rope. They asked Harry if he would like to accompany them; thinking he would be bringing the prisoner good news, he willingly agreed.

Harry happened to be at the head of the party as the provost read out the letter stating the purpose of their visit and telling Bone his life had been spared. Bone was sitting reading the New Testament as they spoke, and as he took in what was being said he rose to his feet, threw the book to the floor and ran to the corner of the cell with tears streaming down his face. 'I want to die, I want to be with my wife,' he cried. Leaving the chaplin to console the prisoner, Harry left the cell after this harrowing and totally unexpected experience.

After refreshments and a hot meal, Harry was shown around the prison and was asked for his thoughts on the scaffold they had constructed for the execution. He examined the wooden structure, raised some six feet off the ground and accessed via a set of steep steps, and told the officials it was a very poor arrangement. He explained to them the virtues of the English scaffold, where the drop and condemned cell were all on one level. Harry departed for home that night having received his fee in full – a practice the English authorities didn't adopt from their Scottish counterparts. (In England, no execution meant no fee for the hangman.)

Thomas Bone's sentence was commuted to life imprisonment and he was transferred to Perth Gaol to serve out his sentence. Four years later, after smashing all his personal property in his cell, he hanged himself with a bed sheet, achieving the outcome the authorities had denied him at Ayr.

Harry and William Willis were on duty on a sunny July morning when they executed Fred Ballington at Manchester's Strangeways Prison. Ballington was a Glossop butcher who had cut his wife's throat in a carriage at Manchester's London Road railway station after she refused to give him some money to buy more drink.

Like Lawman, whom Harry had hanged at Durham earlier that year, Ballington had also tried to cut his own throat after committing the murder. He was given a drop of 7 feet and died instantly.

A week later Harry carried out two executions in two days. On Tuesday, 4 August, he was at Hull Prison for the execution of Thomas Siddle, who had killed his wife by cutting her throat after she took out a commitment order against him. After hanging Siddle, he travelled north to Durham, where he met up with his brother.

Matthew Dodds was a miner from Hamsterley, near Bishop Auckland who had been convicted of murdering his wife. Mary Dodds had inherited a substantial amount of property and made a will, leaving it all to her husband. Following a series of quarrels she made a new will, this time leaving Dodds just a small allowance, but in January 1908 she was persuaded to make a third will reverting her inheritance back to her husband. A few weeks later Dodds hurried round to a neighbour and said that he had found his wife lying dead in the fireplace. The coroner recorded an open verdict – that death was due to the burns she had received during the fall – and she was buried without a police investigation. Following information received from an anonymous tip-off, however, the body was exhumed, whereupon a pathologist found that cause of death had been strangulation.

At his subsequent trial, Dodds was convicted and sentenced to death. However, the Criminal Appeal Act had recently come into being, and this gave him some hope. Prior to this Act, those condemned did not automatically have the right to appeal and often had to hope that a reprieve or commutation of sentence came from some other means. Matthew Dodds became the first man allowed an appeal under the new Act. His defence claimed that the judge at the original trial had omitted evidence in his summing-up. The appeal was dismissed, however, and the death sentence confirmed. Dodds had been due to be executed on 21 July, but this date was changed when he made the historic appeal. Harry was notified of the new date but wrote back explaining that he was unable to attend on 4 August as he had accepted an engagement at Hull for that day, though he would be free to officiate on the following day.

Unaware that the hangman had extended his life by one extra day, Dodds was reading when Harry peeped into his cell. The first thing Harry noticed, and which he had up until then had no notification of, was that the condemned man had a wooden leg. This required some thought and Harry and Tom retired to their quarters across the corridor, barely six paces from the man waiting to hang, where Harry put on his 'study cap' as he pondered the problem. Consulting the officials he had been told that they believed Dodds was unable to walk without a stick, but when the question was put to the prisoner later that afternoon, he said he would be able to walk if he had his wooden leg. It was decided that in order to avoid the flight of stairs that led down to the gallows room, on the following morning he'd be taken to a holding cell that was on the same level.

Dodds was regularly observed the rest of that evening and seemed in good spirits, chatting to his warders and with the chaplain who made frequent visits. On the morning of his execution, he had a resigned air about him as his wrists were secured and he was led out into the corridor. Moments later the distinctive clump of the wooden leg echoed eerily through the hushed gaol. Entering into the yard, Dodds passed three reporters who had been given permission to witness events. He cast them a cursory glance and limped on without a word. Reaching the drop, Tom strapped the wooden leg to the other as Harry had explained to him, while the prisoner murmured repeatedly: 'Lord have mercy on me.' Seconds later, Dodds was dead.

On 20 August, Harry crossed the Irish Sea to hang John Berryman at Londonderry. Berryman had been convicted of the murder of his brother and sister-in-law after a business dispute. The brothers were joint owners of a farm and after a series of disagreements over a variety of things he had battered them to death with a hammer.

Harry was engaged to carry out the job without an assistant, and was issued with the necessary warrants and a strict timetable to adhere to. Having accepted the role, he then had to turn down an offer from the governor of Perth Gaol to carry out an execution there on the day before the Ireland execution, as it would be impossible to travel from Scotland to be at Londonderry in time. It was then offered to John Ellis, who carried out the execution with Willis as his assistant. Harry travelled to Londonderry via the midnight sailing from Heysham. He described the journey to Belfast as a glorious one, the beautiful calm night sky making many of his travelling companions disinclined to go below deck. Despite being awake most of the night, he met up with the officials from the sheriff's office feeling refreshed and alert.

After a brief rest in his quarters at the gaol, Harry was escorted to the execution chamber, which, he noted, was a long, low-roofed building adjacent to the condemned cell. Having made his calculations for a drop he tested the apparatus and filled a sandbag to stretch the rope. Pulling the lever the drop crashed open and gave the hangman a surprise. Instead of the usual nine- or ten-foot pit below the drop, the gallows had been rigged in a building that overhung the prison yard, and the man was to drop into a chasm with the floor some twenty feet below.

When he entered the cell on the following morning he found Berryman lying on his bed in a distressed state. Two priests knelt at his side trying to offer him comfort while praying intently. Harry crossed the room and bent down to help the prisoner to his feet. Berryman seemed puzzled at the stranger who had entered, his state of mind being so confused that he didn't realise it was time for him to leave the cell.

The prisoner refused a stimulant and walked falteringly and painfully slowly as he made his last journey supported by a warder on either side. A large group of dignitaries gathered around the drop, but they kept well back and Berryman was dead moments after stepping onto the trapdoors. With the aid of a warder the body was hauled up, removed from the rope, and placed in a rough, plain coffin that lay across the open trapdoors. Removing the cap, Harry could see that although Berryman's features were much swollen, the expression was one of composure, indicating a painless and instant death.

While Harry was removing the prisoner and tidying away the tackle, the coroner and a jury arrived at the prison to carry out an inquest. Harry had asked the governor if he would refrain from giving his name, so that his anonymity could be maintained. This he agreed to and when questioned by the coroner he kept his word. The jury, however, disagreed with this finding and demanded to know the name of the hangman. A row broke out at the inquest with the jury repeating their demands to be told who the hangman was.

'So help me God, I don't know who he is!' shouted the coroner after their persistent questioning caused him to lose his temper. Another juryman then gave voice to the inquest stating that the rumour was that the hangman was a local man.

'We refuse to deliver a verdict until we know the name of the hangman,' the foreman then announced. However, eventually, and reluctantly, the jury recorded a verdict that the cause of death had been dislocation of the neck caused by judicial hanging.

In November, assisted by his brother, Harry carried out the execution of James Phipps at Knutsford. Phipps had lost an eye and wore a scarf across his face to hide the disfigurement. On 12 October he had asked a young girl to run an errand for him and when she had returned he had asked her to show him where the local lamplighter lived. They had set off together, but a short time later she was found dead. She had been sexually assaulted and had died from drowning after her face was held down in a pool of muddy water.

The 21-year-old Phipps was identified as the man seen with her prior to her death and he was arrested on suspicion of murder. He pleaded insanity at his trial, which took place just a week after he had committed the murder. The jury took only seven minutes to find him guilty and he was hanged one month to the day from carrying out the dreadful crime.

December was to be another busy month for Harry Pierrepoint, with five executions in all parts of the country. On 2 December he travelled to Norwich, where he hanged James Nicholls, a Norfolk labourer who had murdered an old woman at her home in Fertwell. He was assisted by his brother. They then travelled back to Yorkshire, where they were engaged to execute a disgruntled former Bradford clerk who had battered to death a cashier with a poker.

A passer-by had seen a red-faced man standing in the doorway of a Bradford office building. Asked what the matter was, the man replied he was 'having a bit of bother' in the office. He then went back inside, returning minutes later with blood on his hands. When he later heard of the terrible murder that had taken place, the passer-by was able to give police an excellent description of the man he had seen. John William Ellwood was a former employee at the office but had left after a disagreement with a director. Knowing the routine of the offices, he was aware that the cashier paid a visit to the bank each Friday, often with large quantities of cash.

Following Ellwood's conviction, local interest in the case became huge. Harry had to run the gauntlet of curious townsfolk asking if he was to be the hangman who 'topped' Ellwood. He kept tight-lipped about his appointments, and rumour spread that he had refused the job because it meant hanging someone from his hometown. Large crowds milled around the entrance to Armley Gaol, many from Bradford, and Harry saw several people in the crowd he recognised as his inquisitors in the previous weeks. Besides the curious crowds who recognised the hangman, Ellwood had also boasted to his guards that he knew Harry Pierrepoint well, and that he was going to cause him as much trouble as possible in the morning.

Harry spied him in the cell, but had no recollection of ever having set eyes on the condemned man before. A new permanent scaffold had been constructed in the garage where the prison van was stored. After calculating the drop the hangmen made their way back to their quarters in the prison hospital, where they passed two prison officers busy digging a grave in the small plot of land used to bury hanged murderers.

Back in their cell Harry and Tom pondered the threat made by Ellwood. Although many had boasted to their guards that they would kick up a fuss on the morning of their executions, when the time came, more often than not fear took over and they usually submitted placidly. Trouble on the drop was a rarity, but was always planned for. Harry talked through a drill whereby he got two of the escort guards to stand on wooden planks flanking the trapdoors ready to hold the condemned man's arms if he made a struggle.

When the executioners made their way down the corridor

they noticed the usual crowd of witnesses were complemented by several extra uniformed guards. As the party waited for the under-sheriff to arrive outside the cell, Harry took a last opportunity to size up the prisoner. Peeping through the spyhole, he saw him dressed in his own clothes, standing talking to the warders close to the cell door. On the stroke of nine, the door slid open and the hangmen quickly moved to secure his wrists. Ellwood was pinioned before he had chance to register their presence, thus rendering any of his threats to cause mayhem worthless.

As Harry was baring his neck, Ellwood glared viciously at him. 'Harry, you're hanging an innocent man,' he said. The brothers had debated this point while travelling to the gaol, but fully believed he was guilty as charged; nothing they had witnessed since their arrival had caused them to change their mind. The walk to the scaffold was just 20 yards, and Ellwood glared at the officials, turning his head round as he was escorted along.

'I am innocent!' he shouted at the officials before he was led onto the trap. As Tom swooped down to secure his ankles, Harry adjusted the rope around his neck. Looking the hangman straight in the eye, Ellwood repeated his protestations. 'You are killing an innocent man,' he barked. Harry was becoming angry that a man on the very edge of death was prepared to meet his maker with a lie on his lips. As he tightened the noose and went to place the white cap over the prisoner's head, Ellwood spoke for the last time. 'It's too tight,' he complained. An audible sigh went round as Ellwood dropped into the pit and hung silently at the end of the rope.

The final three executions that year all passed by without incident. With Willis as his assistant, Harry went to Maidstone to execute William Bouldrey, who had killed his wife by cutting her throat. Bouldrey had protested his

81

innocence throughout but confessed his crime to his aged mother in the condemned cell on the afternoon before he was hanged. A week later Harry hanged Henry Parker, a Coventry labourer who had battered to death an old bakery owner with whom he had been having a long-running feud. Parker had used a vicious wooden club studded with several large nails to inflict a fearful beating. Ellis assisted at the execution that took place at Warwick Gaol.

Ellis was also the assistant when Harry made another trip to Cardiff to hang Noah Collins, who had killed his fiancée after she jilted him. Collins had stabbed her many times with a large knife. Mr Justice Bucknill described it as one the most cruel and atrocious murders ever heard in a court of law.

The first execution of what was to be Harry's busiest year as a hangman took place at Pentonville a week into the new year of 1909. On 7 November 1908, at the Shaftesbury Avenue offices of Cartnell and Schlitte, bankers and foreign money changers, Frederick Schlitte had looked up to see a man standing before him with a gun levelled at his chest. Without speaking a single word, he fired once. Despite being wounded, Schlitte threw himself at the attacker, knocking the gun from his hand. A scuffle broke out and ended when the man drew a knife and stabbed Schlitte repeatedly. The wounded man managed to throw something through the window, attracting the attention of passers-by who were able to apprehend the fleeing attacker.

Identified as 21-year-old John Esmond Murphy, alias James McDonald, the attacker was finally to be charged with murder when Schlitte died from his injuries. The attempted robbery had been so disastrous Murphy had fled empty handed. His failed defence was insanity.

Harry and William Willis carried out another execution at Durham in February when they hanged miner Jeremiah O'Connor, who had committed an horrific child murder. The young victim, Mary Donnelly, had only recently lost her father in a mining disaster at West Stanley, which had claimed 160 lives.

With his brother again as assistant, Harry hanged Ernest Hutchinson, a Halifax butcher, who had stabbed to death his new girlfriend after a row on Christmas Eve. Hutchinson became the third man to be hanged at Wakefield. Thomas Meade became another date in Harry's diary after being convicted of the murder of Clara Howell, whom he battered to death in Leeds. Meade had lost an appeal at the Court of Criminal Appeal – his council had claimed the trial judge had misdirected on a number of points relating to his client's defence of insanity.

Harry travelled to Liverpool for his next engagement, the execution of a Chinese sailor. See Lee had shot dead a friend, Yung Yap, during a quarrel, but claimed it was an accident. Another killer who used a gun became the next to hang when the brothers travelled to Stafford, where Joseph Jones paid the ultimate penalty for the murder of his wife.

When Harry travelled to South Wales in early May, it was to make a rare appearance at Swansea. William Foy was a vagrant who had murdered his girlfriend and thrown her body down a deep shaft at a deserted furnace near Merthyr. He had later led the police to the site and described how he had killed her after she had told him she was going to inform the authorities that he had been living off her earnings as a prostitute.

Harry chose to travel to the Glamorgan prison via Conwy and the Menai Strait, making an anticlockwise circuit of the Welsh coastline; Ellis travelled with him as his assistant. Reaching the gaol they were shown the scaffold erected in a converted weaving shed. Work had stopped in the shed a few days before the scheduled execution; the pit, which had been bricked over, was reopened and a large beam fixed above it.

After watching the prisoner at exercise, the hangmen spent the rest of the afternoon playing bowls with Governor Gibson and his daughter on the immaculate lawn in front of his residence on the outskirts of the prison. When darkness fell the hangmen retired inside where they had supper with the wardens, who had just come out of the condemned cell, and told of the pitiful last meeting between the prisoner and his sister and father. The sister had cried continuously throughout the meeting while her father fought to compose himself.

As the hangman and his assistant completed their final preparations a crowd began to assemble outside the gaol. As 8 o'clock neared and the party assembled outside the condemned cell, the gathering had swelled and their singing of hymns could be clearly heard from inside the thick prison walls. As Harry and Tom entered, Foy showed no trace of emotion but turned to his guards and made one last request. He asked if he could have another cigarette. The guards looked around for guidance; it was an unusual request, as most condemned men at this point were usually overcome with fear. Given the go-ahead, a lighted cigarette was placed between his lips and he made repeated draws on it as he walked across the prison yard onto the drop. Without wishing to deny him his last request, Harry placed the hood over his head with the cigarette still between Foy's lips, and pulled the lever. The butt was still in place an hour later when the body was taken down. As they departed the prison, Harry noticed that several of the crowd had cameras, which they pointed at both Ellis and Harry as they made their way back to catch the train home.

A rare double execution came Harry's way in May when two Jewish brothers were condemned for the brutal murder of William Sproull, a sailor on shore leave. Twenty-three-year old Morris Reubens and his younger brother Marks had concocted a simple plan. They persuaded two girlfriends to go out looking for a man who might appear to have a few shillings on him. After letting him buy them a few drinks they would then invite him back to their rooms at Whitechapel, where the brothers would steal cash and anything else of value he had about him.

Along with his shipmate, Sproull had met the two women and in due course, after several drinks the four returned to the house. The Reubens brothers appeared, a fight broke out and spilled into the street, where Sproull received a fatal knife wound.

Bloodstains led the police to the house and both men were soon arrested. They each blamed each other for the murder throughout the trial and began to cry for mercy when sentence of death was passed on them.

Having read the newspaper accounts of the brothers' pitiful cries after being sentenced, Harry expected them to be in a distressed state when he went to observe them. He found them both to be calm and composed, however – a manner they kept up to the very end.

'Goodbye Marks, I am sorry!' Morris cried out as Tom strapped his ankles. May was turning out to be a busy month. A week after returning from London, Harry picked up his tweed travelling rug and boarded the express from Leeds to Glasgow, where he had an appointment to hang Oscar Slater. Slater had been convicted of the murder of an old woman in her Glasgow apartment, though many people believed he may have been innocent. Arriving at Duke Street Prison, Harry had already heard a rumour, as his train headed north, that a reprieve had been granted and this was confirmed when he entered the governor's office.

'I should very much like to see the prisoner before I go, if I may?' Harry asked, and the governor allowed him to look upon the man who had escaped his clutches. Harry was told Slater had collapsed when he heard he had been reprieved. After a wash and brush-up, and payment in full, Harry caught a cab to the station and the long trip home.

Harry and Ellis were back in Wales to carry out the execution of John Edmunds at Usk. Edmunds had raped and shot an elderly widow at her isolated farmhouse; he walked to the gallows with a broad smile on his face.

Walter Davis became the fourth person hanged at Wakefield when he was convicted of battering to death a woman he had been having an affair with in Middlesbrough. As on all the previous executions here, Harry carried out the sentence assisted by his brother. The brothers then hanged William Hampton at Bodmin towards the end of July and Manchester strangler Mark Shawcross at Strangeways in August. Coincidentally, Davis, Hampton and Shawcross were all given a drop of 7 feet, despite having a wide age and weight range. And 7 feet was the same drop Harry gave to his next client, Julius Wammer, a Norwegian sailor whom he hanged at Wandsworth for the murder of a prostitute Wammer had shot dead after she stole money from him.

Madar Dal Dhingra was hanged at Pentonville on 17 August. He came to England from the Punjab in November 1906, studying engineering at University College, London. On 1 July 1909, he attended a concert at the Imperial Institute and as the audience departed he shot dead Sir William Curzon-Wylie, the Aide-de-Camp to the Secretary of State for India. Dr Cowas Lalcaca, moved to apprehend the young killer, and the Indian fired two shots into him. He turned the gun on himself too, but when he pulled the trigger it misfired. He was overpowered and taken into custody.

Dhingra refused to be represented at his trial, stating he did not recognise the court. He said the shooting of the doctor was an accident but that Sir William had been assassinated as he was an enemy of his people. Sentenced to death, he said he was proud to lay down his life for his country. A slightly built man, he was given the longest drop Harry had ever administered, and although he had been calm and composed in the cell, he began to shake uncontrollably as Ellis strapped his ankles on the drop.

After leaving Pentonville Harry headed straight to Belfast, where he was engaged to hang Richard Justin who had battered to death his stepdaughter earlier in the year. As with previous trips to Ireland, Harry worked without an assistant; he gave the man a drop of 7 feet 3 inches.

The year ended with a hectic week in which Harry carried out three executions within seven days. On 7 December, assisted by Ellis, he travelled to Hull to hang John Freeman. Freeman lodged with his brother, Robert, and Robert's wife, Florence. Following a drunken argument, during which Robert accused him of having an affair with his wife, a fight broke out that ended with Freeman cutting his sister-in-law's throat. As he was led to the gallows he told a waiting reporter: 'Let this be a warning of the evils of drink.'

Harry travelled up to Durham after leaving Hull to meet up with assistant William Willis. They were engaged to hang the man convicted of what was known in the press as the Chopwell Tragedy. Abel Atherton was a miner, a native of Wigan, who was in lodgings at Chopwell, a pit village a few miles from Newcastle with a Mr and Mrs Patrick. They had a daughter, Frances, and although she was barely 15 years old, half the age of Atherton, he had fallen in love with her. Unable to understand Atherton's advances, she neither encouraged nor repelled them, but her parents saw the danger and warned her to keep Atherton at a distance. She dutifully obeyed.

Atherton was also warned that his attentions were unwelcome, but instead of taking heed of the warning he began to nurse it as a grievance. This grew until he was finally asked to leave the lodgings, although he still made frequent calls to the Patricks' house. One August afternoon, heated words arose between Atherton and Mrs Patrick, ending in his threat to kill her. He was thrown out of the house, returned to his new lodging where he loaded a gun in front of his landlady and said he was going for a bit of sport. Five minutes later he was in Mrs Patrick's kitchen. A terrible struggle ensued, during which a shot rang out. A second shot was heard and Mrs Patrick fell out of the doorway into the street. She died instantly. Seeing what he had done, Atherton tried to cut his own throat, but only managed to make superficial wounds.

A date of 30 November was set for the execution, but after a failed appeal Wednesday, 8 December was set as the new date. Harry got to Durham at 3 p.m. on the Tuesday afternoon and made his way to the hotel opposite the prison. Willis was already waiting in the bar and as they enjoyed a quiet drink, they could overhear scraps of conversation from Atherton's father and sister-in-law who had just made their farewell visit. 'Abel told me he never did it,' they heard his father exclaim, as he produced some letters from his son in which he declared his innocence.

As Harry and Willis left the pub to make their way to the prison, they noticed that Atherton's father and his sister-in-law were standing in the road watching them, having guessed Harry's business. Having reported to the governor, they had received the necessary details about Atherton – height 5 feet 1 ½ inches, aged 30 and weighing 135 pounds – they were taken to their rooms.

Atherton retired at about 10.30 p.m. and slept well. He was woken at 5.30 a.m., washed and dressed in his own clothing, before the chaplain visited and gave him Holy Communion. After eating a fair breakfast, he was taken to a room close to the scaffold known as the doctor's room, where he was joined by the chaplain again, who offered comfort and prayer as the clock ticked slowly towards the appointed hour.

As the nearby factory hooters rang out the hour and broke the silence in the prison, Harry entered the cell. Atherton looked up and the awesomeness of the moment was reflected in his face. He was clearly terrified; Harry reassured him by gently tapping him on the shoulder, whispering quietly: 'Keep your pluck up, lad. I'll get it over as quick as possible.'

The condemned man appeared to take new heart at this and allowed the executioners to fasten his wrists and bare his neck. Atherton walked to the scaffold with no assistance, and even at the sight of the rope waiting for him, he never faltered. As Harry slipped the noose over his head, Atherton spoke in a feeble voice: 'Yer hangin' an innocent man!' Harry continued his task and put the white cap over his head, then, reaching to his left, he pulled the lever that launched Atherton into eternity.

There was one final execution in the diary, on 14 December, when Harry was assisted by his brother to help hang a former soldier who had murdered four people at their home in Nottingham. Samuel Atherley and Matilda Lambert had lived together for seven years and had three children. There had been frequent quarrels between them, however, and she had left home on several occasions. Atherley was a jealous man, believing that his brother-in-law had had an affair with his wife and was the father of the middle child. This led to further rows, which culminated in neighbours finding Atherley trying to stanch a throat wound and gesturing upstairs. There they found the bodies of his wife and three children; all had their throats cut, with the two youngest children, having first been battered with a hammer. The night before his execution, Atherley wrote to his brother that he was innocent of murder and had not known what he was doing at the time he committed the crime.

Signs that 1910 wasn't going to be a good year for Harry Pierrepoint may have been foreshadowed when he travelled to Dublin to hang Richard Hefferman on 4 January. The 27-year-old Hefferman had been convicted of the murder of Mary Walker at Mullingar. The two had been friends for a time and she had even helped him to find a job at the post office where she worked, but seemed unwilling to take their friendship further. She had failed to return home from work one night, however, and was found stabbed to death on a canal bank. Hefferman had aroused suspicion by telling his landlady he had seen a woman murdered. He was subsequently found to be in possession of a bloodstained knife.

Harry and Tom travelled by train to Holyhead to catch the boat across to Kingstown. Reaching Anglesey, the sole topic of conversation at the terminus was the dreadful murder at Holyhead on Christmas Day. Catching the night boat across, Harry was horrified to find that some bureaucratic error had resulted in his name being released to the crew as one of the passengers, and word spread like wildfire across the boat. While some stared at him as if he was some kind of desperate character, others tried to engage him in conversation. Finally, some of the crew on the steamer ushered him into a quiet part of the boat where he was able to enjoy the rest of the voyage undisturbed. His brother Tom's identity had not been revealed, so he was able to enjoy the crossing without any incident.

The two men entered the precincts of Kilmainham Prison without being challenged. The governor proudly showed the brothers around the prison and Harry noted that of the 38 prisons he had visited to date this was by far the cleanest and best kept. The scaffold was also immaculate.

Spying the prisoner taking exercise up and down a corridor close to his cell, Harry found him a distressed and nervous man, clearly scared of the fate that awaited him. Talking to warders, Harry learned that Hefferman had tried to rip out his throat with his hands, and also to fracture his skull by diving head first into a cell wall. He spent some of his time awaiting execution sedated in the prison hospital, and on two occasions had to be restrained when he attacked guards.

As they retired for the night, Harry spoke to his brother: 'We shall have to be very careful with him tomorrow, Tom, the man has a bad history inside, and I have a presentiment that something unusual is going to happen.' The foreboding was correct and something did happen which turned the execution into one of the most dramatic that Harry was ever involved with.

The brothers were visited by two priests before settling down for the night, shortly after they had administered the last rites to the prisoner in his cell. They chatted briefly before parting for the night. The scaffold at the gaol was constructed in a room built at the end of a narrow corridor leading from the condemned cell. Although it was only a few strides for the prisoner to take once he was in the corridor, and on the same level, the actual room itself was claustrophobically small, with barely 18 inches of floor around the large trapdoors for the hangmen, priests and official witnesses to occupy.

On the stroke of eight, Harry led Tom into the cell.

Hefferman was crying hysterically and repeatedly kissing a large cross held aloft by one of the priests, while another was reciting prayers over and over. Reluctant to interrupt the man at prayer, Harry held back a moment, but seeing that no efforts were being made to end the solemn gathering, he moved forward and quietly but expeditiously got his man strapped and into the corridor. The priests followed and kept up their exhortations, clinging to the prisoner and offering the cross for him to kiss as he struggled to walk the last few yards.

They managed to get Hefferman on the drop with his feet in the correct position. Both went to work, but when Tom stepped back Harry was unable to pull the lever as the priests were standing on the trapdoors, hugging the condemned man. They ignored Harry's call to stand clear and Hefferman started to sway in a faint. Signalling for Tom to steady the prisoner Harry used force to push the priests from the trap and, spying the drop was clear, he pushed the lever. The holy men stood looking down at the stilled rope for ten minutes more, reciting prayers for the departed man's soul.

Afterwards, Harry noted that a feeling of intense relief had come over him as he walked away, and later when recording his thoughts, he wondered how close he himself came to breaking down that morning. It is alleged that the brothers never received payment for the execution.

When Harry next put on his bowler hat and best suit to travel to an execution, it was to hang the man convicted of the horrible murder at Holyhead that had been the main source of conversation when he had sailed to Dublin in January.

William Murphy was a former soldier from Leigh, near Bolton, who had moved to Holyhead when he left the army. He lived with Gwen Ellen Jones, who was separated from her husband, and their two children. Unable to find work in

Wales, Murphy moved to Yorkshire, and while he was away she moved back with her former husband. When she refused to come to live with him he cut her throat and threw her into a ditch. He made a full confession to the crime, and his defence at his trial for murder would be that of insanity.

It failed and he was hanged at Caernarfon, becoming the last man to be executed in North Wales. He showed a rare courage on the morning of his execution. As Harry and Willis entered the cell, he stepped up onto a chair and then jumped back down.

'I suppose it will be like that?' he said to his executioners.

'Yes, as easy as that,' Harry replied, and with that Murphy walked cheerfully to the drop.

In the events leading to Harry's next engagement, Joseph Wren had walked into a police station in Burnley and confessed that he had just murdered a child. A police officer went to the spot Wren had indicated and found a boy's body – an attempt had been made to strangle him before his throat had been savagely cut. Wren's defence was insanity, but it proved useless. Harry and Ellis hanged him in Manchester on 22 February.

Although Harry still worked with Ellis on a regular basis, it seems that their relationship, which had been friendly to start with, had now cooled. Harry had always taken a drink, but as the money rolled in from his executions he began to spend more time away from home drinking with friends, or strangers, until the money or time had run out.

In March Harry carried out his 100th execution when he hanged former soldier George Henry Perry at Pentonville. Perry had stabbed to death his girlfriend after she had attended a wedding reception and not invited him.

Harry made his final appearance at Usk Gaol at the end of March, when he and Ellis hanged William Butler, a 62-year-old habitual criminal who had battered to death an old couple in their remote farmhouse during the course of a robbery. As the executioners left the gaol and walked back to the railway station they were approached by a small boy, one of a gang trailing behind a man on the other side of the road carrying a small bag.

'Do you know who that is?' the young boy asked as he walked alongside them.

'No,' replied Harry.

'Well,' the boy said with bated breath, as though imparting a dreadful secret, 'that is the executioner!'

The two men thanked him for that information, and walked on to catch their train, wondering if the crowd had dared to question their 'executioner' as he innocently went about his business.

Harry and Willis carried out another job at Wandsworth in May when they hanged Thomas William Jesshope, a former employee at the Camberwell Empire Music Hall. Jesshope had been sacked from his job as fireman at the music hall at the end of March for being drunk once too often, and a new man was employed instead. As his replacement was being shown how to lock up after his first night on duty, Jesshope appeared from his hiding place under some seats and stabbed to death John Healey, the carpenter and stage hand, who was showing him around the theatre. Jesshope had blamed Healey for his dismissal.

In June, Tom assisted at the execution of James Henry Hancock, a native of Sheffield, at Cambridge. Hancock had stabbed a friend after a drunken quarrel as they walked home from a public house.

The next month, Harry carried out two executions in three days. On 12 July, he travelled to Durham to hang Thomas Craig, who had killed the husband of his former sweetheart. She had left him while he was serving a prison sentence and moved away to live with her new husband. When Craig was released he tracked them down and shot them both with a revolver. She was hit twice but not seriously injured; her husband, hit three times, was killed instantly. Harry noted that Craig showed no fear at the prospect of his death and as he was noosed on the drop he didn't flinch or turn a hair.

On the following day Harry travelled down to Essex to execute Frederick Foreman, who was to be hanged at Chelmsford for the murder of his girlfriend at Wennington, near Grays. Foreman and Elizabeth Ely both worked in the fields on the farms around Grays, in Essex. They lived together in an old, disused railway carriage in a field at Wennington, from where, on the evening of 16 May, screams were heard. On the following morning, Foreman claimed he had found the body of his girlfriend by the side of a footpath that ran through the field. He told police they had argued on Monday night and that she had left him. Although receiving a fearful beating she had died from exposure. Evidence soon linked Foreman with the crime and he was charged with murder.

Harry turned up at the prison in good time on the afternoon before the execution, but it was clear he had had a drink. He met up with Ellis in the gatehouse of the prison, where it was reported that his conduct was very bad. The old rivalry between them, which had simmered for a time, finally reached boiling point. They came to blows and a warder was forced to come in, to try to break up the fight. Harry calmed down and was able to go about his business in a correct manner, working out a drop of 6 feet 8 inches from the prisoner's details. On the following morning, on the stroke of eight, Foreman was hanged (expeditiously, as the newspaper reporter recorded), and the hangmen left the prison later that morning.

No sooner had Ellis returned home than he penned a letter to the Home Office:

The Prison Commissioners
The Home Office
Whitehall
London
Gentlemen,

The governor of HM Prison Chelmsford engaged me to assist at the execution of F Fourman today.
So I arrived at about 3.30 p.m. yesterday. Tuesday, at about 3.45 p.m. Mr H. A. Pierrepoint the executioner, arrived drunk, and appeared on good terms with everyone. They sat him down and we passed the compliments of the day. When the gatekeeper asked him how he was, he stated he was in the pink, got up from his seat, came across and stood by the desk and said this pointing to me was one of the best of pals. We sat talking a few minutes, still the best of friends. The governor came into the room, so Mr Pierrepoint stated he would want the man's Age, Height, and Weight, the governor told him that the Chief Warder would give him any particulars he required, directly after the Chief Warder came in and was telling him the particulars he required. He appeared to be taking no notice what the Chief Warder was saying to him so I pulls a small book out, commences taking the particulars, which I honestly thought I had a right to do for further guidance. I have always book the Ages, Height and Weight down in a book since I assisted at my first execution in 1901.
Whilst I was booking them down, he commenced using the most disgusting language it has ever been my lot

to hear, I will not repeat it as it is not fit to be said, heard or spoken, then he threatened what he would do for me, made a rush at me, but the Chief Warder and Gatekeeper intervened and talked to him and he appeared to quieten down. Their duties caused them to leave the room, as soon as they had gone, he rushed at me, and knocked me off the chair I was sat on. I got up, but was again knocked off, he was going for me again when Warder Nash who had heard the noise came in, and attempted to stop him, but failed, so the blow caught me behind the ear, then he struck me again, behind the ear, in all he struck me four blows, which have caused me a lot of pain, and still troubling me, so the Chief said I had better go to my room which I was very pleased to do. He is the first person that has ever assaulted me in all my life. Never was a fighting man myself. If I cant agree with people I will not have anything to do with them. I assisted Mr Pierrepoint at the first execution he had which was at Shrewsbury on March 8th 1902 and up to yesterday we have never had a cross word. I have always given him the best advice possible, to take drink in moderation, and always turn up at the prisons sober, as when the public saw him drunk it always caused a lot of un-necessary talk, and it gave them the impression that he had to get drunk to do his work, and that they had a bad opinion of us all that are on the Home Office list, and we were the lowest of the low. The following officers are witnesses, Chief Warder Hale, Warder Gilding and Warder Nash.

I shall be very pleased if you will kindly take the matter up.

I am Gentlemen

Your Obedient Servant

John Ellis

And that was it. A report was sent to the Home Secretary detailing the conduct of the executioner and a letter was sent to the warders asking for their account. They concurred with Ellis's version and a week later an official memo was circulated.

195,461/2.
HOME OFFICE
WHITEHALL, S. W.2
2nd July, 1910
Confidential.

Sir,
I am directed by the Secretary of State to acquaint you that he has felt it his duty to order the name of H.A. Pierrepoint to be removed by the Prison Commissioners from the list of persons who have been found to be qualified to act as Executioners.

Mr. Churchill is informed that when Pierrepoint was last employed he arrived at the Prison on the day before the execution in a drunken and quarrelsome state, that he made use of bad language and assaulted his assistant.

He would therefore be glad if you would note that Pierrepoint should not be employed on any future occasion to act as Executioner.

I am,
Sir,
Your obedient servant,

E Blackwell

CHAPTER 4:
RIVALRY AND
CHANGING TIMES

Harry made no reference to the incident at Chelmsford Prison in any of the newspaper reminiscences of his work on the scaffold. Sixty-five years later his son Albert claimed he had no knowledge of why his father retired other than that it wasn't for any professional error. With what we know now about his conduct at Chelmsford, however, Harry must have put two and two together when his brother Tom received instruction that Leeds Prison had two men under sentence of death and was asked whether he was free to officiate as chief executioner.

Tom wrote to confirm his availability and by a strange twist of fate it was the Governor of Leeds Gaol who was left with the dilemma of recruiting an assistant executioner when there was no one available on the list. Since 1905 the only men carrying out executions had been Harry Pierrepoint and John Ellis as chief executioners and Tom Pierrepoint and William Willis as assistants. Up to that time Ellis had conducted just five executions as a number one, with the bulk of his work coming as Harry's assistant.

The problem was solved, as it had been the previous time, by inviting William Warbrick out of retirement. A letter was sent to his home at Bolton asking if he was able to 'carry out duties at Leeds on August 9th'. It had been arranged that a double execution would take place. Warbrick confirmed he was available, but by the time he got to Leeds to meet Tom Pierrepoint, one of the men had been reprieved. The man destined to be Tom's first 'customer' was a fellow Bradfordian, John Coulson, who had murdered his wife and young son; each had been almost decapitated with a carving knife. Tom carried out the execution without a hitch, calculating a drop of 6 feet 1 inch. Death was instantaneous.

A large crowd waited around outside the prison gates in the hope of seeing the executioner emerge, but Tom and Warbrick hit on a simple ruse to throw them off the scent. Arming themselves with small reporters' notebooks, they left the gaol by the front gate, holding the notebooks clearly in their hands as if they were members of the press who had witnessed the execution. To further support this guise they stopped a few feet away from the crowd and made as if to take notes on the event of the day. Satisfied that the two men who had just emerged were press and not the executioners, the crowd turned back to the front gate and waited for the hangmen to emerge.

Harry's indiscretion at Chelmsford had happened at a time when the country's newspapers had been full of the exciting chase across the Atlantic to bring Dr Crippen to justice for the poisoning of his wife. Crippen was finally arrested in Canada and convicted – the first time radiotelegraphy had been used in a murder investigation. The engagement went to John Ellis, now the undisputed number one executioner, assisted by William Willis. Crippen had tried to cheat the hangman by cutting his throat with a piece of his spectacles, but was thwarted.

Noah Woolf had been convicted of the murder of a man at a home for aged Hebrews in Holloway. He stabbed him to death after being dismissed from the home following a quarrel, and carried out the attack in revenge, blaming the victim for his plight. Woolf spent the first week of his time in the condemned cell adjacent to Crippen, one of three other men who were awaiting the gallows when Crippen was hanged. Two others were later reprieved and it was Woolf alone who faced hangman Ellis. Tom assisted, and Woolf, who was given a drop of 7 feet 9 inches, died instantly. Following Harry's dismissal, the Home Office had gone to work quickly recruiting new assistants. Curiously, two were from Ellis's home county, the other from Tom's home town of Bradford. Tom carried out his second job as chief executioner, again at Leeds, a few days after Christmas, when he dispatched Henry Ison who had battered to death his common-law wife with a poker following a drunken quarrel.

Although now receiving work as chief executioner, Tom found, as Ellis had a few years earlier once he had gained promotion, that most under-sheriffs preferred to use the most experienced man on the list. Thus, apart from a few county officials going against this, work only came along when the number one had accepted an engagement elsewhere.

Work was sporadic for Tom in 1911. There were two executions in May, when he assisted Ellis at the execution of Thomas Seymour at Liverpool, and Michael Collins at Pentonville. Neither produced any incident of note, nor did the next execution Tom assisted at that year, when Ellis hanged Frederick Thomas at Wandsworth.

In May 1911, Harry Pierrepoint decided to put pen to paper and find out once and for all whether his career was completely at an end.

> Prison Commissioners
> Whitehall
> 'Home Office'
> To the Home Secretary.

> Dear Sir.
> It is with deep regret that I am compelled to write and ask you to consider the following matter which I hope you will kindly consider.
> I have had my name on the Home Office list for about ten years, and for about the last five year's I held the then position of recognised Executioner. I have always been credited for the way I have carried out all executions and have not had a single error in any one of them. I have always been told by those on whose behalf I have been officiating that I should be recommended for the way I have carried out all executions.
> I have had nothing wrong with any 'Sheriff' or 'governor' of any prison or prison official.
> I have not been engaged for an execution since I carried out the one at Chelmsford Prison, on the 14th day of July last year when I had Ellis for my assistant and with whom I had a few words and he said at the time he would report me. It came to my notice that he had been showing correspondence concerning myself in a public house in Manchester, where he used to call nearly every Tuesday afternoon when in

Manchester. I was told by three different sources. Of course I took no notice on the first two occasions but when I was told by a most respectable friend who saw Ellis himself with the letter or postcard, I was quite convinced.

The greeting I got when I saw these three people was do you allow Ellis to show letters, he is trying to do you out of your work. I made as little of it before then as I could, but as soon as I saw Ellis at Chelmsford I accused him of it and he denied it, which I knew was a direct lie.

And of course I lost my temper with him. I was only defending my position. Whether he has reported me for it to Mr Metcalf, the 'Under Sheriff' or to the Prison Commissioners I don't know.

I would have reported him many times had I taken the trouble but I never did a man out of his work, under handed nor never will. I have strong reason to think he has been very under minding for a long time.

I have a wife and five young children to keep and I can assure you I have had a lot to bear. I should be pleased if you would communicate with the Rev. Benjamin Gregory of the Huddersfield Mission and inquire about me since I came to Huddersfield this last few months.

Trusting you will do your utmost to have me re-instated.

I am, Sir.

Your Obedient Servent

Henry Albert Pierrepoint

When he received no reply to his letter Harry knew that his indiscretion and violent attack had cost him the position he loved and the substantial income it brought with it.At the end of the year Tom was engaged as a number one, almost a year to the day from his last senior appointment, when he travelled to Stafford to hang George Loake, a retired engine driver who had stabbed to death his estranged wife at Walsall.

The trial of Frederick Seddon was one of the most sensational in the pre-war years. Seddon, a north-London insurance agent, had plotted to swindle his wealthy lodger out of her property. When the old lady died her relatives found that her will had recently been amended to leave all her possessions, a considerable sum, to the Seddons. Their suspicions caused them to inform Scotland Yard who, following an investigation, arranged for an exhumation. When traces of poison were found, Seddon and his wife were charged with murder. The trial showed that Seddon was an avaricious man who was driven by greed. The jury returned a verdict that found Mrs Seddon not guilty and Seddon alone was convicted. As Mr Justice Bucknill was about to pass sentence, Seddon made a Masonic sign, declaring to him before the Great Architect that he was innocent. The judge told him it was a painful thing to sentence a brother Mason, but he believed the verdict was the right one. As Tom travelled down to Pentonville, on 17 April 1912, to assist at the execution, the newspapers were full of news of the *Titanic*, which had sunk two days beforehand. The hangmen had arrived just as Seddon had received word from his solicitor that no reprieve would be granted and he accepted the news in a detached manner, being more upset when he later heard that items of his personal property sold that day had fetched a far smaller return than he envisaged.

When the execution party went to collect him in the morning, Seddon was sitting behind a table in his own clothes with a dejected look on his face. Ellis strapped his wrists behind his back, then left the prisoner in the care of his assistant while he hurried ahead to receive him when he reached the drop. As Tom walked slowly behind Seddon, who walked firmly flanked by warders, a coach-and-four was passing on the outside of the prison wall. Not realising the drama inside the prison walls, the coach driver blew a merry blast on a trumpet horn, its shrill sound echoing eerily down the corridor. As they turned the corner, Seddon saw Ellis waiting for him beside the noose hanging down from the heavy oak beam. The sight unnerved him and Tom had to gently encourage him forward the final few yards. Seddon closed his eyes for the last few paces and the hangmen carried out their last tasks with alacrity. The governor timed the execution at 25 seconds, a record time for an execution at Pentonville.

After assisting at an execution at Wandsworth in October, Tom carried out two executions as chief in the following month. On 5 November he hanged Robert Galloway, a sailor who had strangled a woman in Norfolk, at Norwich Prison. He was helped by one of the new assistants, George Brown. Three weeks later, Tom hanged Gilbert Smith at Gloucester Prison for the murder of his wife. Another of the new assistants, Albert Lumb, was his assistant on this job, and the two travelled together from Bradford to carry out the work. A month later he was the chief executioner at Wakefield, where William Galbraith was hanged for the murder of his wife.

1913 was a good year for Tom Pierrepoint. All the engagements he participated in were as chief executioner, bringing in a healthy income to the household. At the end of January, with Ellis engaged elsewhere, he went to Pentonville to hang Edward Hopwood, who had shot dead a woman in a taxi; two months later he hanged Edward Palmer, a boxer who had cut his wife's throat at her home in Bristol. It was the first execution at the city's Horfield Prison for almost 25 years, and a large crowd waited for a glimpse of the hangman, but Tom was able to slip away unnoticed. Further executions included visits to Dorchester, Newcastle and Cambridge, before Tom carried out an execution on New Year's Eve at Wakefield. The condemned man was George Law, a Sheffield engineer who had strangled his landlady. It was the second execution Tom had carried out at the gaol that year, and on both occasions he was assisted by Lumb.

In contrast to the previous year, 1914 was quiet for Tom. His first four engagements – at Stafford, Winchester and Lewes – were all as assistant to Ellis. In fact, Tom actually assisted at the last two executions to take place at Lewes. In the first, Herbert Booker was hanged for the murder of a woman on a train at Three Bridges, Crawley. Both of them had been wearing Liverpool Football Club rosettes, having just watched their team lose in the FA Cup Final at Crystal Palace, and after a drunken quarrel he had cut her throat, before repeatedly stabbing her. In November, Tom carried out his first execution at Shepton Mallet: Henry Quartley was a builder hanged for the murder of Henry Pugsley, whom he had blasted to death with a shotgun.

The first half of 1915 was a bleak time for the hangmen. Neither Tom nor Ellis carried out any executions in the first six months of the year and when Tom did receive an engagement it was, for the first time in his career, to hang someone who had been sentenced to death for an offence other than murder. Robert Rosenthal was a 23-year-old German-American who had been convicted of treason at Middlesex. He had been arrested on board ship from Newcastle to Copenhagen just as it left British territory, on his way to pass secrets of naval formations to his German contacts. The trial was held 'in camera' (in secret) so that the enemy did not know of his arrest and conviction.

Tom executed Rosenthal at Wandsworth Gaol on 15 July, just nine days after sentencing, aided by a new assistant Robert Baxter. Rosenthal was the only spy to be hanged during the First World War, though eleven more spies were shot dead at the Tower. Rosenthal was hanged and not shot because, unlike the other prisoners, a civilian court and not a military one had tried him.

The year did pick up for Tom at the end of December, when he hanged two men a week apart at Wakefield. On 22 December he hanged Harry Thompson, who had murdered a soldier's wife at Huddersfield, and, a week later, John McCartney, who had cut the throat of a woman he had bigamously married. After just nine years Wakefield, despite having a purpose-built gallows, now ceased as a place of execution.

Tom carried out no executions in 1916. The only appointment in his diary, a job at Leeds, was cancelled when the condemned man was reprieved a week before he was due to die. The name of Pierrepoint did feature regularly throughout the year, however, as the first of Harry's newspaper serialisations appeared in the weekly news. Harry had been working at Huddersfield gasworks following his dismissal from the list. Shortly after the newspaper account of his memoirs began its six-month run in July 1916, Harry was able to move his family to a new house on Mill Street, Failsworth, Manchester. He stayed at the gasworks while his wife left her job in a munitions factory to look after the young family. The fees from the newspaper accounts afforded them the small luxury of Mrs Pierrepoint not having to find work urgently.

Tom was not much busier in 1917 than he had been in the previous year. At the end of March he travelled to Leeds to hang John Thompson, a shepherd who had cut the throat of a teenage girl at Beverley, and a month later he was back at Leeds, where Robert Gadsby paid the ultimate penalty for cutting the throat of his paramour. A week before Christmas, Tom hanged William Cavanagh at Newcastle; Cavanagh had stabbed a sailor following a brawl.

The armistice had been signed, and the First World War brought to an end, before Tom was next in action. John Walsh was a collier who had strangled his sweetheart at Wakefield. Walsh was hanged at Leeds a week before Christmas 1918, having been convicted at West Yorkshire Assizes, one of four men sentenced to death that winter.

Tom hanged three people in two days in early January 1919. On 7 January, Ben Benson walked calmly to the gallows to pay the price for the murder of his girlfriend. He had cut her throat after catching her in bed with a lover when he had arrived home unannounced from the war. Baxter was Tom's assistant. In August 1918 a brutal robbery had taken place at a Pontefract jeweller's shop. The shopkeeper was battered about the head and died on the following day. Four days later two young deserters were arrested in London while selling rings in an East End public house. Some of the rings still had blood-splattered price tickets attached to them. Percy Barrett and George Cardwell each blamed the other for the attack but were both deemed equally guilty in the eyes of the law and they were hanged together.

A number of cancelled executions meant Tom had to wait almost a year to the day before he was next in action. Lewis Massey had been convicted at Leeds Assizes in December 1919 for the murder of his wife. They had separated and despite his repeated requests she would not have him back. He finally lost patience with her refusing to come back, discovered where she was living and beat her to death. Willis was the assistant and the execution at Leeds passed off without incident.

At Lincoln, on Tom's second hanging of the year he was again assisted by Willis. William Wright, a tailor, was convicted of the murder of his pregnant girlfriend, who was found strangled at her cottage. Wright confessed he had throttled her following a quarrel over a brooch he claimed had been given to her by another man.

In April 1920, Tom and Edward Taylor travelled to Leeds, where they hanged Miles McHugh, who had cut the throat of his girlfriend following a jealous quarrel. Three weeks later there was another execution at Leeds, where Thomas Hargreaves Wilson was hanged for the murder of his wife.

Tom and Edward Taylor headed for Durham Gaol on 30 November 1920. James Riley, a miner, had been convicted of the murder of his wife at West Auckland. He was hanged despite a petition for reprieve signed by over thirty-two thousand people.

The busiest day in the bloody history of capital punishment was 30 December 1920, when three executions took place on the same day. Ellis was engaged at Birmingham, Willis carried out his first senior execution at Pentonville, while Tom was on duty at Leeds to deal with Edwin Sowerby, who had been sentenced to death at Leeds Assizes for the murder of his former girlfriend after she had broken off their relationship.

1921 was only a week old when Tom was at Maidstone, where former Sergeant Major George Lever was hanged for cutting his wife's throat.

In August 1920, two men and a young girl were seen walking in the direction of the Crumbles, a stretch of beach between Eastbourne and Pevensey Bay. On the following day the body of a young woman was found partially buried in shingle. She had been battered to death. The body was later identified as that of Irene Munro, a London typist who was holidaying alone in the area. Two men who had been seen with her shortly before her death were soon traced. They claimed to have an alibi, but were convicted at the Old Bailey, before Mr Justice Avory, and sentenced to death.

At their appeal the two men changed their stories – each now blamed the other for the murder. It did them no good: 19-year-old Jack Fields, and William Gray, ten years his senior, were hanged side by side, having come face to face with each other as they met up in the corridor seconds before they were led to their deaths.

On 7 June, Tom and Robert Baxter carried out the execution of three men at Dublin. At 7 a.m. they hanged

Patrick Maher and Edmund Foley, who had been convicted of the murder of a police sergeant during an attempted rescue of prisoners in 1919. An hour later they hanged William Mitchell, who had shot dead a justice of the peace during a robbery. Anxious to keep Tom's identity secret, as Ireland was going through a politically volatile period, the newspaper announced the name of the hangman as Mr Harte.

It was to be the spring of 1922 before Tom was next in action, carrying out another execution at Durham. The condemned man, James Williamson, was another wife killer who had dispatched his spouse with a cutthroat razor following a quarrel. It was an extremely violent murder, the victim's head almost being severed.

Tom's only other execution in 1922 was at Lincoln Gaol, where he carried out a double execution. George Robinson and Frank Fowler, two farm labourers, had been convicted at Lincolnshire Assizes of separate offences, but it was decided they would hang together, for convenience. Robinson had killed his young girlfriend after she jilted him, while Fowler shot dead a bride of three days, against whom he bore a jealous grudge.

In the summer of 1922, *Reynolds News* ran a series entitled 'Ten Years as Hangman' by Harry Pierrepoint. It was basically a rehash of the *Thompson News* series from six years earlier, but often contradicted statements made in the former. In a cheap notebook purchased for him by his son, Harry also set down his life story under the title of 'My Life Story as Public Executioner': 'Now that the bonds of secrecy are released through relinquishing my post as Public Executioner I now take up my pen to write the details of my executions, and travels as Executioner...'

The pages of the exercise book retold his adventures and

tales of the famous people he dealt with, in no sort of chronological order and in no real details not already recorded in the newspaper accounts. However, it ended with the poignant paragraph:

> Now as I lay my pen aside after recounting my memoirs, I ask myself what did I think of my past as an Executioner? Well in the first place I was very ambitious, for the duty, I also loved my work on the scaffold my mind was fixed on my duties. It was my whole desire to become an expert official which I did through my own energies. Now had my time to come back again I should rather settle into some civil business. Which is not only more pleasant but is looked upon with more respect. Now that I have told the truth in all my series which cannot be denied I close with the hope that I may spend the future in quiet and peaceful ending.

Harry Pierrepoint died on 14 December 1922, the day after Tom returned from Lincoln. He was 48 years old and had been suffering from a terminal illness for several years. His last words in any newspaper were a comment on the inconsistency of reprieves – they were prompted by the reprieve earlier that summer of well-to-do Ronald True, who had murdered a prostitute and was sentenced to death in the same week that 18-year-old Henry Jacoby was sentenced to death for the murder of a wealthy widow in the hotel where he worked. True, who had influential friends, was deemed insane and sent to Broadmoor, while Jacoby, a poor boy with no money or friends of influence, went to the gallows at Pentonville. Harry had also commented on the upcoming trial surrounding the Ilford murders.

In January 1923, two executions took place in London that were the culmination of a murder trial which had filled the headlines since it ended in the convictions of Edith Thompson and her young lover Frederick Bywaters, for the murder of her husband – the Ilford murder. The original dates scheduled coincided with a prior engagement Tom had at Leeds Prison and he therefore had to turn down the offer to execute Bywaters at Pentonville. Following the appeal of both the Leeds killer and Bywaters, the revised dates of execution meant that Tom would have been free to carry out the execution of Bywaters, but the offer had since gone to Willis.

Instead, assisted by the recently appointed assistant Tom Phillips, Tom carried out the execution of Lee Doon, a Chinese laundryman who had battered to death his boss in Sheffield, and then concealed his body in a trunk. He was arrested when a neighbour spotted him dragging the heavy trunk into a garden where he had planned to bury it.

Four days leter Tom Phillips assisted Ellis at the execution of Edith Thompson, who was dragged screaming and fainting to the gallows, while Tom went about his carrier business at home in Bradford, no doubt rueing the missed fee.

Two executions at Durham were the only dates in the diary over spring and summer. A blacksmith who had shot dead his son-in-law was hanged in April, and an African sailor who had shot dead a married woman at South Shields. On both executions he was assisted by recent recruit Robert Wilson.

On 12 December, Tom travelled to Dublin to carry out a double execution, and three days later he carried out a single execution. Unlike the previous visit to Dublin's Mountjoy Gaol, none of these three executions were political – rather, they were prompted by a mixture of greed, revenge and jealousy.

When Tom carried out the execution of Matthew Nunn at Durham in January 1924, there was reportedly a terrible incident on the scaffold when the rope was alleged to have snapped as the trap was sprung. Charles Duff, in *The Handbook of Hanging*, claimed that the prisoner hit the pit floor bound hand and foot, and after a new rope was secured a second, successful execution took place. There is no discernible record of this being true – no word of it appeared in the press – and given the purpose of Duff's book (to support a campaign to abolish the death penalty) it must be treated with some scepticism. There was no such incident when Tom returned to Dublin to hang Jeremiah Gaffney, who had shot dead a man in Kerry.

Due probably to illness and stress, John Ellis tendered his resignation in March 1924 and thereafter Tom began to receive a larger share of work. Willis received promotion to replace Ellis and, in August, Baxter was also promoted to Chief Executioner. Baxter's first job as a chief was to hang Jacques Vaquier, who had poisoned a love rival, an execution that has often been mistakenly credited to Tom.

One afternoon in late August, Tom was having tea at home with his nephew Albert when he read in the paper that John Ellis, some six months retired, had tried to commit suicide, having first tried to kill his wife and family. 'He should have done it bloody years ago,' Tom said crudely. 'It was impossible to work with him!'

One of the most notorious murder cases in the between-the-war years concerned the murder of Emily Kaye by Patrick Mahon at Eastbourne. Mahon's wife had triggered off the murder investigation after she was rummaging through his pockets and found a ticket for a left-luggage locker at Waterloo Station. Suspecting he may be having an affair, she asked a neighbour, a former policeman, to check what was

Henry 'Harry' Pierrepoint (1874–1922), demonstrating the restraining strap he designed to pinion William Hancocks, a one-armed man, hanged at Knutsford in 1905.

Top: Newgate Gaol, 1901. In March, Harry arrived here for training as an executioner.

Bottom: Pentonville prison. In September 1902, Harry, as assistant to William Billington, carried out the first execution here using the giant wooden beams that had previously been in place at Newgate.

EXECUTIONS.—TABLE OF DROPS (October, 1913).

The length of the drop may usually be calculated by dividing 1,000 foot-pounds by the weight of the culprit and his clothing in pounds, which will give the length of the drop in feet, but no drop should exceed 8 feet 6 inches. Thus a person weighing 150 pounds in his clothing will require a drop of 1,000 divided by 150=6⅔ feet, *i.e.*, 6 feet 8 inches. The following table is calculated on this basis up to the weight of 200 pounds :—

TABLE OF DROPS.

Weight of the Prisoner in his Clothes.	Length of the Drop.		Weight of the Prisoner in his Clothes.	Length of the Drop.		Weight of the Prisoner in his Clothes.	Length of the Drop.	
lbs.	ft.	ins.	lbs.	ft.	ins.	lbs.	ft.	ins.
118 and under	8	6	138 and under	7	3	167 and under	6	0
119 ,,	8	5	140 ,,	7	2	169 ,,	5	11
120 ,,	8	4	141 ,,	7	1	171 ,,	5	10
121 ,,	8	3	143 ,,	7	0	174 ,,	5	9
122 ,,	8	2	145 ,,	6	11	176 ,,	5	8
124 ,,	8	1	146 ,,	6	10	179 ,,	5	7
125 ,,	8	0	148 ,,	6	9	182 ,,	5	6
126 ,,	7	11	150 ,,	6	8	185 ,,	5	5
128 ,,	7	10	152 ,,	6	7	188 ,,	5	4
129 ,,	7	9	154 ,,	6	6	190 ,,	5	3
130 ,,	7	8	156 ,,	6	5	194 ,,	5	2
132 ,,	7	7	158 ,,	6	4	197 ,,	5	1
133 ,,	7	6	160 ,,	6	3	200 ,,	5	0
135 ,,	7	5	162 ,,	6	2			
136 ,,	7	4	164 ,,	6	1			

When for any special reason, such as a diseased condition of the neck of the culprit, the Governor and Medical Officer think that there should be a departure from this table, they may inform the executioner, and advise him as to the length of the drop which should be given in that particular case.

Table of Drops. Despite an official table of drops being provided, the hangman still had to rely on experience to ensure a 'perfect execution'.

William Murphy, the last man to be hanged in North Wales, at Caernarfon in 1910. As Harry entered his cell, the cheerful Murphy stepped up onto a chair and then jumped back down. 'I suppose it will be like that?' he said to his executioner. 'Yes, as easy as that,' Harry replied.

Top: Tom Pierrepoint (1870–1954), Harry's older brother served as a hangman for forty years, the longest serving of the family dynasty.

Bottom: Town End, Clayton. Here young Albert Pierrepoint spent his summer holidays; where Harry trained his brother to become a hangman; and where later Tom would teach friends who accompanied him as assistants to Ireland.

Top left: John Ellis. For a time, Harry Pierrepoint and assistant Ellis were the only men on the list of the country's executioners.

Top right: Frederick Seddon, who after a sensational trial was convicted of murdering his lodger by poisoning, and at whose execution in April 1912 Tom assisted.

Bottom left: Robert Baxter, Tom Pierrepoint's assistant at many executions and later a rival for the role of chief.

Bottom right: Patrick Mahon, found guilty in 1924 of murdering his pregnant lover, tried unsuccessfully to cheat the hangman by jumping as the trapdoor lever was pulled.

Right: Ethel Major, who went to the gallows in December 1934 for poisoning her husband with strychnine. Her execution was Albert Pierrepoint's first experience, assisting his uncle Tom in the execution of a woman. Her ghost is reported still to haunt Hull prison.

Left: Max Haslam, the victim of a crippling childhood disease, stood less than five feet tall, was a habitual criminal and was hanged by Tom and Albert in 1937 for the murder of a wealthy widow. Police also found the body of her pet dog suspended from the headboard in her bedroom.

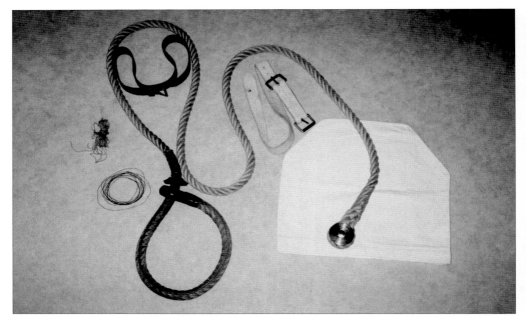

Top: The tools of the hangman's trade: rope, leg and arm straps, white hood and twine.

Bottom left: The rope was suspended by chain from the heavy oak beams. This is a view of the execution chamber at Wandsworth prison.

Bottom right: The night before a scheduled hanging, the rope was stretched by suspending a weight equivalent to that of the condemned, to reduce the chance of it stretching and thus giving the condemned a longer drop than intended.

being stored at the left-luggage office. He presented the ticket and found it related to a Gladstone bag, which contained bloodstained clothing, a kitchen knife and a tennis-racquet case marked with the initials E.B.K. The neighbour informed Scotland Yard, who posted a man to question Mahon when he came to collect it, and on 2 May, as Mahon handed over the ticket, he was approached by detectives and asked to account for the contents of the bag.

After sitting silently in Kennington police station under the watchful gaze of Chief Inspector Savage, Mahon finally revealed that the bloodstained clothing belonged to 38-year-old Emily Beilby Kaye, a woman with whom he had been having an adulterous relationship. He claimed that while they were staying at a cottage at Eastbourne, on 11 April, she had fallen and struck her head on the hearth, receiving fatal injuries. Fearing the repercussions on his home life if he reported the accident, he had decided to dismember the body and dispose of the dissected body parts. Police hurried to the house, situated on the Crumbles, a stone's throw from where the body of Irene Munro had been discovered a few years earlier, and discovered the dismembered corpse in a trunk, with saucepans on the stove filled with boiled body parts.

A postmortem found that Kaye had been pregnant when she died, suggesting a motive for murder. Mahon denied committing murder and his trial in July lasted five days. As he was giving evidence on the final day, describing how he had dissected the body, a terrific thunderstorm broke outside the courtroom, and a lightning flash lit up the sombre courtroom. The accused turned a ghastly shade of white.

Tom arrived at Wandsworth Gaol on the afternoon of Tuesday, 2 September, and was given the details of the condemned man. Mahon weighed 141 pounds, stood just short of six feet tall and was to be allotted a drop of 7 feet 8 inches. Observing him in the condemned cell, Tom saw that he seemed quite composed – in contrast to the first time he had been brought into the cell, when he had had to be carried along the corridor before collapsing on his bunk crying and moaning. During his stay in the shadow of the gallows he lost 9 pounds, as he was unable to eat most of his meals. Mahon appeared to have some knowledge of the execution procedure, for as he was placed on the drop and the noose positioned, he sensed the hangman was reaching for the lever and jumped with bound feet as the floor beneath him collapsed. It was alleged he jerked backwards and struck his back on the edge of the scaffold. Although Tom later told his nephew of this incident, there is no record of it in assistant William Willis's account of the execution. Coroner Sir Bernard Spilsbury also made no record of any other bruises on the body when he performed the autopsy later that morning, although it was noted that the neck had been broken in two places, which was unusual in a standard execution.

The year 1925 was relatively busy, with 18 executions carried out in Great Britain and Ireland, including three double executions. Tom was responsible for 11 of them; the rest were split between Willis and Baxter. At a double execution at Durham on 15 April, one of the condemned men sang loudly as he walked to the drop. The governor of Durham Gaol, fearful that there may be trouble, had requested that the four executioners be employed, a practice that soon became standard procedure.

On 5 August, Tom was in Ireland to carry out two executions at Dublin on the same morning. At 8 a.m., 24-year-old Michael Talbot walked to the gallows in the men's prison at Mountjoy, for the murder of Edward Walsh, the husband of Annie Walsh, his aunt, and with whom he had been having an affair. Walsh was murdered in his bed, allegedly for the insurance money. Mrs Walsh blamed her nephew for the killing; he later confessed to the crime, but said that he had committed it in league with her. Both were convicted and 90 minutes after her lover walked to the gallows, Annie Walsh was hanged in the women's prison, spending her last hour crying and praying.

Tom was accompanied by a friend from Bradford, whom he had trained up in the same stable his brother had trained him in 20 years before. Such was the rivalry between the executioners that Tom, who was at liberty to appoint his own assistant, didn't want to bring anyone off the official list whose names would then be recorded in official circles and who could potentially take job offers that would otherwise have gone to him. The unnamed assistant went under the name of Robinson, and on subsequent trips to Ireland, over the next six or seven years, the persons who accompanied Tom changed from time to time but always signed in as Robinson.

There were twenty executions in 1926, eleven of which were carried out by Tom. His work involved three trips to Ireland, and was to mark the first time he hanged a woman in an English prison.

Louie Calvert was a 33-year-old part-time prostitute and petty thief. In the spring of 1925, she moved in with Arthur Calvert, who was unaware of her past. After telling him she had fallen pregnant, Calvert persuaded him to marry her. As autumn approached she left her home in Leeds and travelled to Dewsbury; she had told her husband that she would stay under the care of her sister until the child was born. No sooner had she arrived in Dewsbury than she went back to earning money as a prostitute, finding lodgings with Lily Waterhouse, an old lady she had known previously. She then placed an advertisement offering to take in a child for adoption, which she hoped to then return back to Leeds with and show off as her newborn baby. She was soon contacted and took into her care a baby girl.

The plan may have worked had she not fallen back into her old thieving ways. Her landlady noticed items of her own property missing and reported it to the police, who advised her to take out a summons. When Calvert failed to turn up in court, officers went to her house and found the landlady battered and strangled in a bedroom. A letter in the house was addressed to Louie Calvert in Leeds and, aware that she was the subject of the summons, the police travelled to her home, where they discovered items belonging to the murdered woman. Mrs Calvert, when she opened the door to the police, was wearing her landlady's clothes and boots.

Asked at her trial if she had anything to say before sentence of death was passed, Calvert replied: 'Yes sir, I am pregnant!' Medical examinations later established that this wasn't the case and Calvert's execution went ahead as scheduled. Although the sentence was to be carried out at Manchester's Strangeways Prison, whose regular hangman was William Willis, the job went to Tom, with Willis being nominated as assistant – presumably because she was convicted at Leeds and it was the under-sheriff of Yorkshire who appointed the hangman. The national strike was in full flow at the time, causing a lack of newspapers, and so, in contrast to the case of almost every other woman executed in the twentieth century, Louie Calvert went to the gallows with barely a murmur from the general public.

Whether Willis raised any objection to what could be construed as a demotion for the execution is unclear, but in any case his behaviour was beginning to cause concern among prison officials. Three days following Mrs Calvert's execution, he was again only employed as an assistant, this time to Robert Baxter, a man whom he claimed almost ten years' seniority on. His conduct was recorded as aggressive, irritable and full of self-importance. When he failed to secure the leg strap on the condemned man satisfactorily tightly, he was dismissed.

The nine executions carried out in 1927 were split fairly between Tom and Baxter, with four each in Great Britain. Tom gained an extra 10 guineas fee when he carried out the last execution of the year at Dublin, hanging 19-year-old William O'Neill, who had carried out a brutal murder in County Wicklow.

1928 got off to a record start and brought in a healthy sum to the pockets of both Tom and Baxter. They each carried out five executions in the first month. Tom carried out four in five days, travelling to Manchester, Lincoln and then, after a day at home, up to Durham. By now the government was becoming increasingly reticent about releasing information relating to executions, and when the inquest jury asked after the execution how long had elapsed from the hangman entering the cell to the execution being carried out, they were informed by the prison governor that he was not permitted to disclose that information. Both the Manchester and Durham engagements had originally been to carry out double executions. Leaving Durham, Tom travelled down to Leeds, where he hanged a Sheffield miner who had strangled the woman he was having an affair with.

On 31 January, Tom carried out the execution of James Power, a former policeman who had impersonated a detective before raping and murdering a young woman by throwing her into a canal, where she drowned. Power was hanged at Birmingham's Winson Green Gaol, which overlooked the canal bank where he committed his crime.

Probably the most famous name to enter Tom's diary of engagements this year was that of Patrick Kennedy, who – along with his accomplice, Frederick Browne – had been convicted of the murder of PC George Gutteridge, shot dead on a quiet country lane in Essex. Kennedy, allegedly a former member of the IRA, was a petty thief who regularly teamed up with Browne, the owner of a garage that specialised in dealing with stolen cars. They had been stopped as they drove a stolen car down the Ongar to Romford road and, fearful that the policeman's eyes might hold their reflection after they had shot him dead, they blasted him in both eyes.

Tom hanged Kennedy at Wandsworth at the same moment Baxter hanged Browne at Pentonville. Although both Tom and Baxter were receiving a fair share of executions, they were both warned that 'touting for business' – offering to carry out an execution rather than wait to be asked – was contrary to their terms of engagement and could lead to dismissal. It had become a clear divide of work: Tom received engagements predominantly in the north; Baxter, a resident of Hertfordshire, carried out most of the work in London and the south. In January, Tom had had to reject the offer to hang a man at Glasgow, as it clashed with the Lincoln engagement, and as his diary was full on dates either side, he reluctantly had to turn it down. In shades of what happened in 1923, when he lost out on the Bywaters execution, Tom again found himself sitting at home while the Glasgow job was passed to Baxter. Perhaps even more galling was the fact that two other men were later condemned in Scotland that year and Baxter, well-respected and capable as he was, received the call to carry out those jobs too.

Tom made the by-now familiar round of northern gaols in 1929, with executions at Durham, Liverpool, Manchester and Leeds, plus the seemingly perennial trip across to Ireland. The year was also to see the start of a debate that raged in Parliament for the next 18 months, and which threatened to hinder seriously the hangman's earning potential.

CHAPTER 5:
OUR ALBERT AND UNCLE TOM

With the dawn of the new decade came the first major referendum on capital punishment in modern times. The debate, which had started at the end of the previous decade, filled the papers for weeks and was split between those wanting to keep it as a deterrent while not simply keeping it for retribution, and those advocating total abolition. Recent cases were reviewed to support both sides of the debate, and for a while Labour Home Secretary J. R. Clynes sanctioned a large number of reprieves. Clynes was the first home secretary in modern times to be an abolitionist. At the end of the report the committee recommended that the death penalty should be suspended for a trial period of five years. The Conservative members of the committee refused to sign the report, however, and the government's failure to bring in any amended legislation effectively defeated it.

In February 1930, Tom gave an interview to the *Yorkshire Observer* and the reporter was able to glean a couple of quotes from the normally reticent and secretive executioner.

Describing Tom as 60 years of age, but looking younger and in excellent health, the reporter caught up with him at Haley's Foundry, where he had recently started work.

'Why should a murderer be nursed for the rest of his life?' Tom said, demonstrating his advocacy of the retention of capital punishment. 'I think it would be encouraging people to murder if the death penalty were abolished, but it would make no difference to me either way.'

In fact, the last sentence was clearly contrary to his way of thinking, and to his financial demands. He was known to be quite vocal in his annoyance when a date in his diary was crossed out. 'There'll come a day when they'll all get a bloody reprieve,' he had mumbled angrily to his nephew in the previous year. Money was clearly an overriding factor to Tom, as he made clear in the final quote in the article: 'I am quite prepared to give evidence before the Select Committee if they should ask me,' he told the reporter, adding as an afterthought, 'providing, of course, if they made it worth my while.'

For Tom's first execution of the new decade he travelled across to Belfast to execute Samuel William Cushnan, a 26-year-old farm labourer. Cushnan had been sentenced to death on 9 March, at Antrim Assizes, for the murder of a postman who had been found shot dead in May 1929, with his post-bag, containing over £60, plundered. Convicted largely on circumstantial evidence, Cushnan had betrayed himself while on remand, describing in a letter how a fellow prisoner was going to help him dispose of the stolen money. The jury failed to reach a verdict at his first trial, while at the second trial he was sentenced to death twice over! When the initial death sentence was passed, it was announced that Cushnan was to be 'hanged on April 8th 1929'. The prisoner was taken down from the dock before a court official noticed the mistake with the fateful date. He was then brought back into court and re-sentenced. An appeal for a reprieve on the grounds of mental anguish was quickly dismissed and he was hanged at Crumlin Road, Belfast.

Over in England, at the same moment Cushnan walked firmly to his death, Sydney Fox, the notorious Margate matricide murderer, was being dragged kicking and screaming to the gallows, where he was hanged by Robert Baxter.

There were just two further executions in 1930 – at Wandsworth and Winchester – both carried out by Tom; another six dates in the diary came to nothing while the parliamentary debate raged on. At Winchester he hanged William Podmore, convicted on circumstantial evidence of the murder of a Southampton garage owner. He declared his innocence throughout and moves were made to secure a reprieve right up to the last moment.

1931

In March 1931, Tom travelled down to Bedford to hang Alfred Arthur Rouse, a bigamist who had committed a brutal murder and then left the body in a burning car in the hope of starting a new life. Known as the Blazing Car Murderer, Rouse was a travelling salesman, convicted of the murder of an unknown man whose body was found inside the burnt-out car at Hardingstone, Northamptonshire. On 5 November 1930, two young men spoke to a man as he passed them walking away from a blaze, which they assumed was a bonfire. As they approached, they discovered that it was a burning car. Fire officers were called and when the blaze was extinguished they found the charred remains of a man on the front seat. Despite the car being a charred shell, the number plate was hardly damaged and the car was quickly traced to Rouse, who lived in north London.

He had already left London and travelled to Wales to be

with a girlfriend when police named him in the newspapers and, under pressure from her parents, he returned home to answer questions. Rouse said that he was giving a hitchhiker a lift to Leicester when they had run out of fuel. He asked the passenger to fill the tank from a spare can of fuel in the boot while he went to relieve himself in the bushes. This he did while smoking a cigar Rouse had given him. Rouse said as he had walked a little way down the road he saw the car suddenly explode into flames. He panicked and fled, but not before realising that this accident had given him a chance to lose his identity and free himself of his many debts and tangled love life. He then fled to his mistress in South Wales.

He maintained throughout his trial that the fire was an accident, but on 31 January he was convicted after evidence emerged that suggested the car had been tampered with. His wife stood by him throughout the trial, believing his pleas of innocence. It was known, but not revealed in court, that Mrs Rouse knew of the plan to commit murder so they could both benefit from a £1,000 insurance policy. Rouse was the third of eight men Tom executed that year.

On 16 April, Tom carried out an execution at Manchester. Three days later, without his knowledge, his nephew came home from work and sat down to pen a letter to the Home Secretary.

The Prison Commissioners
Home Office, London
19.4.1931

Dear Sir,
I beg to offer you my services as an Assistant
Executioner to my uncle T.W. Pierrepoint at any
time he or any other retire from their position. My

age is 26 and I am strong in health and build
during the last few years I have thoroughly
studied out the carrying out of an execution and
the Calculating of drops etc. learned from the
diary of my late father Mr H.A. Pierrepoint.Hoping
this letter will meet your kind approval
I am dear Sir,
Your obedient servant
Albert Pierrepoint
41, Mill Street
Failsworth
Manchester

Within days he received a reply. Tearing open the slim brown
envelope he read that the sender was directed to inform him
there were no vacancies at the moment.

Albert was the middle child of Harry and Mary
Pierrepoint. Born on 30 March 1905 at Clayton, Bradford, he
attended Beaumont Street School at Huddersfield after the
family moved from Bradford when Harry ended his career as
an executioner in 1910. During a lesson in his class, the
children were asked what they wanted to do upon leaving
school. The 11-year-old Albert wrote: 'When I leave school I
should like to be the Official Executioner...'

Throughout his early years he spent his summer holidays
with his Uncle Tom and Aunt Lizzie at Clayton, and their
closeness increased when Albert's father passed away.
Although Tom was unwilling to discuss his role as an
executioner in front of the family, Aunt Lizzie was far more
talkative and when her husband was away on an execution
she invited Albert to read through the diary that he kept in
the lounge. In the winter of 1917 the family moved to
Failsworth, Manchester, where Albert attended the Holy

Trinity School. In those days it was possible for children at the age of 12 ½ to work half-time at the local cotton mills. On 30 September, Albert reached the required age and was able to start work at the nearby Marlborough Mills, where a week's shift from six in the morning until fifteen minutes to noon brought home the princely sum of six shillings a week. He handed the money to his mother, who returned to him the going rate of one penny in the shilling.

Following the death of his father, Albert, as the eldest son, took possession of his papers and diary, which he studied at length over the next few years. He continued working in the mills until a change of career at the end of the 1920s, when using his experience and love of horses he gained a position at a wholesale grocer's. Working as a horse drayman he delivered the goods that the travelling salesman had taken orders for. By 1930 he was trained to drive a car and a lorry and was earning a weekly wage of two pounds five shillings. Six months after he had received the rejection to his application as assistant hangman, another letter was sent to the house on Mill Street.

There were always at least six names retained on the short list of approved executioners from which the governors and under-sheriffs selected hangmen and assistants.

In the autumn of 1931 a vacancy arose when Lionel Mann, an assistant of five years and the veteran of a dozen executions, offered his resignation. His full-time employers had told Mann that his work on the scaffold was holding back any chance of promotion. In the late autumn, Albert came home from a long day delivering groceries to find an official letter waiting on the mantelshelf. Having seen scores of these same long, OHMS-stamped, buff envelopes during her husband's tenure as chief executioner, Mary Pierrepoint realised what she had always suspected yet hoped against.Mary confronted Albert when he sat down to read the letter. She was concerned that Albert wanted to follow in his father's footsteps. For a dozen years she had watched her eldest study his father's papers and, as he was the nephew of the country's chief executioner, it was no surprise to her. But still, it was something she wasn't happy to accept.

At 3 p.m. on the first Saturday in December 1931, Albert stood on the corner of Southall Street and surveyed the entrance to Manchester's Strangeways Prison. He knew that behind the high, sombre brick walls, waiting in two condemned cells, were local men Solomon Stein and Peter McVay whose crimes had been thoroughly reported in the local press and whose court appearances had made the headlines across the country when both, incredibly, chose to plead guilty as charged. Sentenced to death by Mr Justice Finlay, the men were scheduled to hang a week apart and were the next appointments in Uncle Tom's diary.

As Albert approached the main entrance, the smaller wicket gate opened and out stumbled a middle-aged man, neatly dressed but appearing to be the worse for drink. Presenting the letter to the warder at the gate Albert was shocked to find he was one of a dozen applicants to be interviewed that afternoon. During the stern interview, geared up to weed out anyone whose motives for applying were morbid or ghoulish, Albert was asked if he didn't think he was too young to apply. When the governor queried the response that his father had been a chief executioner at 24 years of age, Albert reaffirmed that his father had indeed been that age and asked him to check his father's record to confirm this. Although it's clear that the reasons for Harry Pierrepoint's dismissal were well known to prison governors, the calm, assured way the young Pierrepoint conducted himself was enough to see him safely over the first hurdle.

While Albert waited to learn his fate following the interview, Tom arrived at Strangeways to carry out what would be his last engagement of 1931. Solomon Stein had booked into a local hotel room to celebrate his 21st birthday with a girl he had recently met. She enraged Stein by stealing money from him as he dozed on the bed, then telling him she had to leave as she had made another date for later that night. Stein strangled her with a tie and gave himself up to the police on the following morning. Nothing untoward happened at the execution and it was noted it took just five seconds from the time Stein was pinioned to the drop falling. In what appears to be an arbitrary show of mercy, McVay was reprieved three days after Stein's execution.

The first execution of 1932 took place at Crumlin Road, Belfast, when Edward Cullens, a 28-year-old fairground entrepreneur, was hanged for what the press dubbed a 'mafia-style' gun murder of a business rival. On the morning of Monday, 13 January, Tom and assistant Robert Wilson arrived in Belfast off the Liverpool night boat and carried out the execution without a hitch at 8 a.m. on the following morning.

Most men facing the gallows tried to put on a brave face to friends and relatives; 32-year-old George Alfred Rice, convicted of the dreadful rape and murder of nine-year-old Constance Inman in a Manchester park, was no exception. His counsel's plea that the girl was suffocated accidentally during the sex act, and that Rice was only guilty of manslaughter, was rejected. It was reportedly a harrowing trial, with Rice collapsing in tears on hearing the guilty verdict. Mr Justice Finlay, distressed by the evidence heard in his court, was also in tears as he passed sentence of death.

Despite the revulsion felt around the city, Rice was still visited regularly by friends and family, and on his last visit he told his friends he was prepared to meet his end bravely. It was to be an idle boast. At 8 a.m., Rice sat in the cell listening intently to the words of the priest and as the door opened he went to pieces, shrieking and crying, begging for mercy. As the assistant helped Tom strap his wrists, Rice collapsed in a heap and had to be carried shrieking and moaning across the corridor and supported on the trap.

Twenty-two-year-old George Pople was the next name in Tom's diary. He was paying the penalty for the murder and robbery of a woman on a road outside Oxford. Tom carried out two executions in two days at the end of April, the first at Hull when black sailor and bigamist George Michael stabbed to death his Danish-born wife on New Year's Eve in full view of a policeman. On the following day, Tom carried out a double execution at Leeds, when Thomas Riley and John Roberts were hanged side by side for two separate murders linked only in that in each case they had battered their victims to death with a hammer.

By the time Tom travelled again to Manchester, to dispatch Darwen-based child-killer 18-year-old Charles Cowle, Albert had received word that his interview had been successful and he was invited to attend Pentonville Prison for a medical examination and a week's instruction and training in the apparatus and methods used for execution.

For this first trip to London, the young Pierrepoint had to first make arrangements with his bosses at work to take a week's unpaid leave and he then confided in a friend the nature of his 'business trip'. Catching the midnight train from Manchester's London Road station, he arrived at Euston at 6 a.m., recalling how the magical place names he had heard a hundred times in the musical halls filled him with excitement as he set out on his new adventure. After a breakfast-time tour of the city he finally asked a policeman for help in finding Pentonville Prison. Given directions to 'The Ville', at a few minutes to 9 a.m. he presented himself at the main gate. Also on the training course was 42-year-old Stanley William Cross, a Londoner living in Fulham.

Albert had imagined himself making this journey so many times as he read and re-read his father's papers and accounts. Two things took him by surprise: firstly the spotlessly clean and highly polished execution suite, and secondly the sight of a noose hanging shackled to the chain that hung down from the giant beams. The engineer gave both trainees a step-by-step guide to the equipment and procedure, only briefly looking down at his hand-written prompts, leading Albert to assume that assistants must leave the list pretty frequently. Interestingly, prior to Lionel Mann's departure the list had carried the same names for the previous seven years, an unusual longevity of assistants, with the last addition being in the autumn of 1928.

Given rooms in the prison and the freedom to spend a few hours outside after the days' sessions ended, Cross and Albert spent several evenings seeing various sights and drinking in public houses, but on the penultimate night of the course Albert stayed in his quarters and wrote to his uncle explaining he was on the training course and hoped he would pass and soon be assisting at executions. The four-day training course ended with both trainees carrying out a dummy execution in front of the governor, then sitting a written exam in which they calculated a variety of drops and explained the execution procedure from start to finish. Both left the prison uncertain whether they had passed or failed. John Ellis, who had just finished a stint on seaside fairgrounds in which he carried out dummy executions and explained the procedures of carrying out executions, committed suicide at the second attempt on Tuesday, 20 September. A week later, notification that the name of Albert Pierrepoint had been added to the official list was received.

26th September 1932
A.1125/27

Sir,

With reference to your application for employment as Assistant Executioner, I am directed by the Prison Commissioners to inform you that your name has now been added to the list of persons competent to act in that capacity.
Assistant Executioners are employed as occasion requires by the governor of Prisons where executions take place, and when your services are required in connection with any execution a communication will be sent to you. You should notify the Secretary, Prison Commission, Home Office, S.W.1., of any change of address.

There is no necessity for you to write to any Sheriff or Under-Sheriff asking for employment in connection with an execution and any such application may result in your name being struck off the list.Enclosed for your information is a copy of the rules to which persons acting as Assistant Executioners are required to conform.

These rules are confidential and should not be communicated to any other person. Your particular attention is drawn to Rules 5 and 8, and the Prison Commissioners desire to emphasise the importance of complete reticence in regard to

your official duties. The remuneration is set out
in Rules 4 and 6, in addition to which necessary
travelling expenses will be paid on each occasion
on which your services are required.

I am, Sir,
Your obedient servant
L.W. Fox
Secretary

RULES FOR ASSISTANT EXECUTIONERS

1. Every person acting as an assistant
   executioner is required to conform to any
   instructions he may receive from or on behalf
   of the High Sheriff as to the day and hour and
   route for going to and leaving the place of
   execution.

2. He is required to report himself at the prison at
   which an execution is to take place, and for
   which he has been engaged, not later than
   4 o'clock on the afternoon preceeding the day
   of execution.

3. He is required to remain in the prison from
   the time of his arrival until the completion
   of the execution, and until permission is
   given him to leave.

4. During the time he is in the prison he will be
   provided with lodging and board.

5. He should clearly understand that his conduct and general behaviour should be respectable, not only at the place and time of the execution, but before and subsequently, that he should avoid attracting public attention in going to or from the prison, and he is prohibited from giving to any person particulars on the subject of his duty for publication.

6. His remuneration as an Assistant Executioner will be £1.11.6d for the performance of the duty required of him, to which will be added £1.11.6d if his conduct and behaviour are satisfactory, during and subsequent to the execution. These fees will not be payable until a fortnight after the execution has taken place.

7. Records will be kept of his conduct and efficiency on each occasion of his being employed, and this record will be at the disposal of any High Sheriff who may have to engage an executioner.

8. The name of any person who does not give satisfaction or whose conduct is in any way objectionable so as to cast discredit on himself, either in connection with the duties or otherwise, will be removed from the list. It will be considered as objectionable conduct for any person to make an application to a sheriff or under-sheriff for employment in connection with an execution, and such conduct may involve removal of such person's name from the list.

9. The Assistant Executioner will give such
information or make such record of the
occurrences as the governor of the prison may
require.

Albert was delighted when he received the letter and quickly penned a reply:

Prison Commissioners,
Home Office,
Whitehall,
LondonS.W.1
1st Oct. 1932
A.1125/27.

Dear Sir,
I am in receipt of your letter of the 30th inst.,
and I am very pleased to hear that I am been
placed on the list to act at executions. I have
read the rules carefully and I will try my utmost
to carry them out.
I am Sir,
Your Faithful Servant
Albert Pierrepoint

The summer and autumn of 1932 were lean months for the hangman; Tom had just one engagement in his diary during that time, to go to Winchester prison to hang a sailor who had murdered his girlfriend, but a week before the scheduled execution a reprieve was granted. The last execution of 1932 in England took place at Oxford, when Ernest Hutchinson was hanged for the murder by suffocation of his live-in lover. Surprisingly, neither Tom Pierrepoint nor his main rival Baxter received the offer to carry out the execution. Neither did long-serving assistants Robert Wilson, Tom Phillips or Henry Pollard, with over thirty years' service between them. Instead, surprisingly, the man appointed to carry out the task was Fred Allen of Wolverhampton, the newest recruit to the list and whose record to date consisted of just a handful of assists. He even had the ignominious experience of falling through the trapdoors at his first execution in 1928, when Baxter pulled the lever before he was fully clear of the trapdoors. Quite why Allen was appointed in preference to the senior assistants is something of a mystery; maybe he had impressed observers with his conduct on a previous visit in December 1931 when he assisted Tom in the execution of travelling salesman Henry Seymour. Nevertheless, there was now a new rival as chief executioner for both Tom Pierrepoint and Robert Baxter.

Three offers landed on Albert Pierrepoint's doormat in December. He had been informed that although he was now qualified to assist at an execution, he would first be required to witness an execution as an observer, to see if his nerve would hold and ensure he would not become ill or faint at the sight of someone being executed. First was the offer to witness the execution of Leeds domestic servant Kate Collins, who had drowned her illegitimate newborn child, but she was reprieved just a week after sentence was passed. Engagements at Durham and Birmingham also came to nothing and just when it appeared the year would end without the chance to put his skills into practice, he received a hand-written offer from Uncle Tom to assist at Dublin's Mountjoy Prison. Tom was to officiate on Thursday, 29 December, and the trip was to mean three days away from home.

Having got this far with his ambition, Albert now had to make some serious decisions about his future. On Christmas Eve, he finished his deliveries and then told boss Percy Sellers he was handing in his notice in order to begin a career he had wanted to be kept secret, but of which the employer had learned about through a workmate's gossip. Sellers admired Albert's conscientious attitude to work and an agreement was quickly reached that allowed him to take time off work when necessary.

The first sign that the life of an executioner might carry a hint of danger revealed itself to Albert when Uncle Tom arrived at his Manchester terrace house and pulled out a revolver and leather washbag full of .45 bullets. There had been a considerable amount of protestations and campaigning about the innocence of the man they were crossing the water to execute.

Patrick McDermott was a 26-year-old farmer convicted of the murder of his brother. In the early hours of Monday, 4 September, John McDermott was found shot in the gateway to his home, seven miles from Roscommon. Hearing two gunshots, his brother and sister, with whom he lived, rushed from the house and found John dead from wounds seemingly inflicted with a double-barrel shotgun. John was eldest of the children and all three had separate rooms in the house. Their father had died two years earlier and John had taken charge of the farm, worth £700. The other two children were left £100 each. On the night of the murder John had left the house and gone to visit a friend. He was shot as he returned home. Detectives investigating the crime asked Patrick if he had seen a flash of fire when he heard the shots, and he said that he could not see the spot where his brother died from his window. This was found to be untrue. He denied having a gun but a friend told police that he had recently borrowed a gun from him, allegedly to shoot crows that were attacking crops. Three days after the murder of his brother, police charged the younger brother. At his four-day Dublin trial it was alleged the motive was so that Patrick could inherit the farm, which he intended to sell, using the money to emigrate to America.

On Tuesday 27 December Albert and his uncle took the last tram from Newton Heath into Manchester City Centre and headed for Victoria Station and the midnight boat train to Holyhead. They transferred to the overnight mail boat, on which Tom had reserved a cabin. It was a journey he had made over a dozen times in the last decade and he was a familiar sight to a number of the stewards and other members of the crew. Once the journey was underway Tom suggested they go to the bar, where they soon fell in with a crowd of priests who were providing a vocal entertainment to the rest of the travellers while enjoying a glass of Guinness.

Albert – the very image of the assistant hangman in the 1962 film *The Quare Fellow* – joined in with the singing, putting his light baritone voice to work on a number of sentimental Irish songs: 'Mother Machree', 'The Rose of Tralee' and 'The Mountains of Mourne'. The whole experience, from the singing and the travel, to the adventure and the danger, built up the self-esteem of the young Albert as he embarked on the first step to follow in his father's footsteps.

Albert recalled an escapade on the trip during which they had been taken into the bosom of a burly sea lawyer who seemingly was unaware of the identity of his new friends, for when a group of rowdy, drunken troublemakers waited at the terminal for the embarkation of the hangman, he unwittingly gave them a safe ride to Dublin city centre by informing anyone interested to know that he knew Pierrepoint and could confirm he wasn't on this train. With Tom secretly nursing his revolver, he and Albert travelled the last few miles into Dublin in silence.

Presenting his young nephew to the prison governor, Tom

was given the details of the prisoner, and after breakfast they were taken to the scaffold to make the necessary preparations. After checking all was in order they retired to their quarters, where Tom was soon asleep on his bunk. Later that afternoon they were allowed to see the prisoner at exercise and after calculating a drop of 7 feet 5 inches, they filled a sandbag with an equal weight and tested the drop in the presence of the governor and chief engineer. With the rope stretching, they retired to their room and waited.

Although Tom had told him everything about the job, there was no attempt to build up any importance in Albert's role in the execution: he was to help secure the wrists if needed, but primarily to strap the ankles when the condemned man was on the drop, before stepping back as fast as he could.

At a few minutes before eight, with all the preparations having been carried out in the condemned cell, Albert stood beside his uncle and waited. He never saw his uncle any different outside the condemned cell: arm strap in his hand, a flat sweet in his mouth and the white cap folded in his breast pocket, like a handkerchief, waiting for the signal to go into action.

As the minute hand rolled over to the hour, the signal was given and they went to work. They moved at a pace – Albert noticed a priest and a warder but was too preoccupied watching his uncle to take in much else. After a few short paces they reached the scaffold. Albert dropped to his knees and secured the man's ankles, as he had practised scores of times. With barely time to regain his balance after stepping off the drop, there was a bang then silence. The rope hung straight and true and Patrick McDermott was dead. Tom walked across to a staircase at the side of the drop and descended into the pit to open the man's shirt for the doctor to place the stethoscope. As death was confirmed and the acknowledgement that the hangmen had done their job, a bottle of whisky appeared and glasses were offered to all who had been present. While others eagerly accepted their tot, Tom spoke for Albert in refusing alcohol while engaged on official business.

Once they had taken the body down and stowed away the equipment, Tom and Albert reported to the governor, where the drop and other measurements were officially recorded. As they prepared to leave, the governor, after congratulating them on their efficiency, warned that there was a hostile crowd waiting, some holding banners that bore statements such as: 'British hangman destroys Irishman'. They slipped out of the gaol into the crowded street, but no one challenged them as they made their way through the crowd and away from the prison. After a tour of a local Guinness brewery they retired to the quiet of Phoenix Park, where they rested before making their way to the docks to catch the night boat home. Tom was pleased with his nephew's work, and told him so. He said he was glad he had refused a tot after the execution, adding that if he couldn't do the job without whisky he shouldn't do it all.

The boat, and then train, got them into Manchester before the morning trams had started to run, so they commenced the walk back to Failsworth, where Albert's relieved mother was waiting for their return. As Tom ate a breakfast of pobs (bread soaked in warm milk), Albert washed, changed, then went out to do a full day's work.

In January 1933, Albert wrote to the Home Office advising them that although he had yet to formally witness an execution in England he had acted as assistant in Ireland. By return the Home Office wrote that he would still be required to act as an official witness at an execution in Great Britain before he could be offered the chance to formally assist. Within the week another letter landed on his mat, offering Albert the chance to witness an execution at Birmingham.

One afternoon in October 1932, Jeremiah Hanbury, a widower and unemployed foundry puddler, entered the house of Mrs Jessie Payne, the mother of four young children, at Newtown Brockmoor, and struck her two blows with a hammer, knocking her unconscious. He then cut her throat so severely she was almost decapitated, before giving himself up to a policeman. At his trial it was alleged that Hanbury and Mrs Payne had been having an affair, but that in July she had ended the relationship and refused to see him. As a result he became depressed and his counsel, offering a defence of insanity, suggested it was during this depression he had committed murder.

On the afternoon of Monday, 1 February 1933, Albert travelled to Winson Green Prison, Birmingham, in the company of his uncle. There, they met up with Robert Wilson, who had been engaged as the assistant. As they sat in the gatehouse waiting to be admitted into the main body of the prison, a group of visitors arrived. It was Hanbury's sister and some other relations. At the end of the farewell meeting Hanbury tried to put his family's minds to rest by showing his bravery. He told them not to put the house into mourning, but at 8 o'clock he asked them to pull down the blind cord and let it flick back and then say, 'Poor Jerry, he's gone.' On the following morning, Hanbury ate the large breakfast he had requested, and while the hangmen completed their preparations in the adjacent gallows room, he sang loudly in the remaining minutes that he had left. On the stroke of eight they went for him, and as he took his place on the drop he spoke in a firm clear voice: 'Be good everybody, thank you for your trouble.' Wilson stepped back off the drop and in an instant Tom pulled the lever. Albert had observed the execution without disgracing himself.

In August 1932, schoolchildren in Armagh stumbled across the body of a woman hidden in some bushes. She was identified as 23-year-old Minnie Reid, a domestic servant from County Armagh; her throat had been cut, and police found a bloodstained razor nearby. Investigations led police to Harry Courtney, a lorry driver. He admitted that he had known the victim for four years, though he denied that they had been lovers. Courtney could offer no alibi for the time detectives believed Reid was murdered and traces of her blood were found on some of his clothing. At his trial it was suggested that Reid had become pregnant, naming him as the father, but as he was already engaged to another girl, he had committed the murder hoping the trail would not lead to him. In the face of overwhelming evidence, Courtney finally admitted that he had had a relationship with Reid. His defence was that while he had agreed to meeting with the girl he told her he did not want any further contact with either her or the baby, whereupon she committed suicide by cutting her own throat. The jury dismissed his defence and, finding him guilty, the judge sentenced him to death. Albert assisted his uncle at the execution and Courtney was given a drop of 6 feet 5 inches. He died instantly.

In June 1933, Albert was engaged by the governor of Walton Prison, Liverpool, to act as assistant at the execution of Richard Hetherington. It was the fourth execution to take place that year, and the third to feature both Tom and Albert Pierrepoint. Hetherington was a Westmorland farmer who had been involved in a long-running dispute with his neighbours, Joseph and Mary Dixon. The quarrel was over money owed for work done by Hetherington on the Dixons' farm for which the old man was refusing to pay. The bodies of Mr and Mrs Dixon were discovered in the burnt-out shell of their bungalow and when Hetherington was arrested he had in his possession money and papers belonging to the dead couple. He made a full confession.

Tom carried out three executions in December, at Durham, Manchester and Birmingham. On the last execution he was again assisted by his nephew. In the early hours of 27 August, Charles Fox was stabbed to death after disturbing someone burgling his house at West Bromwich. The killer fled leaving footprints outside the house, and spots of blood from a cut sustained while gaining entry to the house. At another burglary committed a few days later at nearby Newton, the thief left fingerprints which were eventually traced to Stanley Hobday, an electrician already known to the police as a petty thief. A stolen car was recovered in Cheshire, which had Hobday's fingerprints on the steering wheel. Detectives used the BBC to appeal for information on the whereabouts of the wanted man and he was arrested at Gretna Green. The most damning evidence against Hobday were the footprints left at the murder scene. Plaster casts made of these found they were from a size-four shoe, an unusually small size for an adult. Hobday wore size-four shoes. And he weighed just 128 pounds; Tom worked out a drop of 8 feet 7 inches, one of the longest drops permitted by the Home Office.

Tom carried out 80 per cent of all the executions which took place in England in 1934. In early January he travelled to Hull, where he hanged Roy Gregory, a Scarborough boot maker who had murdered a young child. From Hull he travelled straight to Ireland, where he carried out an execution at Dublin – for some reason, without the aid of an assistant. In the spring, Tom carried out two jobs at Leeds and one at Bristol, before he received the offer of carrying out an execution at Wandsworth. It was unusual for Tom to get work in London, which was mainly the domain of Robert Baxter, but the Sheriff of Sussex was responsible for selecting the number one and opted for Tom ahead of Baxter. The execution of Frederick Parker and Albert Probert was notable in that it was the last time that members of the press were able to witness an execution.

On the night of 13 November 1933, 80-year-old shopkeeper Joseph Bedford was found on the floor of his general store at Portslade; he had head injuries. Bedford was taken to hospital, where it was quickly found that the old man had not fallen, as was at first thought, but had been struck over the head. He died the following morning. Witnesses reported two men seen near the shop on the evening of the murder and on the following day detectives questioned two men they had in custody who had been picked up for loitering. Parker, a criminal, bully and casual labourer from Hove, and Probert, a fitter from Dover, were questioned separately, unaware that Bedford had since died. Parker admitted helping Probert to rob the shop, but was insistent it was his friend that had committed the assault. 'I wish it had been a bigger job,' he rued, adding the haul had yielded just £6. Despite Probert denying any involvement, the two men were then charged with murder. Both died bravely without giving any trouble. Tom was assisted by Tom Phillips, Stanley Cross and his nephew. As they relaxed in their quarters on the evening before the execution, Phillips was asked by Albert what had really happened at the execution of Mrs Thompson at Holloway back in 1923. Phillips denied that the horrendous scenes reported in the press had taken place, but said it was a very upsetting execution, especially for the female prison officers who accompanied the condemned woman as she fainted on her last walk.

Albert had his first experience at the execution of a woman when he was engaged by the governor of Hull Prison to assist his uncle to hang Ethel Lillie Major, the daughter of a Lincolnshire gamekeeper. In May 1934, Arthur Major, her husband, complained of stomach pains after eating corned beef. He was in agony for two days before he died. The death certificate stated death was due to status epilepticus. As the widow arranged the funeral, police received a letter urging them to investigate the death, as a neighbour's dog had also died after eating the scraps of a meal prepared by Mrs Major. The funeral was halted as the guests began to arrive at the house, and when police questioned Mrs Major she made a fatal slip by admitting her husband had died of strychnine poison although no mention had been made up to this point of the cause of death.

The hangmen reached Hull on the afternoon of 18 December 1934 and as they went down to the execution chamber to rig the drop the chief warder gave them the condemned woman's details. Mrs Major was 42 years old, stood 4 feet 11 ½ inches tall and weighed just 122 pounds. They worked out a drop of 8 feet 6 inches. When they returned to their quarters, Albert questioned his uncle.

'What are women like?' he asked. 'What do you have to do, anything special?'

Smiling slowly, his uncle asked, 'Why lad, you're not afraid are you?'

'No,' he replied, 'I was just wondering.'

Tom put his hand on his nephew's shoulder and reassured him there was nothing to worry about: 'I shall be very surprised if Mrs Major isn't calmer than any man you have seen so far.'

Albert watched his uncle strap the woman's hands as they entered the cell on the following morning. He saw that the pinion was only strapped loosely, having learned from his uncle he did this because unlike men, he had never known a woman to resist the inevitable, and all had gone bravely to the drop. Ethel Major didn't resist. She was the last person hanged at Hull Gaol and her ghost is still said to haunt the prison.

1935 brought mixed fortunes for Tom and Albert Pierrepoint. Tom had spent the final day of the old year in quarters at Leeds Prison in the company of assistant Stanley Cross. At 8 o'clock on New Year's Day they carried out the execution of Frederick Rushworth who, along with his girlfriend Lydia Binks, had killed their newborn baby. Binks was reprieved just a few days before she was due to hang. Tom carried out further jobs as far afield as Durham, Wandsworth and Gloucester without any problems being recorded.

The first letter that Albert received in 1935 was for an engagement in Bristol in March and, opening it, he found it was asking him to carry out the role as number-one executioner. Reginald Woolmington had been convicted for the murder of his young wife, but after legal history was made when the conviction was quashed in the House of Lords, Albert received a further letter saying his services would not be required at Bristol Gaol after all.

Albert did get to assist his uncle when they travelled to Bedford for the execution of Walter Worthington. A retired poultry farmer from Huntingdon, Worthington had been convicted of the murder of his third wife by shooting her after a row about her infidelity. The murder was witnessed by two of his sons and immediately after committing the crime he walked to the local vicarage and confessed to the vicar, who in turn called the police. It was Albert's only execution date in his diary that year. A week later Tom carried out an execution at Durham, before he too had a lean spell that lasted until the spring of 1936.

Following the death of her husband, 36-year-old mother-of-four Dorothea Nancy Leech took the name Waddingham, and, posing as a qualified nurse, set up an old people's home in Nottingham, which she ran with the help of her lover Ronald Sullivan. In January 1935, Mrs Louisa Baguley, an 89-year-old widow and her spinster daughter Ada, aged 50, arrived on the recommendation of Nottingham council as their first patients. Early in May, Ada, who was obese and bedridden, instructed her solicitor to change her will in favour of Nurse Waddingham, who had promised to care for both women till the end of their days. A week later the old lady died, followed a few months later by her daughter. Waddingham's haste to have Ada Baguley cremated alerted the attention of the same doctor who had signed the death certificate of the mother. He arranged for an autopsy to be carried out and when this revealed an excessive amount of morphine, an exhumation was also ordered on Mrs Baguley. When this also revealed excessive amounts of morphine had been administered, Waddingham and her lover were charged together.

They stood trial before Mr Justice Goddard at Nottingham Assizes in February, but it was decided there was not enough evidence to proceed with charges against Sullivan and he was acquitted. After a two-week trial, 'Nurse' Waddingham, who had recently given birth to her fifth child, was convicted on overwhelming evidence and sentenced to death. The jury surprisingly added a recommendation for mercy when returning a guilty verdict.

When Albert and Uncle Tom arrived at Winson Green Prison on the afternoon of 15 April, they found that demonstrations, led by the wealthy abolitionist Mrs Van der Elst, were already well underway. They received the prisoner's details and found they were almost identical to those of Mrs Major. Although six years younger than the Lincolnshire murderess, Nurse Waddingham was just half an inch shorter, but weighed a pound and a half more. She was to be allowed a drop of 8 feet 5 inches, 1 inch less than Mrs Major.

The demonstrations that had started on the previous afternoon had grown to a crowd of over five thousand, many carrying sandwich boards protesting that the hanging of a mother of five children was barbaric. Inside the prison the sound of the hymns sung by the crowd could clearly be heard as the execution was speedily carried out.

Parsee doctor Buck Ruxton, who had been convicted of the murder of his wife Isabella and her maid, 20-year-old Mary Rogerson, at Lancaster, was the next name in Tom's diary. The women had disappeared in September 1935, and Ruxton told relatives his wife had taken Mary away to have a pregnancy terminated. While police investigations were being carried out in Lancashire, two dismembered bodies were discovered in a ravine in Dumfriesshire. They had been wrapped in a copy of a Sunday paper available only in Lancaster and Morecambe and this led police to Ruxton. His house was searched and traces of blood were found in the bathroom where he had dismembered the two women, after strangling them.

1936 was to be a unique year in modern times: two women went to the gallows. Less than three months after the execution of Nurse Waddingham, Charlotte Bryant followed her to the gallows. Bryant was an Irishwoman who had met her husband Fred while he was serving in Londonderry in the Black and Tans. She accompanied him back to Dorset, but she soon became disillusioned with life on a farm and began a steady stream of affairs with local farm hands and labourers. It seemed her husband chose to ignore her behaviour and in 1933, Leonard Parsons, one of her lovers moved in with the Bryants and their five children and began to live with her as man and wife. Somewhat amazingly, Parsons and Fred Bryant became good friends. In December 1935, after Parsons had moved out, Bryant began to complain of stomach pains and when he died on 22 December an inquest was ordered. It was discovered that he had died of arsenic poison and a tin found to have contained arsenic was discovered in the garden.

Mr Justice Mackinnon at Dorchester Assizes sentenced Charlotte Bryant to death at the end of May. It was alleged that her striking black hair turned white as she awaited execution. She had written a letter to the new king, Edward VIII: 'Mighty King. Have pity on your afflicted subject. Don't let them kill me on Wednesday.' It was in vain.

The name of long-time rival to Tom Pierrepoint, Robert Baxter, had been removed from the list of hangmen at the end of 1935, when illness brought his career to an end. He had been succeeded briefly by Alfred Allen, who had carried out one execution in 1936, and one in 1937 before he died. Albert assisted his uncle at the end of 1936 at Durham and again in February 1937 when they were engaged to hang a dwarf who had been convicted of a gruesome murder at Nelson in Lancashire.

Max Mayer Haslam was born with a crippling bone disease that left him unable to walk until he was nine, by which time he had grown bow-legged. Reaching his early twenties he stood a little over 4 feet tall and his disability caused him to become a surly loner. After a number of convictions and prison terms for bungled robberies, he was released from Manchester's Strangeways Gaol in May 1936. On Friday, 19 June, Haslam broke into the house of Miss Ruth Clarkson, a wealthy 74-year-old recluse, who lived alone with her dog in Nelson. Despite outward appearances, Miss Clarkson was a wealthy woman who owned property and collected antique jewellery and when word reached police that a dwarf was selling some stolen jewellery in Nelson they called at her house, to be greeted by a fearful sight. Miss Clarkson had been battered 17 times with a bloodstained tyre lever found beside the body, while upstairs, suspended from the headboard of the bed, was the body of her pet dog.

Haslam's alibi, that he was at a cricket match when the crime was committed, failed to convince the jury. He was due to hang alongside George Royle, a Stockport man who had strangled a hitchhiker, but just hours before the scheduled double execution Royle was reprieved and Haslam alone faced hangmen. He weighed 127 pounds; Tom worked out a drop of 8 feet 6 ½ inches, after taking into account the abnormal muscle formation of the 23-year-old.

In June, Tom and Albert carried out an execution at Dublin and by the time Tom and his young nephew travelled down to Exeter to hang Ernest Moss, Tom was now the unrivalled chief executioner. Moss, a 26-year-old former Brixham policeman, had left the force and become a taxi driver after his marriage collapsed. He moved to Exeter where he met 18-year-old Kitty Constance Bennett. The two swiftly became lovers and moved into a bungalow at Woolacombe. Soon, however, Moss realised he no longer wished to live with Kitty and decided that the easiest way to end the relationship would be by committing suicide. He had an abrupt change of mind, however, picked up a shotgun and battered her to death with its butt. He then confessed to the police and insisted on pleading guilty when he appeared before Mr Justice Hawke at Devon Assizes in November.

It was Albert's first visit to Exeter, the scene of a unique incident in the annals of capital punishment. In 1885, hangman James Berry had attempted to hang a man convicted of the murder of his employer. Three times, John Lee was led onto the drop, three times Berry pulled the lever and three times the trapdoors held firm and refused to open. The sentence was later commuted to life imprisonment and Lee went on to outlive his would-be executioner.

Two doors down from the grocery store where Albert was employed was a sweet shop and tobacconist managed by Anne Fletcher, an attractive blonde lady originally from Bolton now living with her aunt in Newton Heath. They soon became a couple and Anne often accompanied Albert on his cross-Pennine jaunts in his recently purchased wire-wheeled Ford 8. Tom and his wife had given up the general store in Clayton and were now living a mile or so down the hill at Lidget Green.

Tom Pierrepoint officiated at every execution carried out in 1938, the first time in over 20 years that one hangman had carried out all capital sentences in one calendar year. He travelled as far afield as Norwich, Durham, Liverpool, Manchester and Wandsworth. (Nephew Albert assisted on visits to the last three prisons.) It was a year that saw over a dozen reprieves including three women.

In March 1939, Albert received a letter asking him to assist at an execution at Wandsworth Prison. The executioner was not his uncle, who had accepted an engagement scheduled to take place at Pentonville on the same day; instead it was to be the debut execution of Tom Phillips. Phillips had been an assistant dating back to the days when Ellis was the chief executioner and had worked as Tom's assistant on over a score of occasions.

On 2 January 1939, the body of 17-year-old Peggy Irene Pentecost was found in a Lambeth hotel room. She had been strangled and a bed quilt had been forced into her mouth. She had checked into the hotel on New Year's Eve with a man who had signed the register Mr and Mrs Armstrong of Seaford.

Armstrong was traced and found to be a parlour-man of Seaford, with a number of previous convictions, including attempted murder. He admitted that he had become engaged to Peggy shortly after Christmas, and at his two-day trial before Mr Justice Humphries at the Old Bailey, in March, it was alleged he had killed her after he had discovered she was also seeing another man. Armstrong's execution was the first of five that took place at Wandsworth that year. Four days later Tom Pierrepoint, with Phillips as his assistant, carried out the execution of William Butler, who had stabbed a shopkeeper to death during a robbery. The final three executions all took place in October, a month after war had broken out in Europe. In two days at the end of October Tom hanged two soldiers from the North Staffordshire Regiment on consecutive days for the rape and murder of a hotel worker close to where they were stationed in Surrey.

In February 1940, the Pierrepoints, along with Phillips and Cross, were in action at Birmingham when they carried out the double execution of two members of the IRA who had been convicted of a bomb outrage in Coventry. In the summer of 1939, the IRA formulated the 'S' Plan, a bombing campaign on the British mainland aimed at focusing attention on the requests for the withdrawal of British troops from Ulster. In July that year, James Richards travelled to the mainland and lodged with an Irish family on Clara Street, Coventry. The house quickly became a terrorist HQ, and explosives were stored and prepared there. On 21 August, Peter Barnes also travelled to Clara Street, and over the next few days a woman who was also staying at the house purchased a suitcase while Richards and another man obtained a bicycle from Halfords in Coventry. On 24 August, Richards made a bomb in the front room of the house and on the following day the bicycle was left on the busy Broadgate at Coventry, where it exploded in the early afternoon killing five people, among them 21-year-old Elsie Ansell, who was due to be married in a few days' time. The serial number found on the bicycle led police to Richards and arrests in London later that night led to Barnes. In total five people were arrested and charged with murder.

At Birmingham Assizes in December, three defendants were acquitted of the charges but Barnes and Richards were convicted of the murder of Elsie Ansell. Although there was no direct evidence that Barnes had planted the bomb, there was enough incriminating evidence against him to prove he had participated in the outrage. Richards claimed it was against the orders of the IRA to kill people and that therefore the explosion was accidental. 'My Lord,' he said as the black cap was draped on Mr Justice Singleton, 'before you pass sentence, I have something to say... I wish to thank sincerely the gentlemen who have defended me during the trial and I wish to state that the part I took in these explosions since I came to England I have done for a just cause... God bless Ireland and God bless the men who have fought and died for her. Thank you, my lord.' On the morning of 7 February 1940, Phillips and Cross led Richards onto the drop. He walked bravely. By contrast, his fellow countryman was assisted to the drop by Tom and Albert in a state of partial collapse.

William Appleby and Vincent Ostler were two petty crooks who in the early hours of Friday, 1 March, were spotted breaking in to a Co-op store at Coxhoe, County Durham. Police Constable William Ralph Shiell was called to the premises with several colleagues and as two men made their getaway, PC Shiell gave pursuit. He was closing in when one announced: 'All right, let him have it!' A shot rang out and the constable fell, fatally wounded. He was able to give his colleagues a vague description of his killers before he died. Left near the scene was a stolen Vauxhall motorcar, and a newspaper appeal resulted in reports that a similar car had been seen in the possession of two local criminals. Appleby, a 27-year-old joiner, was questioned first and confessed that he had taken part in the robbery, though he insisted that he had been unaware that his accomplice, whom he named as Ostler, a 24-year-old ice-cream salesman, was carrying a gun.

Ostler, a father of four, and the son of a serving policeman, was interviewed, unaware that his friend had confessed. He denied any knowledge of the murder, but was arrested and charged with wilful murder. Tried before Mr Justice Hilbery at Leeds Assizes, Appleby denied PC Shiell's deathbed claim that he had shouted 'Let him have it!', instead insisting he told Ostler to 'Give him a clout!' After a four-day trial, both were sentenced to death, with the jury giving Appleby a strong recommendation for mercy. Both men were of similar height and weight, Appleby just under 5 feet 8 inches and 156 pounds; Ostler was an inch taller and a pound heavier. Appleby was given a drop of 7 feet 2 inches, his companion a drop of half an inch less. Tom was assisted by his nephew, along with Stanley Cross and new assistant Alexander Riley from Manchester.

When Albert received his next letter of engagement it was to assist at the execution of Udham Singh, a 37-year-old Sikh assassin who, on 13 March, attended a meeting at London's Caxton Hall and shot dead Sir Michael Francis O'Dwyer. In 1919 O'Dwyer had been the Lieutenant-Governor of the Punjab, where, under the command of General Dyer, scores of Indians were killed as riots were brutally suppressed. As the meeting ended, Singh, also known as Singh Azad, pulled out a revolver and fired six shots at the platform. Sir Michael was killed instantly; others received gunshot wounds, but were not seriously injured. From a diary taken from his room, it seemed the killer had mistaken his victim for General Dyer.

Stanley Cross was nominated to carry out the execution, his first engagement as chief executioner. Tom Phillips had had his short career as a chief executioner terminated following an execution in March, when his conduct was brought into question. Tom Pierrepoint was unavailable, as he had accepted an execution to hang a woman at Liverpool scheduled for the same day. With travel being somewhat erratic, as wartime bomb damage was causing interminable delays on all modes of transport at the time, Cross was offered the engagement, possibly as the journey from his home in Fulham was a fraction of that of any other man on the list, and also because he was now the most senior assistant, if only in age and not in experience.

Arriving at the gaol, Cross found that he had a large number of official witnesses as he and Albert were taken to the execution chamber to rig the drop. They were given the condemned man's details: age 37 years, height 5 feet 8 inches; weight 158 pounds. At exercise they saw that he was of a proportionate build but with a slim neck. Singh had been on a 42-day hunger strike prior to his trial, but had begun to take food again following his conviction. Albert claimed that the chief executioner had made no plans for the drop, and was at a loss as to what the drop should be.

As the governor noticed things were not running as smoothly as expected, Albert took over and with a quick glance at the official table of drops, worked out a drop of 7 feet 1 inch. Confident in the role of assistant executioner, Cross allowed Albert to take the lead. Together they measured off the drop, adjusted the chain, weighed and fixed the sandbag at the same weight as the condemned man. In the presence of the governor and official witnesses that included the under-sheriff, they tested the scaffold and dropped the sandbag to take out the stretch in the rope. The official witnesses departed without a word.

In *Executioner: Pierrepoint*, his 1974 biography, Albert claims Cross thanked him for his help in working out the drop, admitting he got flummoxed in front of such an impressive audience. Later that evening Albert studied the condemned man's details and adjusted the drop to a finer degree, and when the governor asked for a record of the official drop, Cross said it was 7 feet 1 inch. On the following morning, prisoner 6828 Udham Singh was hanged at 8 a.m. As the hangmen left the prison Albert claimed that Cross offered him a sum of money, equal to half of his fee. 'You've got to take it. You got me out of that scrape, you should have the lot really,' Cross is alleged to have said.

Records of the measured details on the official LP C4 sheet, however, showed that all was not well for the new hangman. The second column on the official record sheet, which is filled in and added to a large leather-bound volume that is known to officials as the 'execution book', is headed 'Particulars of the Execution'. The first entry is the drop as determined before an execution and is recorded as the official drop given to the governor after the drop had been calculated and measured. It is recorded as 7 feet 1 inch. The second entry is the length of drop as measured after the execution, from the level of the floor of the scaffold to the heels of the suspended culprit. As the drop causes the spinal column to break, ideally at the second and third vertebrae, this second measurement is usually an inch or two longer than the first measurement, and is usually made up from the stretch of the condemned person's neck. In this case the second measurement is 6 feet 6 ½ inches! Evidently someone had miscalculated, and the blame was put firmly at the feet of the chief executioner. Asked on the official form if they felt the hangman and assistant had performed his duty satisfactorily, Governor Ball and Dr Murdoch stated that in the case of Pierrepoint he had performed his duties satisfactorily, but in the case of Cross they found that he did not, adding: 'He is not a suitable person on account of mental incapacity viz particulars of length of the drop.'

At the end of August 1940, four men attended the hangman's training school at Pentonville. Unusually, all four graduated onto the list, and when Tom and Albert arrived in Bedford for the execution of William Cooper at the end of November, they found that two of the new assistants were in attendance as trainee observers, doing the very role Harry Pierrepoint had been prevented from taking 40 years before.

On 5 July, farmer John Joseph Harrison was found seriously wounded on his farm on the Isle of Ely. He had been battered about the head with a bottle. William Cooper was a former horse keeper at the farm who had been dismissed in April. He was arrested on a charge of assault and when the old man died on 21 July the charge was changed to one of wilful murder. Tried at Cambridge Assizes in October, Cooper claimed he had called at the farm to ask Harrison why he had dismissed him, and that the victim had attacked him first with a hammer.

Cooper claimed that he had merely picked up the bottle in self-defence. The prosecution suggested Cooper had beaten the old man in revenge for his dismissal before stealing a sum of money; the jury believed them.

Cooper was calm in the lead up to the execution and when the hangman and his assistant observed him at exercise there was nothing to suggest he would cause any trouble on the following morning. He even played dominoes with the warders until he retired for the night. With Harry Allen and Steve Wade in attendance, Tom and Albert stood outside the prison door on the stroke of 8 a.m. Receiving the signal to enter, they found that Cooper's whole demeanour had changed during the night. Now clearly terrified, he fainted through sheer terror as the hangmen entered the cell and he had to be carried by warders down the corridor to the execution shed.

The miscalculation of the drop at his first senior execution had evidently not caused Stanley Cross's name to be removed from the official list, for when the first enemy agents were sentenced to death at the end of November, he was engaged to carry out the executions. In September, four enemy agents, travelling in two pairs, landed in Kent. Karl Meir and Jose Waldberg, both German-born, had both had been drinking prior to landing, and to quench their thirst they called into a pub at Lydd where, ignorant of the British licensing laws, they tried to purchase a glass of cider. The suspicious licensee, warned to be on the look out for spies, called the police and they were arrested later that afternoon. Like all subsequent spies caught during the war, they were tried under the 1940 Treason Act; their trials were held 'in camera' so that the enemy would be unaware of their capture. Evidence was heard in court that the two men had sent back radio messages prior to their arrest.

Cross, assisted by Albert Pierrepoint and two other new assistants, Henry Critchell and Harry Kirk, carried out the executions at Pentonville. Again, the official report commented unfavourably on his capacity to carry out the work, and although a week later Cross hanged a third spy, Charles Van Der Keiboom, this turned out to be his last execution as number one.

Tom Pierrepoint was kept busy in the first part of 1941. With his nephew he made another trip over to Dublin in early January to hang David Doherty for the murder of his cousin Hannah Doherty. The two had been clandestine lovers and when Hannah fell pregnant Doherty was asked to procure medicines to induce an abortion. When he turned up at the rendezvous without them they quarrelled, and, fearful that her shouting would attract attention, he strangled his cousin and then battered her about the head with a boulder. They were no protests outside the gaol and Tom and Albert were able to slip in and out without any problems. Although tall and powerfully built, Doherty submitted meekly when they went for him and died without a struggle.

By the time he had invited Albert to accompany him on another visit to Dublin in April, Tom had carried out executions in Manchester, Durham and Liverpool. Henry Gleeson was hanged at Mountjoy, protesting his innocence after being convicted of the murder of Mary McCarthy. It was later alleged that she worked as a prostitute and had been executed by the IRA for antisocial activities. Gleeson was framed for the murder; witnesses who could have testified to his innocence were intimidated and warned against giving evidence. The real killer was suggested to be George Plant, a member of the IRA who was later executed by firing squad in March 1942.

On 9 July, Tom went down to Wandsworth to hang George Armstrong, a Newcastle-born spy who was the first Englishman to be executed for treachery during the war. While Armstrong was awaiting his fate in the condemned cell, a few miles across the city events were taking place that were to have an major impact on the career of the young Pierrepoint.

CHAPTER 6:
WARTIME EXECUTIONER

One night in April 1941 two men called at The Palm Beach Bottle Party club in London's Soho. There was a scuffle at the door and Antonio 'Babe' Mancini, the 39-year-old club manager, promptly barred them. On 1 May, the same men and an accomplice returned to the club and another fracas erupted during which Harry Distleman received a fatal knife wound. He died in hospital after claiming Mancini had stabbed him. Mancini, an Italian-born gangster, was one of three men charged with involvement in the murder. Two others were convicted of attempted murder; Mancini alone was convicted of murder and sentenced to death on 4 July. His first appeal was heard in September and dismissed, as was an appeal before the House of Lords on 16 October. Finally, almost four months after conviction, Mancini was told that no reprieve was forthcoming and he was to be executed on 31 October.

Albert later told how he had received a letter at the end of 1940 stating that the Home Office thought it may be necessary to appoint an assistant executioner to act in future as executioner: 'I have been asked by the Commissioners to enquire whether in that event you would wish your name to be considered.' If this was indeed the case, it seemed a bit of a pointless exercise. It was clear that with the termination of Tom Phillips's brief stint as a chief executioner, and with official documents stating that Cross was not deemed to be a competent candidate to officiate, Albert Pierrepoint was the only suitable person on the list who could have been promoted.

Albert received the original request to carry out the execution of Mancini in early August, but following the appeals, the date was rescheduled on three occasions before it was finally settled. It was coincidence that the first two men he was engaged to execute as number one had their appeals go all the way to the House of Lords. In 1935, Reginald Woolmington had been successful, Mancini was not so fortunate and on the afternoon of Thursday, 30 October, Albert passed through the gates of Pentonville Prison to carry out the execution. In the gatehouse he met assistant Steve Wade and after reporting to the governor they went to their quarters, where they were given the condemned man's details. The engineer asked Albert what he thought the drop would be, and replied that, as he hadn't seen the prisoner yet, he was planning a drop of around six foot. 'Six foot three will be good enough for overnight,' he told the engineer.

'Yes, I guessed it would be very near that myself,' he replied.

They were escorted to the execution chamber, where the long wooden box containing all the equipment was opened. Albert was already experienced enough to see at a glance that all was in order, and taking out the two ropes he examined each one meticulously, from the top where the rope is shackled to the chain, inch by inch along the whole of the ten-foot length, paying particular attention to the noose part, where the leather-clad rope passes through the brass eyelet woven into the hemp. Two ropes were always supplied: a brand-new, pristine clean one from John Edginton & Sons, the official Home Office suppliers, based on the Old Kent Road, and another, which was dirtier in colour and which had been put into use on a number of occasions. By habit most hangmen chose the used one, as there was less stretch in it and it was, therefore, much easier to achieve an accurate drop. Having rigged the estimated drop they fastened the sandbag onto the noose and when the prison engineer returned with the governor Albert carried out a test drop, knowing that unless there was an eleventh-hour reprieve, the next time he pulled the lever it would be to send a man to his death.

Mancini was observed through the spy hole and Albert noted he was handsome and seemed composed as he chatted to the warders who had watched him night and day since he entered the condemned cell. Retiring to their quarters, Albert worked out a drop based on the observations he had made of the prisoner. He now decided to extend the drop to 6 feet 9 inches. Steve Wade was a new assistant with just a handful of jobs to his name, and so Albert made him repeat his role on the following morning over and over before they retired for the night. Albert went to bed early and slept well. At 6.30 a.m. the hangmen were roused by the warder, who shared their quarters. They made their way to the gallows and drew up the sandbag, detaching it from the noose, and disposing of it in a corner in the pit. Albert noted that a stretcher had appeared from somewhere and was in position to one side on the floor. Wade detached the trapdoors from the rubber-clad springs, and standing on a stool, pushed them up flat. Albert slid the bolt into the lever that secured them in place, then located the cotter pin that acted as a security device to prevent the lever being pushed accidentally.

Wade came up by the narrow staircase at the side of the drop that linked the scaffold to the pit and fetched a ladder that was placed against the beam. He took hold of a tape measure as Albert climbed the ladder and adjusted the drop to his new calculation. The rope lay on the closed trapdoors and Albert picked it up, coiled it so the noose hung at head height for the prisoner, and as he held it in place Wade secured it with a piece of thread. They re-chalked the 'T' mark on the trapdoors to which Mancini's toes would be aligned, with the arches of his feet over the gap between the trapdoors. Albert then bent down and gently inched out the cotter pin so that it was just in place but would fall out easily with a gentle push. This would save only a fraction of a second, but it all helped in making the job faster. With everything in order they made an official record of the drop. Then, taking a last look around the green-painted execution chamber, they went for breakfast. After bacon and eggs they returned to their quarters to wait.

At five minutes to nine they received a signal that the official witnesses had assembled and in the company of the prison escort they walked across the prison yard and entered the cellblock that housed the execution chamber. Keeping his nerves in check, Albert realised, as the party assembled outside the cell door, that he was the youngest person present. It was now 25 years since he committed to paper the ambition to follow in his father's footsteps. The governor stood with a stopwatch in hand and as the minute hand reached the hour he raised a finger as the signal to begin.

The chief warder silently opened the cell door and Albert entered with the wrist strap in his right hand. Wade followed a pace behind. Mancini was standing facing the door, and, dressed in his smart suit, he smiled as Albert approached him. After strapping his wrists Albert told the prisoner to 'follow me', stepping through the side door in the cell wall that had silently slid opened after the hangmen had entered. Seven paces took them onto the drop. Albert turned to face the prisoner and stopped him on the chalk mark, and as Wade strapped his ankles, he pulled the white hood from his breast pocket and placed it over Mancini's head.

'Cheerio,' the prisoner said as the noose was placed around his neck. Albert darted to his left, pulled the pin and pushed the lever. The trapdoors crashed opened and held firm in the rubber springs. Mancini dropped into the pit and hung lifeless. Albert Pierrepoint had finally achieved his ambition and was about to embark on a hectic period, travelling the length and breadth of the country putting his new skills into use.

Twelve days later Lionel Watson followed Mancini into the felon's graveyard at Pentonville, paying the penalty for fatally poisoning his girlfriend and her 18-month-old daughter. Tom Pierrepoint officiated. There were four executions in December 1941, with Albert present at them all, officiating at the first two and assisting Uncle Tom at the remainder. Both of Albert's jobs as chief took place at Wandsworth: in the first he hanged John Smith, who had stabbed to death his girlfriend in a lovers' quarrel. Recorded as being carried out 'very expeditiously', it passed off without incident – unlike the next engagement, which was to give Albert what he later described as the toughest job on the scaffold.

Karel Richard Richter was a 29-year-old Sudeten-born German. Dropped by parachute near London Colney, Hertfordshire, on 13 May, he was equipped with £500, $1,000 and a map of East Anglia. His task was twofold: to attempt to assassinate the exiled Czechoslovakian premier, and also to pass on money and information to other enemy agents already in the country. He became a spy the moment he discarded his flying suit and changed into civilian clothes, and after burying the parachute and money he laid low until the following evening while he got his bearings and thought out his plan. At 10.15 p.m. he set out on his mission, but it was compromised almost immediately. Stopped and asked directions by a lorry driver, Richter – who knew the immediate locale but not too much beyond – gave a surly reply, enough for the driver to report him to a policeman a little up the road. PC Scott cycled after the man and asked to see his papers. Richter was carrying an alien's visa card with an address in London. One condition of such a card was that the holder had to be at that address by an 11 p.m. curfew. Scott asked him where he had come from and was told he had walked from Dover and that it had taken him two hours. In fact, the journey, by foot, would probably take around 24 hours. The man spoke with an accent and, suspecting he was a spy, Scott took him into custody. After interrogation at the intelligence centre at Ham Common, it was deemed that Richter was not suitable to be 'turned' into a double agent, and subsequently he found himself before Mr Justice Tucker at the Old Bailey. On 24 October, after a four-day trial held 'in camera', he was sentenced to death.

Observing him in the condemned cell, Albert and assistant Steve Wade could see Richter was a tall, powerfully-built man. Standing a fraction under 6 feet tall and weighing 172 pounds he had a 'bull' neck and a constant scowl on his face. On the morning of 10 December, the official witnesses gathered outside the cell, and at 8.58 a.m. they were given the signal to go to work. They entered swiftly, but as Albert strode over with pinion strap in hand Richter made a bolt for the door. Wade warded him off and the prisoner then charged at the wall, diving headfirst with terrific force. This stunned him for a moment but only made him even more violent. The hangmen seized him, strapping his arms behind his back, and the guards closed in. It appears that a new strap was used – possibly one Albert had acquired himself, and if so presumably against government rules. (Wade later said the strap was faulty, with not enough eyelet holes.) The condemned man twisted his wrists as he struggled and managed to break the strap, the metal tongue on the strap splitting one eyehole and breaking free. Wade shouted to Albert, 'He is loose!' and they turned back as the prisoner clawed and fought for his life. Warders finally held him until the hangmen made him secure, Albert digging his knee into the man's back to draw the strap onto the next free eyelet. Richter fought, charging the wall again repeatedly screaming, 'Help me!'

The struggle progressed from the condemned cell floor across to the scaffold. Reaching the drop, Richter kicked and screamed for his life, managing to get across the trap to the opposite wall with legs splayed. As Albert placed the noose over his neck Wade drew his ankles together. Still the condemned man struggled, and now Wade could see Albert had completed the noosing and was moving across to push the lever. Wade was still vainly trying to get the strap on the legs and shouted, 'Wait! Strap on legs and down he goes!' A warder took hold of one of the legs and forced it against the other, allowing Wade to draw the strap around the ankles before dashing off the trapdoor. With his last act on earth, Richter shook his neck violently from side to side, managing to loosen the safety washer that held the noose in place. At that moment, as the rope slackened, the drop fell. Aghast, they could only watch as the noose unwound, only for the eyelet to catch underneath his nose. The rope swung violently in the pit but the prisoner was hanging limp and lifeless: his neck was broken and he had died instantly. It had taken 17 minutes from entering the cell to the condemned spy hanging beneath the trapdoors. The postmortem later that morning found that cause of death was fracture of the cervical vertebrae in the correct place, and that death had been instant. Steve Wade retired to his quarters and, filling in his diary while Albert made his report to the governor, wrote: 'Execution good in the circumstances. I would not miss this for £50 – well worth it!'

Following his promotion, work came thick and fast for Albert. In 1942 there was a score of executions split equally between uncle and nephew. On top of his work as a chief, Albert's income was supplemented by three jobs assisting his uncle.

Tom's most notable customer that year was probably Harold Hill, hanged for the horrific murder of two young schoolgirls. Doreen Hearne and Kathleen Trendle had vanished while walking home from school at Penn in Buckinghamshire in November 1941, having last been seen asking a soldier for a ride in his army truck. Three days later they were found stabbed to death in a copse. Several clues were found at the scene, the most important being a khaki handkerchief with a laundry number that led police to Hill, a driver in the 86th Regiment. He was hanged at Oxford on 1 May, Albert assisting his uncle in the first execution at the prison for a decade.

In contrast to his uncle's low-key engagements, the first dates in Albert's diary were two notorious wartime murder cases that had filled the thin newspapers and managed briefly to push the war out of the headlines. In March, he travelled to Wandsworth to hang Harold Dorian Trevor, a 62-year-old habitual criminal who had been sentenced to death at the Old Bailey for the murder of 65-year-old Mrs Theodora Jessie Gledhill.

On 14 October 1941, Trevor, who had recently been released from prison, responded to an advert placed by the elderly widow for a room to rent at her West Kensington tower-block home. He agreed to take the room, but as Mrs Gledhill was writing out a receipt, Trevor began to beat her over the head with a beer bottle before strangling her as she lay on the carpet. He then ransacked the house and fled, taking a small amount of cash. When the body was discovered, detectives found a receipt made out to Dr H. D. Trevor lying on the table. Fingerprints had also been left on the broken bottle and a quick check found that the man they were looking for was indeed Harold Trevor. Arrested at Rhyl, Trevor, a Yorkshireman, had spent almost all the previous 40 years in prison on a variety of charges from larceny to fraud. He had no previous record of violence and following conviction doctors assessed whether his sanity was in doubt, but found no grounds for a reprieve on medical grounds. Trevor spent his last days in the condemned cell in a very distressed state, unable to eat or make coherent conversation and on the morning of his execution he shuffled, terrified, the last few paces to the drop.

Another Yorkshireman, Gordon Cummins, a 28-year-old leading aircraftsman and RAF cadet, was responsible for a wave of terror in war-torn London in the early war years that earned him the name of 'the Black-out Ripper', and which led him to a 9 a.m. appointment with Albert Pierrepoint. On 9 February, schoolteacher Evelyn Hamilton was found strangled in a Marylebone air-raid shelter. She had been travelling alone across London to her home in Newcastle. A scarf had been tied across her throat and nose, but fingermarks on the neck suggested that she had been manually strangled and that the killer was left handed. Her handbag containing £80 was stolen but she hadn't been sexually assaulted.

On the following night, Mrs Evelyn Oatley, a prostitute, was found strangled in her Soho flat. Her naked body had then been mutilated with a tin opener and fingerprints recovered again suggested a left-handed killer, though the prints didn't match any on file. On 13 February, the naked body of prostitute Margaret Florence Lowe was found in her flat close to Tottenham Court Road. This attack was even more horrific than that on the previous victims: the lower part of her body had been subjected to a frenzied attack from a knife and razor. While detectives were at the scene investigating, news came through of another murder. Mrs Doris Jouannet, the wife of an elderly hotel manager, had been found strangled and mutilated in her flat near Paddington. Later that day a young woman was accosted in a public house near Piccadilly. As she left, a man followed her outside, pushed her into a doorway and tried to strangle her. The attack was thwarted by a passer-by and the attacker fled, leaving behind a belt and gas mask. The number on the mask was traced to Cummins, stationed at St John's Wood. Police interviewed him and although he gave them an alibi for the times of the murders he was found to be missing a belt from his uniform. Taken into custody he made a detailed statement and when he was asked to sign it, Cummins picked up the pen with his left hand.

At his two-day trial at the Old Bailey he was indicted on just the murder of Evelyn Oatley. It was shown in court that although he was clearly a sexual deviant, Cummins had also committed the murders for gain. He was hanged during an air raid and was given a drop of 7 feet 1 inch.

Albert was back at Wandsworth within the month to carry

out his first double execution as a chief. José Estelle Key was a 34-year-old British subject, born in Gibraltar, and charged under the Emergency Powers (Defence) Act. He had been arrested on suspicion of espionage, and detained trying to leave Gibraltar for central Spain – allegedly to see his brothers, who worked in the dockyards. He was searched, and found to have in his possession information on the movements of the British forces, warships and aircraft in and around Gibraltar. As Key had been arrested in a British territory, it was decided to take him to London for trial. Hanged alongside him was Alphons Louis Eugene Timmerman, a Belgian arrested as a spy after arriving at Glasgow from Portugal, posing as a Belgian refugee.

Travelling home by train later that morning with assistant Steve Wade, Albert shared a carriage with a couple of pompous city gentlemen who scoffed at the announcement in their newspaper that two spies had been hanged at Wandsworth that morning, declaring loudly they had been shot in the Tower. Pursuing his claim that they had been shot, one of them addressed Wade, telling him they had actually been shot, just like the ones who had been executed in the First World War. Wade stayed noncommittal and as the train reached its destination, he whispered to Albert that he should present him with a business card to show who he was. Unlike many of his predecessors, Albert had no cards, nor did he have customised headed notepaper like James Berry and John Ellis, among others.

On Easter Sunday 1942, an RUC patrol, patrolling the Kashmir district of Belfast, had been ambushed by members of an IRA gang. They gave chase and later stormed a house at nearby Clonard. The first officer to approach the house was PC Murphy. As he entered, via the back door, a shot rang out and he fell fatally wounded. Six men were arrested, including 19-year-old Thomas Joseph Williams, who had himself received three gunshot wounds during the incident. The six, all aged between eighteen and twenty-one, stood trial at Antrim and were each sentenced to death. Tom Pierrepoint was engaged to carry out the executions and recruited his nephew to assist him. Discussions were held as to the best way to carry out the executions and they came to the conclusion that proceedings should mirror those that Ellis had arranged 20 years earlier when faced with six men condemned to die on the same day. At Dublin's Mountjoy Gaol, Ellis and his assistants had carried out three double executions, timed at 6.00 a.m., 7.00 a.m. and 8.00 a.m.

In Belfast the condemned men were housed in pairs in the condemned cells; just four days before the scheduled executions, however, they were taken out of their cells and escorted to an interview with their solicitor. 'I have good news for you all, with one exception,' he told them. Five were to be reprieved, though for reasons not disclosed – but presumably because his hand had fired the fatal shot that killed the policeman, Williams was not to be spared. The others bade him a tearful goodbye before being transferred to another part of the gaol. Tom was wired immediately that his trip across the water was not to be as lucrative as first planned. Williams was hanged on 2 September: he went to his death bravely and was given the longest drop administered in modern times. He weighed 127 ½ pounds and stood just 5 feet 6 inches; the aged Pierrepoint had decided that 8 foot 9 inches was the drop required for instant death.

By this time the temperament, reaction, agility and conduct of the 72-year-old hangman was being questioned and when he travelled to Wandsworth to hang Herbert Bounds in November an official complaint was made about him. Bounds was a hawker who lived with his wife in Croydon. He suffered with nerves and the two had a violent, unhappy relationship. Earlier that year, following an argument, he accused her of trying to poison him. In August, during a row she picked up a bread knife and threatened to kill him. Bounds picked up his razor, in self-defence he claimed, and during the struggle she received wounds to her neck from which she later died.

Assisted by Harry Critchell, Tom carried out the execution at Wandsworth on 6 November. Within a week the governor sent a letter to the Prison Commission outlining his concerns as to the hangman's conduct:

11.11.42
Executions

At the execution of a recent prisoner on 6.11.42. I was not favourably impressed by the attitude of T. W. Pierrepoint the executioner.

The execution was carried out with expedition and satisfactorily performed. I have the greatest admiration for the way in which the Minister prepared the prisoner for his end, and the comfort the latter receives from the former enables him, in average cases, to meet his end with admirable decorum.

But if the end of the Minister's influence over the prisoner is brought to a close too abruptly, a more unhappy scene is witnessed than, in my opinion is necessary.

I formed the opinion that Mr Pierrepoint at his advanced age, I believe his age is 72 years - has passed his peak of efficiency and is becoming less tactful and more abrupt in his methods. It

impressed me as though he had turned what I
would call an unpleasant episode of drastic
efficiency, into a more unpleasant one.

B.E.N. Grew
Governor

It was neither the first nor the last time that official correspondence on Mr Pierrepoint passed between official channels, and it was no coincidence that once his young nephew had graduated to the role of senior executioner, more and more governors were opting for the younger Pierrepoint.

The majority of wartime executions took place in London, with most of them taking place at Wandsworth and, following the unsavoury incident in November, Tom was overlooked on the next engagements there. On New Year's Eve, Albert and Steve Wade hanged Johannes Dronkers, a Dutch spy, and less than a month later Fransiscus Winter, another spy, this time a Belgian, convicted like all other enemy agents under the Treachery Act.

Winter was hanged on 26 January 1943. Albert left the prison before lunch but returned later that afternoon as he had another appointment, this time to hang a murderer whose crime had heralded the career of brilliant Home Office pathologist Professor Keith Simpson, whose painstaking forensic work helped bring to justice a brutal wife murderer.

In the summer of 1942, workmen clearing a bombed chapel in Lambeth unearthed the remains of a mummified body. Keith Simpson was able to tell detectives they were investigating a murder: the body was that of a woman who had been strangled approximately 18 months before.

Through dental records, they were soon able to identify the corpse as that of Rachel Dobkin, who had disappeared in April 1941. Her estranged husband, Harry Dobkin, a 45-year-old Jewish firewatcher, was contacted and his arrogant and dismissive behaviour immediately made him a suspect. He said he had last seen his wife alive in the previous year and they had parted on friendly terms. He also denied any knowledge of the Lambeth chapel, though it was known to the police that he had been recently employed there as a firewatcher. Tried before Mr Justice Wrottesley at the Old Bailey in November, Dobkin was alleged to have killed his wife after a dispute over maintenance payments. Weighing over 200 pounds, and standing a few inches over 5 feet tall, he was given a relatively short drop of 5 feet 9 inches. At the autopsy, Simpson's secretary, Molly Lefebure, noted that Dobkin had a peaceful demeanour about him and that he had died quietly and bravely, praying ardently.

On 27 December 1942, David Cobb, a 21-year-old black soldier from Alabama, USA, was serving in the 827th Engineer Battalion (Aviation), at Desborough, Northamptonshire. Leaving his post at the guard hut he approached Lieutenant Robert Cobner to complain about the length of time he had been on duty. The lieutenant reprimanded Cobb for carrying his rifle in an improper manner and told him to stand to attention when addressing an officer. Cobb said that as he was already confined to barracks for an earlier offence he did not care about this, at which Cobner called for a sergeant to arrest Cobb. As the sergeant approached, Cobb pulled down his rifle and refused to hand it over. Lieutenant Cobner stepped forward to take it and received a fatal shot to the heart. He died instantly. David Cobb was tried by General Court Martial at Cambridge in January 1943. His defence was that he did not recognise the officer and had refused to hand over the rifle until proper identification procedure had been followed. It was a weak defence, though, and he was sentenced to death by hanging. The American military were allowed to retain most of the traditional formalities of an American execution, apart from the actual method of execution, which had to conform to British practice. Standard American practice was to use a 'cowboy coil' knot and a standard drop of around five feet. This rarely caused instant death, more often causing the prisoner to suffer death by asphyxia in a slow, painful process.

Cobb was the first American serviceman to be sentenced to death in Britain and his execution was scheduled to take place at Shepton Mallet Gaol on 12 March. There hadn't been an execution here since Bombardier John Lincoln had been hanged 17 years before. Tom Pierrepoint, who had carried out that execution, was contacted by the American authorities and his nephew was engaged to act as assistant.

Arriving at the prison on the afternoon before the execution, the hangmen were informed that in line with American custom the execution was to take place on the first hour of the scheduled date. A few things differed from the procedure at a British execution. In those days of rationings and shortages, an American execution was one of the rare occasions at which food and drink were served in abundance. Another difference, and the one that Albert found the most disturbing, was the length of time the condemned man spent in the company of his executioners. In a routine execution in a British prison, the condemned was usually hanging dead on the end of the rope between ten and sixty seconds. For this, and each subsequent execution carried out at Shepton Mallet, the prisoner was escorted to the drop, and once placed upon the trap he had to wait for around five minutes while the

Above: Albert Pierrepoint (1905-1992), the most famous British hangman of the twentieth century.

Left: Shortly after he retired in 1955, Albert bought a pony, which he named Trio, possibly in reference to the family threesome who had shared the same profession.

Left: Club owner Antonio Mancini, the first man hanged by Albert in his official capacity as Chief Executioner in October 1941.

Right: Gordon Cummins, an RAF cadet, was responsible for a wave of terror in war-torn London in the early war years that earned him the name of 'the Black-out Ripper', and which led him to a 9 a.m. appointment with Albert Pierrepoint on 25 June 1942.

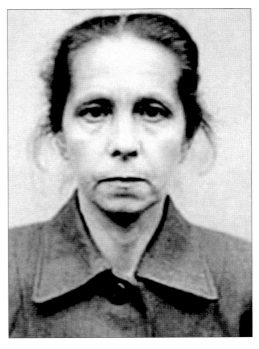

Albert travelled to Germany in December 1945 to hang a number of Nazi war criminals. Among them were four staff responsible for mass murder at Bergen-Belsen and Auschwitz concentration camps. *Clockwise from top left:* Elizabeth Volkenrath, senior supervisor at Auschwitz; Irma Grese, a sadistic compound commander at Belsen and perhaps the most notorious of all female war criminals; Juana Bormann, a short but ferocious guard at both camps; and Josef Kramer, the camp commandant and 'Beast of Belsen'.

Top left: On the morning of his execution, traitor John Amery said: 'I've always wanted to meet you, Mr Pierrepoint. But not, of course, under these circumstances!'

Top right: In March 1950, Timothy Evans was hanged at Pentonville Prison for murders which his neighbour, John Reginald Christie, seen here, was responsible. Christie was hanged by Albert in July 1953.

Bottom: In 1946, Albert took ownership of an aptly-named public house, 'Help the Poor Struggler', between Oldham and Manchester.

'Capital Punishment Amendment Act, 1868'

(31 & 32 *Vict. c. 24, s. 7*)

The sentence of the law passed

upon DEREK WILLIAM BENTLEY

found guilty of murder, will be

carried into execution at 9 a.m.

to-morrow.

C R Wigan Under Sheriff of THE COUNTY OF SURREY

_____ Governor.

27th JANUARY 1953

WANDSWORTH Prison.

No. 278

(C23368—6) 100 3/48

Derek Bentley was convicted of murder in a
controversial trial which still divides opinion today.

Left: Louisa Merrifield, along with her husband, was charged with the murder by phosphorous poisoning of their elderly benefactor. Louisa went to her death in September 1953 but her husband was released.

Right: Ruth Ellis was hanged at Holloway in July 1955 for the shooting of a former lover. A large public clamouring for her reprieve was heightened by a hoax telephone call purporting to be from the Home Office.

Albert Pierrepoint with his wife Anne in the late 1980s.

Albert Pierrepoint – in a career lasting 23 years, he hanged over 400 men and women.

charge was re-read, spelt out and the prisoner was asked if he had any last statement. Cobb, the first of three men that Tom hanged at Shepton Mallet that year, marched erectly from the death cell to the execution chamber and stood calm and cool as he listened to the words of the chaplain, which were spoken in tandem with those of the military official who read out the sentence of the court-martial.

Three weeks after the execution of David Cobb, Albert carried out a job at Wandsworth, assisted by Steve Wade. His task was to execute Dudley Raynor, a Burmese sergeant in the Pioneer Corps convicted of the murder of his new teenage bride Josephine, whom he had kicked to death following a jealous quarrel. He pleaded guilty at his trial at the Old Bailey, and the trial lasted just nine minutes. Following the execution, the hangmen left the prison and Wade told Albert that they had been summoned to the inquest. Reluctantly Albert accompanied him to the mortuary, where they were introduced to pathologist Keith Simpson, who was about to commence the autopsy. After getting over the initial shock of finding Miss Lefebure sitting beside the body of the recently executed man typing up the report as Professor Simpson dictated his findings, Albert became absorbed as he was shown where the knot had separated the spine between the second and third vertebrae, which was deemed the ideal spot for the break.

In June, Albert accompanied his uncle to Dublin, where they hanged Bernard Kirwan, who had been awaiting execution, when Irish playwright Brendan Behan had been imprisoned at Mountjoy. Behan later wrote a bestselling play about his experiences in gaol, The Quare Fellow, based around the atmosphere in the gaol while an inmate awaits execution. The hangman is depicted as a northern working-class man who sings Irish songs on the boat across the Irish Sea.

A month later Tom was back at Wandsworth when he carried out the execution of Charles Arthur Raymond, who had battered about the head WAAF Marguerite Burge with a blunt instrument. She had also been sexually assaulted. Raymond, a French Canadian soldier, was charged with the murder after he talked too much and aroused the suspicious of his colleagues. At the Old Bailey in May, after a five-day trial, he was sentenced to death, through an interpreter.

Again the hangman's conduct was questioned, this time due to his lack of dexterity and speed. An official reply was penned to the governor in response to this.

20.7.43
Re: Thomas William Pierrepoint

The commissioners thank you for your report on the above named who acted as executioner in the case of Charles Arthur Raymond on 10.7.43. Owing to wartime difficulties of replacements and favourable reports from other prisons, the Commissioners are inclined to allow Mr Pierrepoint to act. Particular attention should be paid to his technique.

On 29 August 1943, Albert married Anne Fletcher at St Wilfred's Church, Newton Heath, Manchester. They had become closer following the death of first his sister Ivy, who had worked as a nurse at Winwick Hospital, Warrington, before she collapsed and died of exhaustion, and then his mother, who passed away suddenly a year later. Returning from their honeymoon in Blackpool, they settled into the house at East Street, a few blocks from his previous house on Mill Street.

Tom carried out four executions in a fortnight in December. On 14 December he was at Shepton Mallet; on the following day he carried out an execution at Pentonville; and a week later he pulled the lever at Wandsworth for the last time. The final execution was at Liverpool, where Thomas James, a ship's fireman, paid with his life for the murder of a prostitute. On 17 August, the body of Geraldine Sweeney was found in the cellar of a bombed house in Liverpool. She had been viciously assaulted with a bottle and a broom handle, but the cause of death was strangulation. James had confessed to a friend that he had killed her, and his friend's wife subsequently told the police. James denied killing the woman, adding that if he was to kill someone he would he would stab and not strangle them. His defence claimed that James had drunk 22 pints on the day of the murder and could not remember anything, but this did not prevent him from being sentenced to death by Mr Justice Wrottesley at Liverpool Assizes.

James was scheduled to hang alongside Joseph Gibbons, who had been convicted at the same assizes for a murder in Chester. The prison doctor at Walton was concerned about the conduct of Thomas James, however, and in a confidential memo he asked for more staff to be sent to the prison as James knew he had no chance of being reprieved and was determined to cause as much trouble as possible in the condemned cell and at his execution. It was also decided to employ four executioners, but as it turned out Gibbons was reprieved and James went to the gallows alone.

In early January 1944, Albert received a telegram summoning him to London. Arriving at the Home Office, he discovered his services were required to hang two young saboteurs in

Gibraltar. Albert, who had never spoken to his wife about his work as an executioner, had to wire Anne to say he would be away from home for three days. Later that afternoon, along with Harry Kirk who was to be his assistant, they travelled to an aerodrome near Bristol, from where their flight was to depart. The route via Lisbon meant crossing over the Channel and so was carefully worked out as dog-fighting and air raids were still a regular occurrence. Arriving at Lisbon airport, the hangmen were astonished to find many planes sporting the swastika livery. As a neutral airport, aircraft of all nationalities were welcomed and as such it was a popular departure and arrival port for spies and enemy agents. From Lisbon the two flew along the Spanish coast before reaching Gibraltar. The double execution of 22-year-old Louis Cordon-Cuenca and 19-year-old Jose Martin Munez took place at the Moorish Castle, with both men being given identical drops of 6 feet 10 inches.

On his return he discussed the journey with his new wife and also talked frankly of his 'other career'. Although she had obviously known about it for many years, the name Pierrepoint is not an easy one to hide behind; she had refused to question him on it, waiting for Albert to be the one to broach the subject.

The year 1944 was to be the last in which Tom Pierrepoint held the mantle of senior executioner, being appointed number one at all executions carried out in Great Britain and Ireland, with the exception of five in London at which his nephew officiated. On 11 August, Tom carried out a double execution at Shepton Mallet, when two Americans, serving with a Quartermaster Service Company, became the first to be executed for rape for almost a hundred years. On the evening of 4 March, Dorothy Holmes had left a Gloucestershire dance hall with her American soldier boyfriend. Eliga Brinson and Willie Smith, two black soldiers, followed them and as Dorothy and her boyfriend kissed goodnight, they were attacked. The white soldier was hit in the face with a bottle as Dorothy was dragged into woods. He ran to get help but by the time he returned both men had raped the terrified woman. They were court-martialled at Cheltenham in April, accused of rape of a civilian – which carried a capital sentence during wartime. It was the fourth of five visits Tom made to Shepton Mallet that year.

On 1 December, Tom and Albert made another journey to Dublin for an execution. Charles Kerins, a native of Tralee, had been sentenced to death by the Special Criminal Court for the murder of Detective Sergeant Denis O'Brien in September 1942. O'Brien had been ambushed and shot dead by a gang of men wearing dark glasses and carrying Tommy guns as he left home to go on duty at Dublin Castle. Kerins, a member of the IRA, stated he didn't recognise the court and refused to put forward any defence or to make any further statements. After carrying out the sentence, the IRA was alleged to have passed a death sentence on the hangmen.

In February 1945, Albert was contacted by the Irish authorities and asked if he would be willing to train an Irish executioner. Having received permission from the Home Office, he travelled into Manchester city centre, where he met Thomas Johnstone, who had travelled over for two days' training at Manchester's Strangeways Gaol. Albert could tell at once that the man was not really a suitable candidate, describing him as old, short and timid, but nevertheless he trained him for two days and when a few days later he was engaged to carry out an execution at Dublin, Johnstone was to be his assistant. Despite concerns for the Irishman's safety, the execution of Montreal-born James Lehman passed off without incident.

Tom had a busy few months carrying out a dozen executions, including that of Aniceto Martinez at Shepton Mallet on 15 June. Martinez, an Hispanic, had broken into the house of a 75-year-old woman and savagely raped her. When the frail old lady staggered to the police station she told police she thought her attacker was an American and investigations soon pointed the finger at Private Martinez. He admitted the crime but claimed that he had been drunk and had entered the house thinking it was a brothel. The execution was significant in that it was the last time Albert acted as an assistant hangman, and the last time he worked with his Uncle Tom.

In October, Albert was asked to officiate at the execution of five German soldiers who had been convicted of murder in a Scottish army camp. Sergeant Major Rosterg had been a prisoner of war since September 1944. He was a regular soldier in the German army, not a Nazi like the majority of the prisoners. Sent to a camp near Devizes, his high standard of education soon earmarked him for the role of camp interpreter. In the winter of 1944 a number of fellow prisoners planned a mass breakout and when word reached the British guards the ringleaders were removed to the high security Comrie Camp in Perthshire, Scotland.

Unfortunately for Rosterg, he too was transferred to Comrie, and although word of the planned escape had not come from him, he was suspected, tried by kangaroo court, sentenced to death and in the early hours of 23 December, mercilessly beaten and kicked before being hanged in the hut latrine. Five men – Joachim Goltz, Heinz Brueling, Josef Mertens, Kurt Zuehlsdorff and Erich Pallme Koenig – were convicted of the murder and sentenced to death. Brueling and

Mertens were 21 years old, the rest a year younger. It was alleged that under the guidance of Koenig, Zuehlsdorff had put the rope around the man's neck and hanged him; the others had all beaten and kicked Rosterg before he died.

Arriving at Pentonville, for what would turn out to be the largest mass execution in modern penal history, Albert was met by assistant Steve Wade, and also Harry Allen, who had been invited back onto the list of assistant executioners following a period away, probably on some kind of active service. It was decided that they would be hanged in five single executions, as this would lessen any chance of a struggle or scene on the scaffold. None made any attempt to struggle and only Koenig, the last to go to the gallows, made any kind of statement, shouting, 'Long live the Fatherland!' as the rope was placed around his neck.

They were the first Germans to be executed for non-espionage crimes and it had been good practice having to deal with multiple executions on one day, as this was to form the bulk of the work Albert was engaged to carry out over the next four years. In all he was to stand face to face with over two hundred more convicted Germans, as retribution and the war crimes trials were to keep him busy over the next few years while Europe settled back into peacetime.

CHAPTER 7:
HANGMAN'S HOLIDAY

Six weeks after the multiple executions at Pentonville, Albert was back at the north London gaol to carry out the double hanging of another two German prisoners of war, Arnim Kuelne and Emil Schmittendorf, whose crimes had been remarkably similar to those of their five compatriots. A month or so before the war ended, inmates at a German POW camp on the outskirts of Sheffield were enraged when a tunnel they had long been working on was uncovered just days from completion. Believing an informer was at work they found a suspect – incorrect, as it turned out – in the form of Gerhardt Rettig, who had been seen near the tunnel entrance chatting to guards. Unlike the majority of prisoners, Rettig wasn't a National Socialist and when it was learned that threats had been made, it was decided to remove him to another camp. But while plans were being drawn up for his transfer, an angry mob attacked the suspect and kicked him to death. Four men were identified as ringleaders: two were later acquitted and two were hanged side by side on 16 November.

Following the Allied victory in the Second World War, Nazi

leaders were charged with war crimes and convicted at the Nuremberg trials, which were overseen by the American military. Taking place at the same time were a number of other war-crime trials, the first which concerned the British being that of those Nazis charged with crimes committed at the Bergen-Belsen concentration camp.

Its name usually shortened to 'Belsen', the camp was situated near the city of Celle, and set up in October 1942 as a transit centre. Later turned into a concentration camp by its second commandant, 39-year-old SS-Hauptsturmführer Josef Kramer, it housed prisoners who had become too weak to work as forced labour in German factories, and who were put to death in the gas chambers. The camp was liberated by the British army in April 1945; soldiers found over ten thousand unburied corpses and a further forty thousand sick and dying prisoners, of whom over twenty-eight thousand would subsequently die. As a result of these atrocities former members of staff from Belsen, including inmates who had taken part in acts of brutality against other prisoners, were charged with either being responsible for the murder of Allied nationals or the suffering of those in Belsen.

The Belsen trial was conducted by a British military tribunal in the converted gymnasium of a cavalry barracks at No. 30 Lindentrasse, Lünburg, Germany and began on 17 September 1945. It was to run for 53 days. President Major-General HMP Berney-Ficklin headed the panel, and four military lawyers handled the case for the prosecution. The accused comprised sixteen men including Josef Kramer, sixteen women, plus twelve former prisoners (seven men and five women). All were tried together and sat in the large dock, each with a number fixed to their chest.

There were two charges. The first was that a number of named members of staff, in violation of the law and usages of war, caused the death of persons interned at Belsen between 1 October 1942 and 30 April 1945, when responsible for the well-being of the persons interned there. The second count concerned atrocities carried out at the Auschwitz concentration camp in Poland. The two were heard together, as some defendants were charged with both counts.

On the afternoon of 16 November, the verdicts were delivered. Thirty-one prisoners were convicted on one or both counts and fourteen acquitted of all charges. On the following day the sentences were read out to the prisoners. Eleven were sentenced to death by hanging; nineteen others were sentenced to various terms of imprisonment.

Josef Kramer, Fritz Klein, Peter Weingartner, Franz Hoessler, Karl Francioh, Ansgar Pichen, Franz Stofel, Wilhelm Dorr, Juana Bormann, Elisabeth Volkenrath and Irma Grese were sentenced to death by hanging. The sentence was translated for them into German as 'Tode durch den strang', meaning literally 'death by the rope'.

Kramer was the Belsen camp commandant, Klein officiated as the camp doctor and Hoessler was both compound commandant and also in charge of No. 2 Camp. The remainder of the men were mostly conscripts, holding subordinate positions, with duties that included supervising working parties, kitchens and ration stores. Only Kramer, Klein and Hoessler were officers, the remainder being mostly NCOs.

Irma Grese, a compound commander at Belsen, was perhaps the most notorious of the female Nazi war criminals. Born in October 1923, she left school in 1938 at the age of 15 and, following a short stint working in a hospital, she was sent to work at the Ravensbrück Women's Concentration Camp near Berlin in 1940, becoming a guard at the age of 19. In March 1943, she was transferred to Auschwitz, later rising to the rank of Senior SS Supervisor, the second highest rank that SS female concentration camp personnel could attain. In January 1945, she returned to Ravensbrück before being transferred to Belsen in March. At her trial survivors gave details of the murder, torture and cruelty that she engaged in during her time at Auschwitz and Ravensbrück, and later at Belsen. The court heard testimonies of acts of sadism, beatings, arbitrary shootings, and the savaging of prisoners by her trained dogs. She also selected prisoners for the gas chambers. She chose to dress in jackboots, habitually carried a whip and pistol and was said to enjoy shooting prisoners in cold blood. In her hut, following the camp liberation, soldiers found a lampshade that had been made from the skins of a number of inmates.

Forty-two-year-old Juana Bormann had said at her trial that she had joined the SS auxiliary in the summer of 1938 to earn more money. She first served at the Lichtenburg concentration camp in Saxony and, in 1939, she was assigned to oversee a work crew at the new Ravensbrück women's camp. In March 1942 she was one of a handful of women selected for guard duty at Auschwitz No. 1 Camp in Poland. Standing a little over five feet tall, she was notorious for her cruelty and was known in the camp as the 'Weisel' and 'the woman with the dogs'. She had a habit of unleashing her German shepherd dog, 'the big bad wolfhound' as she called it, on helpless prisoners. Later that year she moved to Auschwitz Birkenau as an Aufseherin (supervisor). She came under the command of Irma Grese, moving to Hindenburg in 1944, before arriving at Belsen in March 1945.

Twenty-six-year-old Elisabeth Volkenrath had claimed she did not volunteer into the SS, and that the role of Oberaufseherin (senior supervisor) she held at Belsen was not an important one; she had no administrative control in the camp, and the job mainly consisted of detailing other overseers to particular jobs. She was responsible for the actions of those under her as well as for allocating their duties. The allegations against her for her crimes at Auschwitz were so numerous that the authorities stopped collecting any more evidence at a very early stage of their enquiries. At the trial it was testified that during 1942 Volkenrath had made selections and given orders that prisoners be loaded onto lorries and transported to the gas chamber. In her testimony, she denied having made gas chamber selections herself, but claimed that she had attended selections because she had to be present as she was in charge of the women's camp. She maintained that her role was merely to see that the prisoners were kept quiet and orderly.

The eleven sentenced to death all lodged an appeal to the convening officer, which was in turn forwarded to Field Marshal Montgomery. All appeals for clemency were rejected.

After a number of messy executions by firing squad, the British authorities at Lunburg were keen that the executions they sanctioned should be carried out efficiently. It was agreed that Albert should officiate at Hameln and so, shortly after lunch on Tuesday, 11 December, he caught a plane from Northolt aerodrome for a flight to Buckeburg in Germany.

The plane landed in the early evening and was met by an officer and his driver, who escorted Albert on a windswept 40-minute drive through war-torn Germany to the fairy-tale setting of Hameln. Arriving at the jail in Westphalia, Albert was ushered into a meeting with a number of senior dignitaries seconded from the prison service back home, who were discussing the scheduled executions that had become their responsibility.

Albert was to hang thirteen people, eleven from Belsen along with two others – Georg Otto Sandrock and Ludwig Schweinberger, convicted at Luneburg by the War Crimes

Commission for the murder of Pilot Officer Gerald Hood, a British prisoner of war at Almelo, Holland, on 21 March 1945. The arrangements were left to the hangman's discretion and were scheduled to take place on Thursday morning. Albert was billeted outside the prison and after a good night's sleep, at a little before 9 a.m. on Wednesday, he reported at the gaol to prepare for his duty. He knocked at the gate and was immediately greeted by a surly, gruff, German prisoner officer who enquired as to his business. Unable to explain to the non-English-speaking guard why he was there, he was rescued by Regimental Sergeant Major Richard O'Neill, a member of the Control Commission, seconded to be his assistant for the duration of the visit.

That afternoon each prisoner was weighed and measured so that the correct drops could be calculated. The multiple executions were to take place in a purpose-built execution room at the end of one of the prison's wings, on a gallows specially constructed by the Royal Engineers to a Home Office blueprint. Armed with the prisoners' personal details Albert retired to his quarters, where he worked out the drops and the order in which the prisoners would be put to death. It was decided to hang the three women in three single executions followed by double executions for the men. This was done in a chivalrous attempt to spare the women prisoners from hearing the repeated drops, as the tiny cells they were held in were just along the corridor from the drop room. With the calculations and death list completed, Albert and his new assistant filled a sandbag and carried out a test drop, leaving the rope to stretch.

On the following morning, under the guidance of Brigadier Paton-Walsh and Deputy Governor Wilson of Wandsworth and Strangeways prisons respectively, the official party assembled. Satisfied that all was ready, Albert walked into the corridor and called for Elisabeth Volkenrath. She exited her tiny cell and walked down the corridor escorted by two German guards. Out in the corridor, Albert pinioned her arms and as she was led onto the scaffold, O'Neill swiftly strapped her ankles as the rope was secured around her slim neck. Seeing all was ready Albert pulled the lever, giving her a drop of 7 feet 5 inches. The doctor followed the hangman into the pit and recorded that death had been instant. The time of execution was given as 9.34 a.m. The body was left to hang for just 20 minutes before being removed from the rope and placed in a coffin. The drop was reset and prepared for Irma Grese. Her last word was 'Schnell!' as she took her place on the trapdoor. She went to her death at 10.03 a.m. and Juana Bormann followed her onto the drop at 10.38 a.m.

Another rope was fixed to the beam and, following a break for refreshment, all was made ready for Josef Kramer and 57-year-old Doctor Fritz Klein. At 205 pounds and standing 6 feet 2 inches, 39-year-old Kramer was the very image of his press nickname, 'the Beast of Belsen'. He towered over the doctor and was given a drop of 6 feet, which was 17 inches shorter than the older man. The double execution took place 11 minutes after noon, and was timed at 25 seconds. Franzich and Weingartner were hanged at 12.46 p.m. Following a break for lunch, Sandrock and Schweinsburger were executed at 1.59 p.m., Pineken and Hohsler at 2.37 p.m., and finally Stakel and Dorr at 4.16 p.m.

With his duties complete, Albert left the gaol and returned to his billet. After resting and a wash and change he was entertained at a mess party that night before returning to England, where he had a forthcoming appointment at Wandsworth with the first man to be executed for treason in England following the end of hostilities.

John Amery was the Harrow-educated son of Leopold

Amery, the Secretary of State for India and a leading figure in Churchill's wartime cabinet. Amery had left England in 1935 and worked as a film producer in Spain. In 1940, while living in France, he became caught up in the invasion. Amery approached the head of the 'English Service' in Germany and offered to broadcast propaganda messages. He then made regular visits to prisoner-of-war camps in France, trying to persuade captured soldiers to change sides.

Arrested in northern Italy in April 1945, he was charged with treason at the Old Bailey in November. Amery's defence put forward the claim that he had taken Spanish nationality and there were lengthy discussions as to whether he should stand trial for treason. On hearing there would have to be an inquiry, Amery chose to spare his family further embarrassment and opted to plead guilty. His trial lasted just eight minutes.

He was hanged on 19 December, and as Albert and assistant Harry Critchell entered the cell and led the traitor to the drop, Amery found the courage to speak to the hangman: 'I've always wanted to meet you, Mr Pierrepoint. But not, of course, under these circumstances!'

Two days later he travelled back across to Pentonville for a double execution before rounding off the year with his fifth visit to Wandsworth, where he dispatched 24-year-old Robert Blaine, who had murdered a Canadian soldier on leave in London.

Tom's engagement diary was beginning to get much thinner: apart from the executions allocated to him by the American authorities at Shepton Mallet, entries for 1945 contained just two dates at Leeds and trips to Norwich, Cardiff and a last visit to Pentonville, where he hanged American deserter Karl Hulten for the murder of a London taxi driver. Albert was due to execute Hulten's partner in crime, 21-year-old Elizabeth Jones, at Holloway, but she was granted a reprieve a few days before she was due to hang, much to the anger of Winston Churchill, who believed she was equally as guilty and deserved the full penalty of the law.

The year 1946 marked the fortieth anniversary of Tom's appointment as a hangman and it was also to be his final year. The first execution of the new year, carried out by Albert, was to be one of the most controversial during the aftermath of the war. William Joyce was born in New York of Irish-American parents. Raised in Ireland, in 1922 his family moved to England, where he was educated at a London university. In 1933 he joined the British Union of Fascists, and secured a British passport by falsely claiming to have been born in Galway. In 1937, after being expelled from Oswald Mosley's Fascist party, Joyce started his own British Nazi party and shortly before the war broke out he fled to Germany. Between September 1939 and April 1945, Joyce found lasting notoriety when he earned the nickname 'Lord Haw Haw' for his 'Germany Calling....' radio broadcasts, a stream of anti-British messages and falsehoods recorded in and broadcast from Hamburg. They were designed to undermine morale on the home front, but soon became treated as nothing more than a joke and his upper-crust voice was the source of mocking and ridicule by music-hall and radio comedians of the day.

As hostilities drew to a close Joyce was wounded and captured by British troops as he tried to flee Germany via the Danish border, trapped by his instantly recognisable voice. At his three-day trial, held at the Old Bailey in September, his defence drew on the issue of nationality: they claimed that as he was born in America he could not be a traitor, as he did not hold allegiance to the crown. Two of the three counts on which he was to have been tried were dismissed, but he was convicted of treason because of the passport he had lied to obtain. As the British passport he held did not expire until July 1940, technically, from the moment war was declared until his British passport expired – a period of some nine months – he was a British citizen. Therefore, as he had been working for the enemy during this time, he had been committing treason and for this he was convicted. Given a drop of 7 feet 4 inches he went to the gallows without a struggle and died instantly.

Later that morning, Albert and assistant Alex Riley travelled across London to Pentonville, where they had another appointment with a traitor. This time it was to hang Theodore John William Schurch, a 27-year-old private in the RASC, court-martialled at Chelsea in September on nine charges of treachery and one of desertion with intent to join the enemy.

Schurch was a former member of the British Union of Fascists, born in London of Swiss parents, who joined the British Army in 1936. While serving in Tobruk he volunteered to join a front-line unit in order to desert, and when he was taken prisoner he asked his Italian guards to put him in touch with intelligence officers. Schurch told them he was a Swiss subject and that, although born in London, his father had registered him as Swiss. He then gave them information he had gathered from British prisoners of war in Italy. His defence claimed he was a poor uneducated fool, but Schurch was found guilty on all ten charges. He was the last person executed for treachery in Great Britain.

On 8 February, Tom carried out the first execution to take place in Glasgow for almost 20 years. Twenty-one-year-old John Lyon was convicted before Lord Mackay at Glasgow

High Court, in December 1945, of the murder of 19-year-old John Thomas Brady, a recently demobbed Royal Navy sailor. On the night of 20 October 1945, Lyon was one of a crowd of eight youths who ventured into Glasgow's Argyle Street looking for trouble. Coming across members of a rival gang they set upon one youth who managed to outrun them before attacking Brady, an innocent bystander, unconnected to any gang, who was stabbed to death with a bayonet and a wood chisel. During the ferocious attack he received 40 stab wounds. Although five of the gang were arrested, only four were brought to trial; three of these were found guilty and sentenced to death. The youngest of those convicted was liable for the death penalty, as his 18th birthday had fallen on the final day of the trial. He and another man were reprieved and Lyon was left to face the hangman alone, becoming the first man executed at Barlinnie Prison. Tom carried out the execution, assisted, it is believed, by Steve Wade.

A month later Tom carried out his last execution at Durham, when he hanged former soldier Charles Prescott who had shot dead his girlfriend's sister following the break-up of his relationship. The victim was not the one he had intended, and at his trial he claimed the gun had gone off accidentally when he had been startled by a horse.

While his uncle went to work at Durham, Albert made his second visit to Germany, where on the afternoon of 8 March he hanged eight men convicted by the War Crimes Commission. In four double executions he hanged Renoth Hans and August Buhning at 2.40 p.m., Friedrich Konig and Otto Franke at 3.10 p.m., Alfred Butner and Willy Mackensen at 3.45 p.m. and finally Erich Heyer and Johann Braschoss at 4.10 p.m.

Three weeks after Charles Prescott met his end on the scaffold at Durham, South African seaman Arthur Charles followed in his footsteps. This execution marked the debut of Stephen Wade as number one. The promotion of Wade was another sign that the career of the aged Tom Pierrepoint was drawing to a close, but the end of the road hadn't quite been reached. On 6 April he was back at Glasgow, where he was engaged to hang hard-man and habitual criminal Patrick Carraher.

The 39-year-old Carraher, 'the fiend of the Gorbals', had been sentenced to death at what was his third murder trial. In 1938 he had been jailed for three years after his trial for murder ended with a conviction for culpable homicide. Carraher had slit the throat of a man who had attempted to break up an argument he had been involved in. Following his release, Carraher continued to earn his living from theft and housebreaking, often using violence. In 1943, he faced a second murder trial, and this time he was sent to prison for the attempted murder of a man with a razor. As before, he served a meagre sentence, earning his freedom in the autumn of 1945. However, he was to be at liberty for just a few weeks. On 23 November, upon hearing that his brother-in-law was involved in a street fight, Carraher rushed to help. Watching the fight was John Gordon, a recently demobbed former prisoner of war who had seen more than twenty years' service with the Seaforth Highlanders. Carraher mistakenly assumed Gordon was connected with the fight and plunged a carving knife deep into his neck; Gordon died in hospital. Carraher was asleep in bed when detectives came to arrest him. Although he initially denied the attack, several former friends testified against him. His defence was that the knife he carried had a short blade and could therefore not have caused the fatal deep wound. This was dismissed when medical evidence showed that with force his knife could easily have penetrated to the depth of the wound.

On 2 March, Carraher's luck ran out and he was sentenced to death. It was claimed that as Tom went to pinion him in the cell, Carraher turned on his guards and during a struggle managed to punch a warder, breaking his nose.

Tom was called into action three times in April, his busiest period for several years. Besides the visit to Glasgow he made two trips to Manchester, where he hanged Harold Berry on 9 April for the murder of a Manchester moneylender, and two weeks later Martin Coffey, who had shot dead the proprietor of a city-centre pawnshop.

Albert was engaged in two executions in one day at Wandsworth on 2 April, when he hanged two Polish army deserters for the murder of a Russian black marketeer. Fearing trouble on the drop, it was decided the two men would hang an hour apart, a practice the authorities chose to adopt on a number of subsequent executions.

On 15 May, Albert carried out the execution of ten Germans convicted of war crimes: Erich Hoffmann and Friedrich Uhrig were hanged at 3.20 p.m. Ludwig Lang and Hermann Lommes followed at 3.55 p.m. At 4.23 p.m. Wilhelm Scharschmidt and Emil Gunther were hanged. Bruno Bothcer and Otto Bopf went to the gallows at 4.56 p.m.; Karl Amberger and Franz Kircher at 5.30 p.m.

On the following morning he carried out another three doubles and one single execution: Eberhard Schoengrath and Erwin Knop at 9.45am; Herbert Gernoth and Wilhelm Hadler at 10.15am; Friedrich Beeck was hanged alone at 10.40am, and finally two doctors, Bruno Tesch and Karl Weinbacher, were hanged side by side at 11.23am. No problems were recorded at any of the executions.

On 28 May, Tom carried out an execution at Lincoln, hanging Leonard Holmes for the murder of his wife. It was the aged hangman's last execution inside an English prison.

Tom was now walking with a stick and becoming more disabled with arthritis, and with official correspondence concerning his conduct flying to-and-fro from various sources, the end was moving closer and closer.

On 10 August, Tom travelled to Glasgow where he hanged 20-year-old John Caldwell. On 26 March, a couple had asked their neighbour James Straiton, a retired detective, to accompany them back to their house, where they suspected a burglar was at work. Noticing the back window open, he climbed through. Inside were two youths, who made their escape after shooting Straiton dead. Detectives suspected the killer might be the same man responsible for break-ins at a number of houses in the area recently and at which a clear set of fingerprints had been left. This led police to Caldwell who was arrested, along with his father. At his trial before Lord Mackay at Glasgow High Court in June, it was shown that Caldwell senior acted as a fence, who sold on goods that his son and his younger accomplice stole. The trial ended with Caldwell condemned to death, while his accomplice on the night the murder took place, a 15-year-old youth, was detained at His Majesty's Pleasure. Caldwell's father and girlfriend were also convicted, but of the lesser charge of receiving stolen goods.

Details of this, the last execution carried out by Tom Pierrepoint, are sketchy: the assistant, if one was indeed used, was again named as Steve Wade.

Like his brother 36 years before, Tom was never informed his services were no longer required; it was simply a case of the letters drying up. Rumours in the press circulated that the Home Office had asked Tom to retire, but in another interview shortly after the death of his wife, he refused to answer questions, or to confirm or deny anything, telling the reporter the Home Office forbade him to even confirm his name. Three days after his uncle's last execution Albert was at work again at Hameln Prison. Unusually, this visit was to carry out just a single execution, that of Teofil Walasek, instead of the multiple drops he had carried out on previous visits.

Albert had recently left the grocery business and had taken over the running of a public house on Manchester Road, Hollinwood, between Oldham and Manchester. The pub had the memorable name of Help the Poor Struggler, a name sure to give journalists plenty of puns when writing about the hangman.

On 6 September, Albert and assistants Harry Critchell and Harry Allen carried out two executions at Wandsworth. Sydney Smith had shot dead a wealthy horse- and cattle-dealer at his home at Hollington, near Hastings. He was convicted at Sussex Assizes in July. Sussex no longer housed a prison that carried out executions, so Smith was sent to south London.

David Baillie Mason was a Surrey engineer sentenced to death at the Old Bailey for the murder of his wife by strangling. Coincidentally, although the two men's ages differed by 15 years, they had the same height and weight, and working out the calculations Albert gave them an identical drop of 7 feet 7 inches.

Smith went to the gallows at 9.00 a.m. without incident. Mason followed at 10.15 a.m. Harry Allen noted in his diary that Mason's execution was very poor and the hangmen were very grateful of the work done by the 'screws'. Mason had, in fact, managed to struggle free as they went to secure his arms in the condemned cell, and was able to punch assistant Critchell in the face before being restrained and dragged to the gallows.

Three weeks after the Wandsworth execution, Albert travelled to Austria. After a frightening episode on his first night in the capital, Vienna, when he was almost mugged by two Russian soldiers, Albert travelled on to Karlou Gaol in Graz, where he was engaged to train an Austrian executioner and two assistants in the British method of execution. Previous execution procedure in Austria was reminiscent of 19th-century British executions when hangman William Calcraft would strangle to death condemned persons with short drops of just a few feet. Eight young men were hanged in four double executions at 30-minute intervals, with the trainees acting as assistants. Within a few weeks, the Austrian authorities wrote that they had been very impressed with the British hangman's skill and that the Austrian hangmen whom Albert had taught were refusing to carry out any further executions unless the British system was copied over there.

October was to be Albert's busiest month as an executioner. On the 8th he hanged 16 war criminals at Zuchthaus Hameln. Starting at 10.27 a.m. with the double execution of Walter Grimm and Karl Mumm, he carried out four more double executions before lunch; two doubles after and finished off with two single executions, the final one being the execution of Ludwig Knorr at 3.36 p.m.

Three days later he carried out another dozen executions: At 8.59 a.m. Karl Reddehase and Walter Quakernack were hanged together. Then followed five more double executions, ending with Johann Frahm and Ewald Jauch, who dropped to their deaths at 11.26 a.m.

On 16 October, the American authorities carried out the executions of the main German leaders who had been convicted at Nuremberg. Reports in the press suggested that Albert was engaged to carry out the sentences, but they were actually carried out by Master Sergeant Woods in a converted gymnasium. Three scaffolds were used, along with the standard cowboy coil noose and a fixed 5-feet drop. Reports leaked out later that the executions were horrific, some of the trapdoors on the gallows being too small for the bodies to drop into without striking the sides, and a number of the condemned men lived for many minutes on the rope, suffering death by painful strangulation.

At the time, Albert and assistant Harry Kirk were at Pentonville to bring to an end a gruesome murder case that had shocked the country earlier that summer. On the afternoon of 21 June, the body of 32-year-old film extra Margery Gardner was found in a Notting Hill hotel room. She had been bound at the ankles, bitten, whipped and then savagely mutilated; the cause of death was asphyxiation. The room had been booked to a Mr and Mrs N. G. C. Heath with an address in Hampshire. Police suspected the killer may have been Heath, a former airforce officer with a long criminal past, but neglected to release his photograph in the press, fearing it may prejudice the case when it came to court.

Reading about the discovery of the body, Heath wrote to detectives and stated that he had loaned Margery the key to his room so she could 'entertain a friend'. Meanwhile, now posing as Group Captain Rupert Brooke, Heath had travelled to Bournemouth where he met Doreen Marshall, a former Wren, who was convalescing at the seaside resort following an illness. On the evening of 3 July they had dinner at her hotel and later departed together. When Miss Marshall failed to return to her hotel the police were informed. 'Brooke' offered to help the investigation, but when he visited the police station he was recognised as Heath, wanted for the Notting Hill murder and detained. Five days later Doreen Marshall's body was found in some bushes. She had been sexually assaulted, mutilated and her throat cut. Heath's three-day trial began at the Old Bailey on 24 September. Faced with the brutal nature of the crimes, his counsel chose to offer a defence of insanity. The jury took less than an hour to convict him.

Seeing the prisoner in the number 2 condemned cell at Pentonville on the afternoon of Tuesday, 15 October, Albert noted he was the most handsome man he had ever hanged. Five days before, while in Germany, Albert had been entertained in the evening following the 12 executions by a number of RAF officers who had been in Heath's old squadron. Knowing that their erstwhile colleague was to be hanged within the week by the country's chief hangman, they spoke fondly of him, recalling a conversation with Heath about his fascination with women.

'Neville, you must have had hundreds of affairs,' someone had joked at a cocktail party.

Taking the remark seriously, Heath swilled his pink gin and thought studiously for a moment, as if totting up the figures in his head.

'Not hundreds, old boy, but thousands... and the funny thing is I've never been the slightest in love with any of them.'

Prisoner 2059 Neville George Clevely Heath was smoking a pipe as Albert and Harry Kirk entered his cell. Without a word they walked across the room and secured his wrists. Heath looked at the door to the scaffold that had silently slid open and spoke to the warders. 'Come on boys, let's be going!' Contrary to reports that later appeared in the press, there was no hitch and death was instant. Heath was alleged to have asked for a whisky before the hangmen entered the cell, adding: 'In the circumstances, you might make that a double!'

In early 1947 Albert returned to Germany. On Wednesday, 22 January, he hanged a 28-year-old British soldier named Frank Upson, who had been sentenced to death by court martial in

Germany for the murder of a German girl. Assisting Albert was RSM O'Neill, who had been present on all previous executions, and a new assistant, Sergeant Joseph Hunter, an NCO in the Royal Canadian Mounted Police.

On the following day, Albert, with the same two assistants, dispatched a further 11 war criminals. Beginning with a double execution at 8.59 a.m., they then carried out four more double executions at 30-minute intervals, ending with a single execution timed at 11.34 a.m.

Returning to Manchester, Albert found a letter waiting inviting him to carry out the execution of Walter Graham Rowland at Strangeways Prison at the end of February. The name of Rowland had once before featured in Albert's diary, way back in the summer of 1934, when as a new assistant he had been detailed to assist his uncle after Rowland had been convicted of the murder of his daughter. A few days before he was due to go to the gallows, Rowland was reprieved and after serving six years he was released on the proviso he join the army.

On 20 October 1946, the body of Olive Balchin, a 40-year-old Manchester prostitute, had been found on a city-centre bombsite, beaten to death with a cobbler's hammer. Rowland was identified as having bought the type of hammer used, and witnesses reported seeing him arguing with the woman on the night before she died. When questioned, he denied murdering her but confessed he suspected she had infected him with venereal disease.

He strongly denied the charges throughout his five-day trial in December, although the evidence against him was strong and he was convicted. On 22 January, five days before his appeal was due to be heard, David Ware, a prisoner in Liverpool Gaol, confessed that he was the real killer. Ware's account was soon rejected when it was revealed that there was nothing he had said during the confession that hadn't already been reported in the newspapers. Ware later retracted the confession, Rowland's appeal was unsuccessful and on 27 February Albert and assistant Harry Critchell executed him. In 1951, David Ware was convicted of the attempted murder of a woman whom he attacked with a hammer. He committed suicide, by hanging himself with a sheet, in his cell at Broadmoor in 1954.

After carrying out two executions in London in mid-March, Albert travelled across to Dublin at the end of the month for the execution of Joseph McManus, who had shot dead the woman he was having an affair with. Thomas Johnstone, the man Albert had trained briefly at Manchester Prison almost two years earlier, was scheduled to carry out the execution, and at his request the governor of Mountjoy Prison had requested that Albert act in the capacity of assistant executioner, but taking full fee for his trouble.

Meeting the would-be executioner in the prison, Albert could see that Johnstone had forgotten all his training, and at each stage of the preparations, Albert had to step in and put things right. Asked if all was satisfactory, Albert told the governor that he didn't want to take any responsibility for the execution and it was soon decided that the two executioners would swap roles, with Albert taking charge and full accountability. The execution took place without a hitch and Johnstone's brief career as Ireland's executioner came to an end.

Albert made a fleeting trip to Hameln to hang Dr Hans Koerbel on 7 March, before making another more extensive visit at the end of April as the letter below details:

Pierrepoint: A Family of Executioners

Accounts Branch
The Foreign Office
Norfolk House
St James's Square
London SW1

I enclose the certificate required in connection
with the remuneration of Mr. Albert Pierrepoint,
executioner, for his recent services to the Control
Commission in Germany.

I hereby certify that Mr. Albert Pierrepoint,
executioner, arrived in the British Zone on the
30th April 1947 by air and left again by surface
route on the 3rd May 1947.

Mr. Pierrepoint carried out the judicial
sentences of execution by hanging 3 women and 5
men on the 2nd May 1947, and 5 men on the 3rd May
1947, a total of 13 persons (all of whom were war
criminals).

The executions were carried out by this official
efficiently and to my entire satisfaction.

Those executed at the Zuchthaus Hameln on May
2nd were:
Elisabeth Marschall
Grete Bösel
Dorothea Binz
Karl Ebsen
Arthur Gross
Johann Heitz
Heinz Stumpp
Karl Truschel

The following persons were executed on May 3rd:
Gerhard Schidlausky & Johann Schwarzhuber at
08.58 hrs,
Rolf Rosenthal & Gustav Binder at 09.37 hrs,
Ludwig Randohr at 10.03 hrs

The three women Albert hanged on 2 May had been convicted for crimes that took place at Ravensbrück concentration camp near Furstenberg in Germany. It was the only Nazi concentration camp for women and also acted as a training base for female SS supervisors, with over three thousand women undergoing training there. On completion of training, some took on duties at Ravensbrück; the remainder were sent to a number of other camps. Ravensbrück had been established in 1938 and was liberated by the Russian Army at the end of April 1945. It was estimated the number of victims there totalled over ninety-two thousand.

Between December 1946 and February 1947, a court in the British zone tried 16 members of the Ravensbrück staff. All were found guilty except one, who died during the trial. Eleven were sentenced to hang, including four women, and the rest to lengthy periods of imprisonment.

At 60 years of age, Elisabeth Marschall was the eldest of those executed. Greta Bösel, born in 1908, had trained as a nurse before she went to work in Ravensbrück in August 1944. Her role was to supervise female working teams, and she was alleged to have used the edict: 'Let them rot if they can't work.' Dorothea Binz was born in 1920 in Dulstarlake. A single woman, she had joined the staff of Ravensbrück in April 1939 and worked as an Aufseherin in the women's camp. She was arrested in Hamburg in May 1945, before being brought back to stand trial at Ravensbrück.

In the summer Albert made another trip to Germany.

Again, official papers noted him arriving in the British Zone on 25 June and leaving by air on 28 June. He carried out the judicial sentences of execution, by hanging, of one woman and twelve men, a total of thirteen persons, on 26 June. The executions were carried out in his usual most efficient manner and to the entire satisfaction of the commission. The papers again listed the names and times of execution:

```
Following persons executed Zuchthaus
Hameln on June 26th
```

Vera Salvequart	09.03 hrs
Longin Nowakowski & Waclaw Winiarski	09.30 hrs
Kazimierz Bachor & Josef Klinler	10.02 hrs
Albert Luetkemeyer & Wilhelm Keus	10.40 hrs
Gustav Alfred Jepsen & Hans Kieffer	11.22 hrs
Richard Schnur & Karl Haug	11.57 hrs
Kurt Rasche & Alfred Peek	12.27 hrs

Twenty-eight-year-old Vera Salvequart was the fourth woman convicted at the first Ravensbrück trial in February. She had argued that she had not been an SS guard, only a prisoner in Ravensbrück. With a shortage of personnel, the SS frequently made German prisoners supervise other non-German inmates. Like Dorothea Binz she had also first trained as a nurse, before embarking on a life of petty crime. Salvequart had been recruited to guard duties while serving as a prisoner, having been convicted of theft. Sent to Ravensbrück in December 1944, she worked as a nurse in the camp's hospital wing, where it was alleged she had administered poison to some of the patients. She petitioned the King for a reprieve, claiming that her last imprisonment was due to her stealing plans relating to the V2 rocket that she intended to pass to the British secret service. She was granted a stay of execution while the appeal was heard. It was in due course rejected, however, and she was returned to Hameln to await a flying visit from the British hangman.

Albert next arrived in the British Zone on 3 September, again by air, leaving on 6 September. On this visit he carried out the execution of one British soldier, three Polish and ten Germans on the 5 September. The executions were again officially noted as being carried out in the most efficient and discreet manner.

The following persons executed Zuchthaus Hameln on Sept 5:

Charles Edward Patrick	09.03 hrs
Tadeusz Kun (Brunswick/armed robbery)	09.37 hrs
Franciczek Smok (Osnabrück/armed plundering)	09.37 hrs
Edward Kubick (Meppen/firearms)	10.08 hrs
Karl Paul Schwanz (Essen/war crimes)	10.08 hrs
Karl Cremer (Essen/war crimes)	10.41 hrs
Albert Roesner (Essen/war crimes)	10.41 hrs
Stephan Streit (Hamburg/war crimes)	11.09 hrs
Josef Knoth (Iserlohn/war crimes)	11.09 hrs
Michael Rotschopf (Essen/war crimes)	11.36 hrs
Johann Wilhelm Luetfring (Hamburg/war crimes)	14.42 hrs
Wilhelm Dammann (Hamburg/war crimes)	14.42 hrs
Friedrich Hochstattner (Osnabrück/war crimes)	15.17 hrs
Heinz Stellpflug (Osnabrück/war crimes)	15.17 hrs

Corporal Patrick was a soldier serving with the British Army of the Rhine who had been sentenced to death by a military court martial. Assisting Albert and Richard O'Neill for the first time was Edwin James Roper.

On 29 April, while in London on an official visit to the War Office, Albert had been leaving a Soho public house when he came across a crowd of people surrounding a man lying in the road next to a motorcycle. Thinking it was the result of accident he carried on his way and only when he picked up the following morning's newspapers did he realise it was the body of Alec de Antiquis, who had been shot dead as he tried to prevent three armed robbers fleeing from a jewellery shop. Trying to prevent their escape by swinging his motorcycle in their path, he was shot in the head by one of the gang, who escaped in the busy traffic.

A witness told police he had seen two masked men enter a building on Tottenham Court Road, and a search uncovered a raincoat that was traced to 23-year-old Charles Henry Jenkins, who had a long criminal record. Two friends of Jenkins, Christopher James Geraghty and Terence Rolt, were also picked up. Under questioning Geraghty implicated Rolt in the murder and he, in turn, implicated Jenkins.

Mr Justice Hallet, at the Old Bailey, sentenced Jenkins and Geraghty to death, and Albert and his two assistants carried out the sentence at Pentonville on 19 September. The hard line taken in the passing and subsequent carrying out of the death penalty resulted in a large amnesty of weapons among the underworld, and to the disbanding of many criminal gangs.

Albert made one final trip to the Zuchthaus Hameln, Germany in 1947, when on 14 November he hanged sixteen men in eight double executions. Starting at 9.02 a.m., he then carried out the second at 9.36 a.m., another at 10.12 a.m, 10.46 a.m., and the final morning execution at 11.22 a.m. He then broke for lunch and carried out the final three double executions at 2.03 p.m., 2.34 p.m. and 3.08 p.m.

The final execution of the year took place at Bristol when, on 30 December, Albert and Harry Allen hanged a Polish soldier for the rape and murder of an elderly publican.

The year 1948 was to see another parliamentary debate on the subject of capital punishment, and as a result there were only ten executions in Great Britain and Ireland. While this may have had a detrimental effect on the earning power of rival executioner Steve Wade, Albert's bank balance was bolstered by a further heavy workload in Germany. On 29 January he carried out the execution of five war criminals and on the following day he hanged another ten in five double executions.

The following persons were executed at Hameln
Zuchthaus on 30th January 1948:

Marion Osuch als Borovic &	
Peter Bartsch	09.00 hrs
Ansis Zunde & Andrzej Paruszkiewicz	09.30 hrs
Manojlo Nikolic & Miloslaw Pavkovic	10.00 hrs
Mihajle Kordic & Pasaka Mehmedovic	10.31 hrs
Franc Safranauskas &	
Stojadin Mitrasinovic	11.03 hrs

A Hamburg newspaper, HNN, reported the execution in the following day's paper:

'Mass execution at Hameln'

On Thursday in Hameln Albert Pierrepoint,
the official British hangman, commenced the
execution of twenty-one War Criminals sentenced

to death by hanging. The first five to be executed
are Udo Kettenbeil, Otto Fricke, Tessmann, Karl
Schuette and Wilhelm Hennings. Operation
'Pontoon' as the execution is called, is the
greatest mass execution in the British Zone since
the surrender in Germany. Amongst the condemned
are sixteen Gestapo men who have been convicted
of the murder of fifty Allied Airmen.

The newspaper erroneously reported 21 persons executed instead of the correct total of 15. The airmen mentioned were portrayed being executed in cold blood at the end of the classic 1963 war film The Great Escape.

In February, Albert carried out three executions at home. On the 3rd, he travelled down to Cardiff, where he hanged a young collier who had committed the dreadful rape and murder of an old woman in the Rhondda Valley. Three days later, he travelled to Perth for his first execution in Scotland, where he hanged Stanislaw Myszka, a Polish deserter.

On 26 September 1947, 47-year-old Catherine McIntyre failed to turn up as planned at a friend's house. Her friends called at her isolated cottage overlooking Loch Tay, Tayside where she lived with her husband and three children and found her son outside the house, expecting his mother to return and let him in. Forcing entry into the house, they found her dead: bound and gagged with terrible cuts and bruises to her head and throat. Missing from the house were her gold wedding ring and a large amount of cash.

Myszka, who lived nearby in a Polish camp, was an immediate suspect. The bruises had been caused by the butt of a gun recovered in a field and which police believed the Pole had stolen from a house earlier that year. They also found at the murder scene a bloodstained shaving razor that had been used to cut the victim's throat. Traces of stubble found on the razor matched the whiskers on Myszka's face. He was arrested on 2 October, and when searched the stolen wedding ring was found hidden in his shoe. The jury at his trial in January needed less than 20 minutes to find him guilty. Albert and assistant Steve Wade hanged Myszka on the portable gallows erected in a cellar at Perth Prison.

The last execution in Great Britain before a temporary suspension of all death sentences took place at Pentonville, when Walter John Cross, a 21-year-old Dagenham lorry driver, was convicted of the murder of a crippled watchmaker. Neighbours had heard screams coming from a house at Barking on the night of 14 November 1947. They spotted a man leaving the house and when they went to investigate, they found the body of Percy Busby. He had been strangled and his empty wallet was found beside the body. Cross was identified as the man leaving the house. At his trial at the Old Bailey, it was alleged that he had gone to the house with a friend on the pretence that his friend wanted a watch repaired. The friend would leave the door ajar as he left and Cross would enter and steal the money from the wallet.

Albert returned to Hameln in February. Again he travelled by air, and carried out the executions to everyone's satisfaction.

Following prisoners executed Zuchthaus Hameln on 27 Feb 1948:

Hauser Friedrich	09.00 hrs
Friedrich Opitz	09.00 hrs
Alfred Schimmer	09.28 hrs
Walter Herberg	09.28 hrs
Otto Preiss	09.54 hrs

Johannes Post	09.54 hrs
Hans Kaehler	10.23 hrs
Oskar Schmidt	10.23 hrs
Walter Jacobs	10.50 hrs
Erich Zacharias	10.50 hrs
Emil Schulz	11.20 hrs
Emil Weil	11.20 hrs
Eduard Geith	11.46 hrs
Johann Schneider	11.46 hrs
Josef Gmeiner	12.08 hrs

A month later he was back again, this time executing four men in two double executions. Unusually, and quite coincidentally, all were given longer than average drops, each over 8 feet.

This is to certify that Mr Albert Pierrepoint, Official Executioner, arrived in the British Zone by air on the 23rd March 1948 and left again by air on the 25th March 1948.

On the 24th March Mr Pierrepoint carried out four executions by judicial hangings, as follows: One War Criminal plus three Allied Nationals sentenced to death by Control Commission Courts.

Mr Pierrepoint carried out his duties in a satisfactory manner and his conduct was discreet.

The following persons were executed at Hameln on 24th March.

Johannes Lehmann	09.00 hrs
Wasyl Skiba	09.00 hrs
Nikolay Steblinski	09.28 hrs
Zenon Lichotta	09.28 hrs

Up to this time the total number of persons executed in the British Zone since the start of occupation was 357, made up as follows:

Executions by judicial hanging	169
Executions by shooting	97
Executions by guillotine	91

The executions resulted from trials by the military, military government, Control Commission and German courts, and of the persons executed 126 were non-German nationals.

In April, Sydney Silverman MP, recommending the suspension of capital punishment for an experimental period of five years, introduced a Bill to the House of Commons to that effect. Passed by a narrow majority, it lead to reprieves being granted to all condemned murderers during that period, including that of Donald Thomas who was convicted of the murder of a London policeman.

Less than two months later the Bill was thrown out by the House of Lords. Commenting on the recently reprieved Thomas, Lord Schuster said he did not feel inclined to take part in an experiment 'which may be at the expense of the lives of every policeman...' In the same week the Bill was thrown out, Albert travelled back to Germany.

This is to certify that Mr Albert Pierrepoint, Official Executioner, arrived in the British Zone by air on the 7th June 1948 and left again by air on the 10th June 1948

On the 9th June Mr Pierrepoint carried out eight executions by judicial hanging, as follows:

a) WAR CRIMINALS:
Karl Finkenrath
Peter Klos
Georg Griesel
Otto Baumann
Otto Mohr
Heinrich Johann Heeren

b) PRISONERS CONVICTED BY CONTROL COMMISSION
COURTS:
Josef Czerwick
Jurko Dobosc

Mr Pierrepoint carried out his duties in a
satisfactory manner and his conduct was discreet.

On 26 July, Albert flew on another trip to Germany, returning by air on the 29th, after carrying out three executions that morning. Two were war criminals, the other being convicted by Control Commission Court. At 9.00 a.m. he hanged Ruth Clausius, followed by the double execution of Luis Schmidt and Jerzy Trawinski at 9.21 a.m.

Clausius and Schmidt had been convicted of war crimes at the second series of Ravensbrück trials held in April 1947. Ruth Clausius (née Hartmann) was born in July 1920. She was a member of the SS guard at Ravensbrück and had worked there in various capacities from July 1944. Following a spell in the punishment barracks she was promoted to SS Oberaufseherin (senior supervisor), in charge of the youth wing in early 1945, where she worked until the camp was liberated. Clausius was convicted of the torture and murder of men, women and children and of selecting prisoners for the gas chambers.

This is to certify that Mr Albert Pierrepoint,
Official Executioner, arrived in the British Zone
by air on the 15th September 1948 and left again
by air on the 20th September 1948. Mr Pierrepoint
carried out five executions by judicial hangings
as follows:

On 17th September 1948:
Doctor Walter Sonntag, 09.00 hrs
Artur Conrad, 09.00 hrs
Doctor Benno Orendi, 09.25 hrs

20th September 1948:
Gertrude Schreiber
Emma Ida Zimmer

Sixty-year-old Emma Zimmer had been a guard at the
Ravensbrück Concentration Camp. Dismissed from service
near the end of the war, either due to advanced age or chronic
alcoholism, she was tried by a British military court and
sentenced to death on 21 July 1948.

This is to certify that Mr Albert Pierrepoint,
Official Executioner, arrived in the British Zone
by air on the 27th October 1948 and left again by
air on the 29th October 1948. On the 29th October
1948, Mr Pierrepoint executed the under
mentioned war criminal by judicial hanging.

Dikty Gottlieb
Emil Friedrich

Mr Pierrepoint carried out his duties in a
satisfactory manner and his conduct was discreet.

The first person to go to the gallows in Great Britain following the rejection of the Suspension Bill was Stanley Joseph Clarke, a pig breeder from Great Yarmouth who had stabbed to death a chambermaid at a Yarmouth boarding house. After pleading guilty, his trial at Norfolk Assizes had lasted less than five minutes and he was hanged at Norwich on 18 November.

Leaving Norwich, Albert travelled straight to Liverpool, where he hanged a 22-year-old guardsman Peter Griffiths, who in May had carried out the rape and murder of a young girl at Blackburn's Queen's Park Hospital. Griffith's arrest came after a massive fingerprint hunt, involving over forty-six thousand men -- the entire male population of Blackburn. Hanged by Albert and Harry Allen, Griffiths walked bravely to his death and met his end, Albert later recalled, like a soldier.

A week later Albert travelled across to Ireland to hang William Gambon, who had battered a man to death with an iron bar in a Dublin tenement block. It appears there may have been some confusion with the appointment of an assistant executioner for this hanging, as Albert carried out the execution alone, for the only time in Great Britain and Ireland. It's possible that Thomas Johnstone had been the intended assistant, but following his shortcomings on his previous trip to the gaol, perhaps he had a change of heart at the last moment.

Albert travelled back to Germany on 6 December to carry out the executions of one war criminal and three Allied nationals. The men were hanged in two double executions on 9 December, and Albert flew home later that morning.

Although Albert had executed many women during his trips to Germany, he had not yet hanged a woman in a British prison. Engagements to hang Florence Ransom and Elizabeth

Jones during the war had both ended in reprieves, as had the execution of the Bolton mother and daughter he had been engaged to hang at Manchester in 1944. On 12 January 1949, however, Margaret Allen finally ended that trend.

In the early hours of Sunday, 29 August 1948, Mrs Nancy Chadwick was found dead in a road at Rawtenstall, Lancashire. She had been battered to death with a hammer. Allen, a neighbour, was routinely interviewed and after detectives noticed bloodstains on her kitchen walls, she readily confessed to the crime. She was tried at Manchester Assizes in December, where it was alleged she had committed the murder for gain: the victim was reputedly wealthy and Allen, having been forced to give up work, and being short of money, had attacked and robbed her friend. A petition for a reprieve in her home town received a lukewarm response. Denied her last request of being hanged in men's clothing, she went to the gallows in a prison frock, having kicked her last breakfast over saying, 'I don't want it and no one else is going to enjoy it!'

A week later Albert flew back to Germany, where he executed three men on 20 January, and another man on the following day. On 17 February, between trips to Lincoln and Liverpool, he flew back to Germany to carry out a single execution. The days of multiple hangings in Germany were now over, but as remaining war criminals were slowly being hunted down and convicted, he was still receiving the summons to carry out his duties.

When Albert travelled to Birmingham on 29 March, it was to hang one James Farrell, who had strangled a young girl in November 1948. A couple of hours after the body had been discovered, Farrell had walked into a Birmingham police station claiming he was a deserter from his unit and wanting to give himself up. From witnesses who had seen the girl on the previous evening, police already suspected the killer might be a soldier and detained him for further questioning. Farrell eventually confessed. He turned 19 in the condemned cell a few days before he was hanged, and was the youngest man to go the gallows for over 25 years.

Albert made two more flights to Germany in the summer, along with two trips to Pentonville and a rare visit to Winchester. On 4 August he made his first trip to Swansea for the double execution of Rex Harvey Jones, a collier from the Rhondda, and Robert Thomas Mackintosh, a steel worker from Port Talbot.

Jones had strangled his girlfriend while drunk; Mackintosh had also strangled a girl, after what the prosecution had alleged 'the devil of lust' had taken possession of him. Both were convicted on the same day and hanged together for convenience. Albert had travelled to the gaol by car, offering a lift to a new assistant, George Dickinson from Adlington, Lancashire. On the journey home, the execution – Dickinson's first – traumatised him and he was repeatedly ill, to the extent that he tendered his resignation a few days later.

Probably the most notorious murder case of the post-war period was that of John Haigh, dubbed in the press 'The Vampire Killer' or 'The Acid Bath Murderer'. In February 1949, wealthy widow Mrs Olive Durand Deacon went missing after arranging a business trip with Haigh, a fellow guest at the Kensington hotel where they both resided. When a friend became concerned about her whereabouts, Haigh offered to accompany her to the police station, where his manner aroused the suspicions of a female officer. A check into his past found he had a long criminal record and when detectives visited a small workshop/storeroom Haigh rented in Crawley, they found evidence to suggest that Mrs Deacon had been murdered. Haigh confessed he had shot her and dissolved her body in acid. He then admitted to having killed eight other people.

At his trial at Lewes Assizes in July, his defence put forward a plea of insanity. Haigh was made out to be a vampire killer who drank the blood of his victims. The prosecution claimed simply that Haigh had killed his victims for financial reasons and was nothing more than a ruthless killer.

A few days before he was to hang, Haigh had asked the governor if he could have a dummy run, as he was concerned that his slight frame and springy step would give the hangman problems. 'Mr Pierrepoint knows his duties well enough,' he was told by the governor, who refused to consider his request.

On 31 August 1949, Albert carried out a double execution at Hameln. Roman Klinski, a displaced Pole, and Mieczyslaw Antonowitz, a German, were hanged side by side at 8.00 a.m. Albert's final engagement in Germany was on 6 December, when he executed Jerzy Andziak, a German sentenced to death by a Control Commission Court. Again, a note was forwarded to the Foreign Office to the effect that Mr Pierrepoint had carried out his duties in a satisfactory manner and that his conduct had been discreet.

In total, over five thousand men and women were convicted of war crimes between 1945 and 1949 in the American, British and French zones, tried by Allied war crimes tribunals. They included staff from concentration camps, arrested and tried for murder and acts of brutality against their prisoners. Over five hundred were sentenced to death and the vast majority were condemned to hang, although no standard execution protocol was agreed – as we have seen, executions were also carried out by firing squad, or sometimes the guillotine. Those convicted in the Polish and Russian sectors were often executed in public, while a number of the high-profile executions carried out by the Americans at Nuremberg, Dachau and Landsberg were televised and shown on news broadcasts.

Albert Pierrepoint hanged two hundred people convicted of war crimes at Zuchthaus Hameln, along with two British soldiers convicted by court martial.

CHAPTER 8:
FAME AND THE ROYAL COMMISSION REPORT

As a result of the 1948 amendment to the Criminal Justice Bill, on 4 May 1949 the Royal Commission on Capital Punishment sat for the first time, the first of 63 meetings to debate 'whether liability under the criminal law in Great Britain to suffer capital punishment for murder should be limited or modified'. The wording was carefully chosen so that the outcome of the commission would look not at the abolition of the death penalty but merely at alternative methods or protocols pertaining to the current system. Over the next four years, the commission, led by Sir Ernest Gowers, visited Europe and America, looking at alternatives such as electrocution, the gas chamber and also the guillotine, to decide if hanging was still a proper method of dispensing justice in the 20th century. Albert would not be called upon to give evidence until November 1950.

The year 1949 had ended with an execution at Wandsworth, when, assisted by Harry Allen, Albert hanged Ernest Soper Couzins, a 49-year-old assistant caretaker at Canterbury Technical College, who had shot dead an insurance agent following a quarrel. When Couzins, a former Regimental Sergeant Major, appeared in the dock, he was sporting a heavy bandage covering a self-inflicted neck wound. The wound, caused by a failed suicide attempt, was so severe it had almost cost him his life and affected his speech to the extent he was barely able to make himself heard as he gave evidence at his trial. He collapsed as sentence of death was passed.

Gauging the prisoner's condition in the condemned cell, Albert proposed a drop of 7 feet 8 inches, long enough to cause instant death but hopefully not too long as to cause the neck wound to re-open and risk possible decapitation. The calculations still proved too long: the resulting drop tearing open Couzins' neck wound, spraying blood around the pit; the assistant hangman described the execution as 'very messy'. It was a rare mishap.

In January 1950, Albert travelled to Pentonville to hang Daniel Raven, a young Jewish advertising agent, who had used a heavy television aerial base to batter to death his wife's parents. The couple had been visiting Marie Raven in hospital after she had recently given birth to their first grandchild; later that night their bodies were discovered. Summoned to their house, Raven was seen to be wearing a clean shirt and tie and a different suit to the one he had been wearing just an hour beforehand. Detectives went to his house and in the boiler they found a partly burned suit containing bloodstains of the rare 'AB' type, the same as that of his father-in-law. Raven maintained his innocence and his counsel suggested that the killer was either a business rival of Goodman's, or someone taking revenge on his father-in-law, a known police informer.

In early March Albert carried out two executions in two days. On Wednesday, 8 March, he travelled to Norwich to hang James Rivett, who had strangled his girlfriend after her father had tried to split them up. Albert then travelled into London, where he had an engagement to hang a young lorry driver, whose execution was to go a long way towards finally bringing about the abolition of capital punishment in Great Britain.

On the afternoon of 30 November 1949, illiterate, Welsh-born lorry driver Timothy John Evans had walked into Merthyr Vale police station and confessed that he had disposed of his wife in London. He made contradictory statements about what had happened, which nevertheless intimated that he had killed his 20-year-old wife Beryl and their one year-old-baby, Geraldine. Three days later their bodies were discovered in a washhouse at 10 Rillington Place, Notting Hill, London. Both had been strangled. Evans told detectives that Beryl had fallen pregnant and a tenant at the house, Reg Christie, had offered to perform an abortion. Christie had then told him that Beryl had died during the operation and if he told the police Evans would also be blamed for her death. Evans said that Christie, a former policeman, had also offered to find a home for the baby Geraldine. Tried just for the murder of his daughter, Evans appeared at the Old Bailey in January. He stuck to his story that Christie had killed his wife and child. Christie was the chief witness for the prosecution. Faced with the varied accounts Evans had given, the prosecution exposed him as a braggart and a liar, and on the third day of his trial he was convicted. Christie burst into tears as sentence of death was passed.

Nottinghamshire colliery worker Syd Dernley was engaged as assistant executioner, and Albert, spying Evans as he exercised at Pentonville, decided that a long drop of 8 feet was required. Dernley wrote later that on the morning of the execution, Albert appeared a little on edge and snapped at his new assistant as he struggled to secure the noose with the pack-thread as they completed their preparations. He also told a tale that as the prison officer came to notify the hangmen that the official party had set off towards the condemned cell, Albert picked up a cigar, which he lit and smoked for a few seconds before placing it carefully on the edge of an ashtray. Entering the death cell, Evans was terrified as they pinioned his arms and led him to the drop. Dernley also noted that he clearly heard the sound of Evans's neck breaking as the drop fell. Returning to their quarters, Albert picked up the cigar and carried on with the smoke, the cigar staying lit: a trick the hangman often used to impress new assistants, showing a cool, calm air of confidence.

Three weeks later Albert again carried out two executions in two days. On Tuesday, 28 March, he was at Liverpool to hang George Kelly, convicted of the murder of the manager and assistant manager of the Cameo Cinema at Wavertree, Liverpool. In the spring of 1949, Leonard Thomas and John Bernard Catterall had been shot dead during a bungled robbery. A tip-off led police to two local small-time criminals, George Kelly and Charles Connolly. Kelly was said to have been the man who had robbed the cinema and shot the two men, while Connolly supposedly kept watch outside. They were tried together at Liverpool Assizes in January, with Kelly being defended by Miss Rose Heilbron, the first time a woman led for the defence in a murder case. The trial ended with the jury failing to reach a verdict and a retrial was ordered. This time Kelly and Connolly were tried separately. Kelly maintained, as he had throughout the first trial, that he did not know the co-accused. This was not believed, and when Connolly was persuaded to plead guilty to robbery, the fact that Kelly was deemed in league with him convinced the jury of his guilt and he was sentenced accordingly.

Kelly's hard-man reputation was shattered when he lost control as he was led to the gallows and soiled himself. Albert told an assistant that they didn't realise what Kelly had done until they took the body down, adding that the prison officers would make sure the news reached his friends outside the prison. (George Kelly received a posthumous pardon in 2003 when the Court of Criminal Appeal deemed the original verdict was unsafe. It was found that the police had withheld a witness statement at the original trial that could have helped Kelly's defence.)

Piotr Maksimowski was a Polish refugee from Beaconsfield, Buckinghamshire. He had been courting Dilys Campbell of Slough and she had led him to believe she was a war widow. Later she confessed that her husband was alive, and that they were still living together. On 31 December 1949, Maksimowski called at his local police station and, showing them his cut and bleeding wrists, confessed that he had killed a woman in the woods. Police discovered Campbell's body covered in a blanket with both wrists cut. Maksimowski told them they had agreed on a suicide pact: she could not face living a lie, and he could not stand to know she still lived with her husband. He claimed that he had lost his nerve after cutting her wrists, however, and had called the police in the hope that Campbell could get medical attention. He pleaded not guilty on the grounds of insanity at his trial. After the sentence of death had been passed on him, Maksimowski spoke through an interpreter and asked if he could be shot instead of hanged. The judge, Mr Justice Croom-Johnson, told him he had no power to deal with the matter as it had now passed out of his hands.

Maksimowski chose not to appeal, and appeared to have resigned himself to his fate. But just two days before he was due to make the nine o'clock walk to the gallows he made a failed attempt to commit suicide. During a game of cards with his warders he suddenly got to his feet as if to stretch his legs. Jumping up onto the bed he managed to break the narrow window in his cell by punching the glass and making a vain attempt to cut his wrists on the broken glass.

Albert travelled down to Birmingham following the execution of Kelly at Liverpool, where he met up with assistant Syd Dernley in a police officers' social club close to Winson Green Prison. After a few drinks they travelled across the city to the gaol, where they spied their man in his cell, his arm heavily strapped with a crepe bandage. Fearing possible trouble on the following morning, the death-watch officers were taking no chances and as the hangmen entered the cell they closed in on the condemned man; in less than eight seconds he was on the drop. The whole procedure had moved so quickly that assistant executioner Syd Dernley later said he didn't even get chance to look at the prisoner in the face until he helped remove the white cap an hour after the execution had taken place.

Albert made a trip to Swansea in April to hang a farmer who had murdered his landlord after falling into debt, and in early July he travelled to Winchester for the double execution of two young Poles, Zbigniew Gower and Roman Redel, who shot a man dead after he had tried to make a citizen's arrest following their botched attempt to rob a bank. According to Dernley, while they were at Winchester, Albert threw a tantrum when the warder brought their evening tea. As it was a hot summer's day the chef had prepared a ham and cress meal, but seeing the plate filled mostly with cress and lettuce, Albert became enraged and demanded that the chef cook them a proper meal, threatening a hangman's strike if he refused! Dernley said that he believed Albert thought he and his assistants were being treated shabbily, and without respect, and that that was the reason for the outburst.

In the following week Albert travelled up to Durham, to carry out the execution of George Finlay Brown – the only time in his career he officiated at Durham – and two days later he was at Bristol where he hanged Ronald Atwell for the murder of a young woman. July ended with a flight to Africa, where the British military authorities who had sanctioned an execution to take place at Cairo, Egypt, had engaged his services.

On the morning of 7 April, three British soldiers – 29-year-old Gunner John Golby, Gunner Robert Smith, 23, and 22-year-old Driver Edward Hensman of the Royal Army Service Corps, stole a jeep from their base at Fayid in the British Canal Zone. Loading it with a variety of stolen army property, including clothes and munitions, the men headed off to Cairo, about a hundred miles away. Knowing that the military police would be on the lookout for them, they had dumped the army jeep and uniforms, and changed into civilian clothes on arriving in Cairo, where they quickly disposed of the stolen property.

Two days later, after drinking the profits, they were broke and desperate to return to their base, and preparing to face the consequences. They decided they would steal a car and soon came across a garage with a solitary night watchman. The plan was that Hensman would look after the guard, while the other two selected a car and got it started. Approaching the guard, Hensman pulled out a revolver and pointed the gun at him, indicating he wanted him to go into the garage office and telling him to keep quiet. The man refused to move and during a struggle the gun went off.

Fearing for his life, the watchman made his escape, shrieking and running out into the compound, where Hensman's colleagues were already choosing a suitable car. Hensman followed the guard outside, where he coldly shot him through the head, killing him instantly.

All three were arrested a week later and three months later they appeared at a general court martial, held in a canteen at Fayid Barracks. The case for the prosecution was that although Hensman had shot dead the victim, all were equally guilty of murder, because all were party to the attempted robbery of the car. The court martial ended in sentence of death being passed on all three men.

The final decision to hang the soldiers was communicated to the provost marshal in the Suez Canal Zone; he fixed the triple execution for Thursday, 31 August 1950. There was only one prison in the Canal Zone able to carry out hangings: Military Prison No. 3, Fanara, just outside Fayid, and keen that the execution was carried out to the standards expected in England, the authorities appointed Albert as executioner. However, they decided to appoint their own assistants and James Riley and George Jellico Train, both staff sergeants in the Royal Military Police, were given the roles.

A gallows was built from a Home Office blueprint and having tested it and worked out the drops, Albert decided to hang Golby and Smith side by side in a double execution at 6 a.m., with Edward Hensman to follow them to the gallows at 6.45 a.m. All were given long drops and the executions passed off without incident of note. Although the press were informed that the executions had taken place at dawn, they incorrectly reported that the men were hanged one by one.

Back home, Albert carried out an execution at Wandsworth in August, and another in Glasgow at the end of October. The engagement at Barlinnie had originally been to carry out a double execution of two brothers, Paul and Claude Harris, convicted of a gangland murder in Glasgow. On the evening of 7 July, Paul Harris was drinking in a Glasgow public house with his brother Claude and two friends when a fight broke out. They left the pub and later called at the house in the Tradeston district, where a further fight broke out. During the brawl one of the Harris gang smashed a bottle against a wall, then thrust it into the face of Martin Dunleavy.

His wounds were so serious that a police officer was detailed to stay by his bedside and get whatever information he could out of Dunleavy. 'I know the bastards,' Dunleavy told the constable, 'but I'm not telling you. I'll get them myself!' He died from his wounds in the early hours of the following morning.

Paul and Claude Harris, and a third member of the gang, subsequently found themselves before Lord Thomson at Glasgow High Court in September. Each pleaded self-defence but the four-day trial ended with sentence of death being passed upon the brothers. The third man was found not guilty and discharged. Known throughout the Govan district as 'the inseparable Harrises', the brothers were allowed to share the same condemned cell, and as Albert and assistant Steve Wade prepared to make their journey north, lawyers visited the brothers, telling them that if one or the other was to confess he had struck the fatal blow, then the other might come under consideration for clemency. With less than 48 hours before the execution was scheduled, Paul spoke to the governor. He confessed that it was his hand that had wielded the broken bottle. Claude Harris was given a respite of one week while further investigations were made into the death-cell confession. At Claude's request he was allowed to remain with his brother until midnight on Sunday, 29 October.

Paul Harris walked bravely to the drop on the following morning, and a week later it was announced that Claude Harris had been granted a reprieve and his sentence commuted to life imprisonment.

On 28 November, Albert travelled across Manchester to Strangeways Prison, where he had an appointment to hang a man named James Henry Corbitt, a 38-year-old engineer. One Sunday morning in August, the body of Eliza Wood was found in a hotel room at Ashton-under-Lyne; she had been strangled. Written on her forehead was the word 'whore'. Corbitt, her sometime boyfriend, was soon charged with the murder and at his trial at Liverpool Assizes in November he pleaded guilty but insane. The prosecution pointed to a diary in which Corbitt had made a number of entries, detailing how he had planned at various times to kill Eliza and how fate had intervened on more than one occasion. This, they alleged, showed clear premeditation.

Although Albert had read a little about the case in the local papers, he recognised neither the name nor the description of the convicted man. Arriving at the gaol, he was informed by the governor that the condemned man had claimed he was a friend of the hangman's. The Governor seemed convinced the prisoner was more concerned that Albert Pierrepoint would acknowledge their friendship than the fear of the drop. Viewing the prisoner in the death cell, Albert recognised him straight away as a man he had often duetted with at his pub; the two even had nicknames for each other – Tish and Tosh. On the following morning, when Albert entered the cell, he greeted his erstwhile friend with the usual friendly nickname. Corbitt responded to the greeting, seeming to take heart from the exchange, and it gave him the courage to make the final walk unaided.

At the end of the year, Albert and Steve Wade were again

in action at Barlinnie, where they hanged James Ronald Robertson, a Glasgow policeman who had killed a woman he was having an affair with. Catherine McCluskey, an unmarried mother of two, was found lying in the road and, at first glance, it appeared she had been the victim of a hit-and-run. On closer examination, it was found she had been deliberately run over and that the driver, after knocking her down, had then reversed the car over her before speeding off.

Investigations into her background revealed that she had been having an affair with Robertson, who was married with two young children. He was also alleged to have been the father of her children. When interviewed by CID officers at work, Robertson denied any knowledge of the murder. At his six-day trial it was alleged he had gone absent from duty earlier on the night of the murder, telling a colleague that he had a date. He had returned looking dishevelled, claiming the exhaust had fallen off his car. The car was found to be stolen, as were a number of log books found in his room. Robertson admitted he had accidentally knocked Catherine down, after she had jumped out of the car following a quarrel and that as he reversed back up the road to speak to her, she slipped under the wheels. Realising his predicament he had panicked and left the body in the road hoping that it would appear like an accident. He was the only serving policeman in modern times to be hanged for murder.

Three days after returning from Glasgow, Albert hanged Nicholas Crosby at Manchester. The body of Ruth Massey had been found on waste ground in Leeds. She was half-naked and her throat had been cut. Medical investigations indicated that she had recently had sex, a used condom found nearby suggesting that it had taken place with her consent, before being violently assaulted and having her throat cut. Her sister had seen her in the company of Crosby, a gypsy, as they left a Leeds public house on the previous evening and he was charged with her murder on the following day.

Crosby would normally have been hanged at Leeds, but the execution suite at Armley Gaol was being refurbished and he was sent over the Pennines for execution. Assisting Albert was Syd Dernley, but there were also two trainee observers in attendance, one of whom was Robert Leslie Stewart.

Scotsman Stewart was known, predictably enough, as 'Jock', and was a good friend of Albert – initially on account of Stewart's wife being employed as a barmaid at his public house. When Mrs Stewart had discovered her husband's desire to become a hangman she had introduced her husband to Albert, who advised him of the correct procedure for applying. Following a successful interview and training he had come to Manchester to gain experience and to test his nerve.

Crosby was in a highly agitated state in the hours leading up to his execution and it was decided that the two trainees would not go into the execution chamber, where they could get in the way if the man began to resist violently, but would carry out the observation from the doorway. As Albert entered the cell, Crosby leapt to his feet and stared at him in sheer terror. He shrieked as they put the straps on, protesting that he didn't want them, but the men ignored him and proceeded with the pinioning. As two burly warders closed in, Crosby followed the hangman onto the drop where his legs were quickly secured and the lever was pushed, releasing the heavy trapdoors. Not the smoothest of executions for the new men to witness, but it was still a quick and efficient job.

On 9 October 1950, the battered body of a man was found in a trackside hut near Rossendale, Lancashire. He was identified as Radomir Djorovic, a Yugoslavian refugee who lived in Blackburn, and investigations soon revealed that Nenad Kovasevic, another Yugoslavian refugee, had disappeared from his lodging. He was arrested on the following day.

At his trial at Manchester Assizes in December, it was revealed that the two men had quarrelled as they made their way across the moors. As it began to rain they took shelter in the hut, where Djorovic had teased his friend when he became upset as he talked about how his family had been killed by the Germans. Djorovic said that he had sided with the Germans and in a rage Kovasevic picked up an axe and struck his friend over the head. Any chance of getting the jury to accept a lesser charge of manslaughter, on the grounds of provocation, was lost when it was found that after the killing he had stolen some personal items, which he had then sold. Last-minute pleas for clemency by the King of Yugoslavia also failed to prevent the law taking its course. When Albert entered the cell on the morning of 26 January 1951, the prisoner put up a fierce fight, having to be dragged kicking and screaming across to the drop.

In April, Albert and assistant Harry Allen travelled down together to Birmingham to hang William Arthur Watkins, who was profoundly deaf. Many years later Albert was asked to comment on the execution when a book was written on the case. Admitting that he had felt sorry for the man he had had to hang, Albert recalled the events following the time he arrived at the prison. He said that after the hangmen had been shown to their quarters, the chief officer escorted them to the condemned cell, where they peered into the cell through the 'Judas hole'. Watkins was seated in such a way that they could not get a proper look at him, and after waiting for several minutes they realised he was not going to move, so they went on to the execution chamber to check the apparatus was all in order. After rigging a sandbag to an approximate drop based on the prisoner's details, they tested the scaffold.

Returning to their quarters, Albert took another look into the death cell. By now Watkins had moved from his chair and they had a clear view of him. Albert was taken aback. The slip of paper the governor had given him stated the prisoner's age to be 49. The man inside the condemned cell sat silently between two guards looked at least twenty years older, causing Albert to ask the governor if he was sure the age was correct – grey haired, slightly stooped, he wore a dejected air as if he had already lost the will to live. The governor confirmed that the age was indeed correct. Albert recorded later that he felt upset seeing a man looking so sorry and waiting to die.

Knowing nothing about the crime, Albert said he had to keep an open mind, but later over their evening meal, guards told them the whole sad story. Watkins had been sentenced to death at Birmingham Assizes for the murder of his unnamed baby, who had drowned in a bath. His defence was that the child's death was an accident, and that it had slipped out of his hands into the bathtub. The prosecution had claimed it was a premeditated crime and that Watkins and the woman he lived with hadn't planned for the child, had failed to notify anyone when it died, and had killed it to be rid of the unwanted burden of responsibility.

At a few seconds before nine o'clock on the morning of 3 April Watkins was sitting with his back to the door. He was sobbing as he spoke to the chaplain, thanking the prison staff for all their kindness. He was alerted to the hangman's presence when he saw the chaplain rise to his feet and indicate their presence with his eyes. Albert spoke to him in a kindly voice as he pinioned his arms and, with an officer on either side, Watkins was escorted through to the scaffold. As Allen strapped his ankles, Albert gently lifted his drooping chin, placed the white cap and noose, stepped back and pulled the lever. The execution took just 12 seconds.

Watkins was the first of four men Albert hanged that month, the remaining three being at Wandsworth. Joseph Brown and Edward Smith were two 30-year-old crooks convicted of the murder of Frederick Gosling, a Chertsey shopkeeper, who was found dead inside his premises. He had been tied to the bed and beaten, and had died from suffocation caused by an old duster being forced into his mouth. On 25 April they were hanged side-by-side, having been convicted largely on the testimony of Smith's brother, who had initially been a suspect.

Albert stayed in London and along with assistant Dernley he went to a Soho gym to obtain tickets for an upcoming championship fight. Not averse to getting his own way, he teased the promoter that if he didn't find him a pair of tickets he would be 'next for the drop'. The inference was jocular but at the same time backed up with a determination to get what he wanted. Leaving the gym they travelled across London to Scotland Yard, where they met up with Detective Superintendent Daws, a long-time friend of the hangman.

Returning to Wandsworth later that afternoon, they rigged the gallows for 56-year-old James Virrels, who had killed his landlady with an axe following a lovers' tiff. Virrels was terrified when they went for him on the following morning and walked slowly and falteringly to the drop.

On 8 May, Albert and Syd Dernley hanged James Inglis at Manchester. Inglis had killed a woman in Hull and, like Crosby the previous December, had been brought over to Manchester while Leeds Prison was being modernised. Unlike Albert's previous 'customer', Inglis had been on his feet ready for the hangmen when they entered the cell and with his arms pinioned he began to run to the drop, almost treading on Albert's heels in a hurry to put his head in the noose. The execution was timed at seven seconds, and Syd Dernley, a veteran of over a score of executions, later said he could not think how anyone could have been hanged in a faster time, so eager was Inglis to reach the gallows.

Leaving Manchester after stowing away the execution equipment, Albert hurried to London Road station, where he had booked a ticket on the 10.30 a.m. express to Winchester via London. At Winchester Gaol he had an engagement on the following morning to hang William Shaughnessy, who had strangled his wife and daughter in an apparently motiveless murder in Portsmouth.

Over the summer Albert made two more trips to Manchester, and also carried out a double execution at Norwich. In September he hanged Robert Dobie Smith at Edinburgh for the murder of a Dumfries policeman, and in October he was at Pentonville, where John O'Conner paid the penalty for the murder of his elderly landlady at his home in Kensington.

The final execution of 1951 was also one of the most dramatic. On 9 August, Herbert Mills, a 19-year-old unemployed clerk, had telephoned the News of the World newspaper in London, sensationally claiming he had discovered the body of a strangled woman in Nottingham. Mills told the reporter that he had yet to inform the police and offered them an exclusive story if they paid him £250. Mills was phoning from a call box and while the reporter kept him talking, another called the police, who hurried to the scene and questioned Mills. He led them to an orchard at nearby Sherwood Vale, where they found the body of 48-year-old Mrs Mabel Tattershaw, who had been reported as missing from home six days earlier. It appeared that she had been battered to death. Mills was treated as a witness and, with police being unable to establish any link between him and the victim, he was allowed to leave custody after being questioned.

A few days later, his account of the discovery was published in the Sunday newspaper, along with photographs of Mills posing where the body was discovered. Re-reading through his account, detectives picked up on the fact that Mills had mentioned strangulation, something that had only came to light at the recent inquest and which had been impossible to tell from the state of the body when first discovered. Mills had also claimed that the victim's face was white when he found her; after six days of decomposition this had certainly not been the case. In a follow-up interview by newspaper reporters, Mills changed his story, now admitting that he had, in fact, found the body a few days before making the telephone call, when the face had indeed been white. Now convinced that Mills was the real killer, detectives invited him to make further statements, until finally, two weeks after making the original phone call, he slipped up, contradicting himself once too often. Realising he could lie no more, Mills eventually confessed to the crime.

At his two-day trial before Mr Justice Byrne at Nottingham Assizes, Mills was described as a desperately lonely boy, cruel, boastful and vain, who wrote bad poetry. It was alleged Mills had met Mrs Tattershaw when she had sat next to him in a cinema. Around this time he had become obsessed with committing 'the perfect murder' and after luring her to the orchard on some pretext he had killed her. Frustrated that his crime had not been discovered, and wishing to gloat over the police's failure to solve it, he made the call to the Sunday newspaper. The prosecution alleged that the main reason for the murder was exhibitionism.

Mills was hanged at Lincoln Gaol on 11 December, and Albert may have made a rare blunder at this execution. With Mills weighing a slight 126 pounds and standing just 5 feet 5 inches, Albert worked out a long drop of 8 feet 6 inches. Mills was hanged at 9.00 a.m., but it was reported that it took over twenty minutes for his heart to stop beating after the drop fell. Did Albert get his sums wrong? Medical evidence suggests that in a small number of cases although the hanging had been carried out correctly, the heart could continue to go on beating long after a man is by all accounts clinically dead. Whether Albert did or did not get his calculations slightly wrong that chilly December morning, it seems nothing was ever made official and apparently no blemish appeared against his name.

One of the drawbacks with being engaged as a hangman, with no control over the scheduling of the engagements, was that there were occasions when executions were fixed to take place at inconvenient times. This was in part due to the way that the assize courts functioned. There were specific term times that the court sat, and with the three-week rule between sentence and execution – longer, if the condemned appealed – it often meant that people convicted at the autumn assizes awaited their fate in the condemned cell over the festive season.

On New Year's Eve, Albert and assistant Syd Dernley found themselves occupying the hangman's quarters at Birmingham, having accepted the invitation to execute Horace Carter. Carter, a Birmingham labourer, had lured a young girl into his home after promising her some sweets. He took her upstairs, raped her, and then, frightened that she would report him to the police, he strangled her. At nightfall he carried her body outside and dumped it in the corporation yard, close to his own back garden. A neighbour discovered the body the next day and Carter was arrested after he confessed to the crime during a routine police interview.

On New Year's Day 1952, the hangmen shook hands and wished each other a happy new year. Then, at nine o'clock, they hanged the brutal child killer in brisk fashion. Carter didn't say a word as he was led to the drop.

1952 was to be one of the busiest years for executions in almost half a century. Albert carried out the execution of Alfred Bradley at Manchester in January. He was assisted by Jock Stewart, who recorded later that Bradley seemed so unconcerned as he waited for the hangmen to enter the cell on the morning of the execution that anyone would think he was waiting to go to the cinema rather than to the gallows. Bradley had killed a night watchman in what was thought to be a homosexual quarrel.

A month later Albert and Jock were again on duty at Manchester when Herbert Roy Harris was hanged for the murder of his wife. Harris had committed the murder near his home in Flint, North Wales, but was brought to Manchester as executions had been discontinued in North Wales during Albert's father's time as chief executioner.

Probably the most infamous execution of that year took place at Liverpool on 25 April, when two Manchester criminals were hanged for the murder of an old lady at Wavertree, Liverpool. Mrs Beatrice Rimmer had been a recluse for a number of years, since the death of her husband. This secretive life led to local rumours of her having large amounts of money and on more than one occasion her house had been burgled. She had last been seen alive on the night of Sunday, 19 August 1951. On the following evening her son found her lying in a pool of blood on the hall floor. Two different weapons had been used, suggesting two killers. In October, Alfred Burns and Edward Devlin were arrested in Manchester, following a tip-off from a soldier held in Walton Prison, Liverpool.

Their defence at the ten-day trial at Liverpool Assizes was that they could not have been in Liverpool on the night of the murder as they were in Manchester, carrying out a robbery in a factory. This alibi was destroyed in court when the other man who had already been arrested for this offence admitted that the robbery had occurred on 18 August. Large crowds gathered outside the gaol as Albert and three assistants led the two frightened killers to the gallows.

In June, Albert made another trip over to Egypt, to hang Tom Houghton, a 23-year-old private in the Royal Army Supply Corp. Houghton, originally from Hull, had murdered Captain Herbert Mason, shooting him dead with a Sten gun in a jealous rage after the captain had danced with a Greek typist whom Houghton said he was due to marry. Working without an assistant, Albert carried out the execution on the same scaffold at Fayid Prison he had used two years before.

By the time Albert travelled down to Bristol to carry out the execution of Thomas Eames at Plymouth, he had a new address. Leaving the Hollinwood public house, Albert and Anne had taken over the rural Rose and Crown situated on the main road linking Liverpool and Preston at Much Hoole.

Eames was a labourer from Plymouth who had been sentenced to death at Devon Assizes for the murder of Muriel Bent. He had split up from his first wife in 1940, although they remained legally wed. In 1947 he was charged with bigamously marrying Muriel Bent and served a short prison sentence. They reunited on his release and had a child. In early 1952, Muriel left him and moved in with a new lover. He asked her to call at the house to collect her mail and on the following morning he took a knife to work and sharpened it with a file. Calling at the house as arranged, she told Eames she planned to marry her new boyfriend and as she went to kiss him goodbye he stabbed her twice in the back.

Eames had to be dragged fighting and kicking to the gallows on 15 July. But he was not the only condemned man to put up a struggle on the morning of his execution that year. In September, Albert and Jock Stewart hanged Mahmood Hussain Mattan, a Somalian sailor sentenced to death at Glamorgan Assizes for the murder of Mrs Lily Volpert, a Jewish shopkeeper. On 6 March, Mrs Volpert had been working in her outfitters shop in the docklands area of Cardiff when a man entered. During an ensuing struggle her throat was cut and over £100 was stolen from the till. A witness claimed to have seen a man matching Mattan's description outside the shop prior to the murder; he was arrested and traces of blood matching the murdered woman were found on his shoes. Mattan was convicted on circumstantial evidence, and mainly on the testimony of a fellow Somalian.

Mattan was violent and abusive to his guards in the death cell, refusing to dress in anything other than his pyjamas. On one occasion when they tried to forcibly dress him he bit a warder on the leg, so it was decided that he should be allowed to wear whatever he wanted. On the morning of his execution, as the hangman came for him, Mattan said he wanted to get dressed in his own clothes, but was told it was too late. He resisted attempts to pinion him and it took quite a struggle to get him to the trapdoors. He was given a long drop of 8 feet 5 inches.

Mahmood Mattan was granted a posthumous pardon in February 1998. The witness who had identified Mattan at the scene of the crime had also identified another Somalian, Tehar Gass, as being at the shop near the time of the murder. When interviewed by detectives Gass admitted that this was true, but this evidence was withheld from the defence counsel.

Two days after hanging Mattan at Cardiff, Albert and Jock Stewart travelled down to Pentonville, where they hanged John Godar, who had stabbed a woman in a taxi, and at the end of the month they returned to the north-London prison to carry out a double execution. When Albert travelled to Birmingham to hang Leslie Green, who had brutally killed his former employer in Staffordshire, Albert was carrying out his 23rd execution of the year. He had now been a hangman for 20 years, twice as long as his father, and he had already carried out more executions than his uncle and father added together. And there were still a few more sensational twists to come.

CHAPTER 9:
END OF THE ROAD

On 2 January 1953, Albert and assistant Harry Smith carried out an execution at Wandsworth, keeping up the hangman's regular trend of spending the New Year celebrations in the austere surroundings of high prison walls. At the end of the month he was back at Wandsworth to officiate at what was probably the most controversial of all the executions in his career, and which – along with that of Timothy Evans four years earlier – further helped bring about a reformation of the whole system of capital punishment in Great Britain.

PC Sydney Miles was shot dead during a robbery at a Croydon warehouse in November 1952. Nineteen-year-old Derek Bentley and Christopher Craig, aged sixteen, had climbed up the drainpipe at the side of the building trying to gain entry through a skylight when they were spotted by neighbours. The police were called and Bentley was soon placed under arrest, but Craig threatened to shoot officers if they approached and a stand-off occurred. Eventually,

Bentley was alleged to have shouted, 'Let him have it', after which Craig fired and fatally wounded PC Miles before throwing himself off the roof. A greenhouse broke his fall and although he suffered broken limbs he was able to take his place in the dock a little over a month later.

His trial was held before Lord Chief Justice Goddard at the Old Bailey in December. Goddard, a staunch retentionist, was a notorious 'hang 'em and flog 'em' judge who seemed determined from the outset that an example was to be made of the young men in the dock. Many claim he was unfairly biased in favour of the prosecution and while there was no doubt that Craig was guilty of the murder of the police officer, he was legally too young to hang. By law, Bentley, as an accomplice, was deemed to be equally guilty of the murder – although, as his counsel strenuously maintained throughout the trial, complicity in the crime had ended when Bentley was placed under arrest before Craig carried out the murder. The speed at which the case came to trial, barely a month after the incident, prevented enough medical evidence being gathered that could have helped show that Bentley, who was of low intelligence and had a mental age of eleven, was medically unfit to stand trial. On the third day of the trial, Craig was sentenced to be detained at Her Majesty's Pleasure; Bentley was found guilty of murder, with the jury adding a strong recommendation for mercy. Widespread public appeal for clemency failed, and journalists broke the news to his family that there was to be no reprieve. Albert needed an escort into the gaol by police officers on the afternoon of 27 January, as a large mob gathered, hurling abuse as the car made its way through the prison gates. Arriving at the gaol he was taken to see the governor, who seemed strained and restless. Bentley had just had a farewell visit from his family and as realisation dawned on him that no reprieve was forthcoming he seemed to be struggling to grasp what was happening, mumbling repeatedly, 'They can't hang me...'

Harry Allen assisted Albert. (I was told by a member of the family that he contacted the Home Office after accepting the engagement, telling them that although he would be available to carry out the execution, he hoped they would see their way to granting a reprieve.) Albert and Harry spent the night in their quarters with a glass of beer, listening to the radio, which broadcast the news that a late-night sitting of Parliament had not done anything to reverse the judgement and that the execution was to go ahead as planned. A couple of the guards coming off duty in the condemned cell spoke to the hangmen and voiced their concerns that the burly prisoner could give them a tough time if he lost his temper or panicked when they went for him. Albert listened to their concerns but was always ready for anything that could occur on the morning of the execution. Although trouble rarely happened, other than some brief resistance when the straps were fastened, there were always contingency plans and everyone on duty was briefed on what to do should an incident occur.

Rising early, Albert tested the equipment and with everything in readiness they returned to their room, where Albert was served his favourite prison breakfast of fried plaice and potatoes. At a few seconds to nine the hangmen approached the condemned cell and took their place next to the governor.

'Good morning, Pierrepoint,' the governor whispered. 'I see that this has got to be done.'

'That's all right, sir,' Albert replied.

Moments later the signal was given and they entered through the green cell door. Bentley got to his feet and as Harry took hold of his right arm, Albert fastened the wrist strap. Bentley looked around confusedly as the door was thrown open leading to the drop, and he stumbled slowly as he was led to the drop, where he was given a drop of 6 feet 9 inches.

On 30 July 1998, the Court of Appeal overturned the conviction. In an unprecedented and damning attack, the Lord Chief Justice ruled that Bentley's trial judge – his predecessor, Lord Chief Justice Goddard – had denied Bentley 'that fair trial that is the birthright of every British citizen'. Passing judgment, Lord Bingham placed the blame for the miscarriage of justice squarely with Lord Goddard, describing him as 'blatantly prejudiced', adding that he had misdirected the jury and that his summing-up had put pressure on them to convict the prisoner. Christopher Craig served ten years in gaol.

In February 1953, Albert and Harry Smith carried out an execution rare in modern times, that of a man who had been convicted of the murder of both his parents. Charles Giffard, senior partner in a firm of solicitors, had hoped his son would follow into the profession. Rather than find work, however, his son Miles lived on an allowance paid by his parents. He became besotted with a girl he had met in London and of whom his parents strongly disapproved. They told him to end the relationship, threatening that his allowance would cease if he disobeyed them. Miles had no intention of doing so, however, and wrote to his girlfriend telling her of his parents' threats and adding that the only solution to the problem would be to kill them.

On 7 November 1952, he returned to the family home at St Austell and waited in the garage for his father to return home. He battered him with an iron pipe before entering the kitchen and attacking his mother. He then telephoned his girlfriend in London, telling her he would be returning to London that evening. The blows to the head had failed to prove fatal, and finding that both parents were still alive, he placed them one at a time in a wheelbarrow and tipped them over the edge of a nearby cliff.

The bodies were discovered on the following morning, and Miles Giffard was arrested in London later that day. He pleaded insanity at his trial at Bodmin Assizes, his defence claiming that he had been receiving psychiatric care in the past and was unaware of his actions. The jury, however, preferred to believe the prosecution's case of murder for financial gain, after it was proven that Giffard had sold some of his mother's jewellery shortly after the murders.

One month to the day after Albert had returned home from hanging Giffard at Bristol, new tenants at John Reginald Halliday Christie's former home at 10 Rillington Place, Notting Hill, discovered the boarded-up remains of three women in a cupboard. Reg Christie had previously come to the attention of the police in the autumn of 1949, when tenant Timothy Evans had been convicted and hanged for the murder of his wife and child. Evans had gone to his grave inside Pentonville Prison blaming his landlord Christie for the murders.

Christie had moved out of Rillington Place a few days earlier and a subsequent police search unearthed six bodies in total. Two were buried in the garden; three had been discovered in the kitchen, and Christie's wife Ethel was found concealed beneath the living room floor. All had been strangled and, apart from his wife, all had had sexual intercourse around the time of death. Arrested in Putney a week later, Christie immediately confessed. He offered a plea of insanity at his trial but this was rejected, and while claiming he could not remember if he had killed Beryl Evans in 1949, he was adamant that he had not strangled the young child.

Albert and Harry Smith met up in the gatehouse at Pentonville on the afternoon of 14 July. They were given Christie's details as age 55, height 5 feet 8 ½ inches and weight 149 pounds, and took a look at him later that afternoon before preparing the drop. He seemed quite upbeat and not to be feeling the strain of his impending doom. That was all to change overnight.

On the following morning, as Albert and Smith returned to their quarters after completing the preparations, they halted as they passed a small window over the gatehouse that overlooked the Caledonian Road, where a large, raucous crowd had gathered. Smith seemed a bit perplexed by their demeanour, saying that it looked like a Bank Holiday crowd. 'I suppose that's the sort of lot who watched hangings at Tyburn, with blokes selling sweets and hot rum to the crowd!' he declared. Mostly it was the sight of large groups of children that shocked Smith. Seeing the discomfort in his assistant's face, Albert told him to come away from the window. Albert was used to large crowds gathering outside the prison walls, but admitted later that this crowd had disturbed him more than any other he could recall.

Christie had his back to the door as Albert entered the cell after receiving the signal from the governor. As they approached they could see he had a sneer on his face as he listened, tight-lipped, to the words of the chaplain. Smith lifted Christie's skinny wrist and Albert secured it before removing his spectacles, which he carefully placed on the table. Christie blinked his eyes as he focused on the side door that had mysteriously opened and as he was motioned to move Albert recalled later that his face seemed to melt. 'It was more than terror… at that moment I know Christie would have given anything in his power to postpone his own death.'

Christie approached the drop in a slow, pitiful stagger, his legs barely moving one in front of the other. Sensing the condemned man would not make it to the drop without falling into a faint, he motioned for Smith to stand clear as he moved towards Christie. He slipped the white cap over his balding head, and had the noose in place before he had reached the chalked 'T' on the trapdoors. Without waiting for the leg straps to go on he pulled the lever and the notorious killer of Rillington Place dropped 7 feet 4 inches to his death.

Two weeks later Albert carried out a job at Leeds, normally the territory of his former assistant Steve Wade. Albert received the offer to carry out this rare execution in Yorkshire when Wade was unable to attend due to illness. Flora Gilligan had been found naked outside her home in York one morning in March. At first it seemed she had fallen from the upstairs window, but an autopsy revealed she had been raped, then beaten and strangled before being thrown from the window. A fingerprint was discovered at the scene and investigations at a nearby army camp found a perfect match. Philip Henry, a soldier due to be posted overseas on the following day, denied the murder, but had no alibi for the previous night and splinters of wood found on his clothing matched samples taken from the wooden window frame at the house. Henry's trial was memorable because the jury, during summing up, asked the judge if they could visit the scene of the crime. After a brief visit to the house, they returned to the court, where they needed just a few minutes to find Henry guilty of murder. It was Albert's one and only visit to Leeds as either hangman or assistant – all previous offers to assist his uncle before the war had ended in reprieves.

1953 had already seen a number of high-profile cases that had filled the pages of the national press, bringing coachloads of visitors to the Rose and Crown at Much

Hoole. Realising it was good for business, Albert was always willing to sign autographs and sometimes pose for a photograph. He also had a batch of publicity photographs produced, which he was happy to sign and give out to customers. No sooner had the Christie case disappeared from the front pages than it was replaced by a case closer to home, when the trial took place at Manchester of Louisa Merrifield and her third husband, Alfred, accused of the murder of Mrs Sarah Ann Ricketts in Blackpool.

The Merrifields had taken up positions as live-in housekeeper-companions to the 79-year-old, twice-widowed Mrs Ricketts in March. Within a month she had changed her will in favour of the Merrifields and, by early April, Louisa Merrifield was telling friends she had been left a bungalow in an elderly widow's will. Mrs Ricketts died on 14 April, and when the death was reported in the local newspaper one of the Merrifields' friends contacted the police; a postmortem discovered that Mrs Ricketts had died of phosphorus poisoning.

Both Mrs Merrifield and her husband were charged with her murder, despite no trace of poison being found at the house, and the existence of conflicting medical evidence that suggested cause of death was actually liver failure. Louisa was sentenced to hang at Manchester Assizes after an 11-day trial. In the case of her husband, the jury failed to reach a verdict and he was released, inheriting a half-share in the dead woman's bungalow. Mrs Merrifield was taken to Strangeways Gaol to await execution.

On 5 September, the outcome of the Royal Commission Report was published. The commission concluded that the process of execution currently in operation in Great Britain was preferable to that of the other nations visited and that drastic action was not needed. It did, however, make a few amendments, among them being the suggestion that, 'Sheriffs should vary their selection of executioners, so as to ensure that there are always at least two experienced executioners on the list of qualified persons.'

The Report also recommended slight improvements to the actual execution process. Henceforth, prisoners were no longer required to hang for one hour following execution, but were now to be removed from the rope once certified dead, a practice Albert had carried out in Germany when the sheer volume of executions on some days had prevented the normal hanging for one hour from being a practical option. The peculiarly gruesome practice of measuring the length of distortion in the body after execution, the length that the neck had stretched, was also brought to an end. The Report also recommended that: 'Where two persons were to be executed on the same day and in the same prison they should continue to be executed together, but two executioners should be employed, each with an assistant executioner.'

A few minor alterations to the system of employing assistant executioners in Scotland, and the recommendation that notice of execution was no longer placed on the prison gates but rather in a national newspaper, were all that were to show for the four years the committee had sat.

On 18 September, Louisa Merrifield was hanged at Strangeways Gaol. Jock Stewart assisted Albert and noted that she died very bravely. 'It went very well,' he said later. 'She said goodbye in the cell to the death cell officers... much better than I imagined. She was braver than any man. The female officers on watch appeared a trifle upset.'

Albert carried out an execution in October at Bristol, and a month later Joseph Reynolds became the last man hanged at Leicester when he went to the gallows for the murder of a young girl. The year ended with three executions in the week leading up to Christmas. On 17 December, Albert hanged Stanislaw Juras at Manchester, and five days later he hanged Alfred Whiteway at Wandsworth; Whiteway had raped and killed two young women on the banks of the Thames at Teddington. On the following day, Albert crossed London to Pentonville, where he hanged 21-year-old George Newlands, who had battered to death an old couple he had become friendly with in Essex. At his trial it was alleged that Newlands was influenced by the 'cosh-boy' films that were being shown at the cinema at the time, and that he had committed the murder to steal enough money to buy a new suit for an impending date.

When Albert made the short journey to Manchester on 8 January 1954, it was to hang a man who had committed a murder in Yorkshire, but who like Juras, whom Albert had hanged three weeks before, had been taken across the Pennines for execution because there had been an unprecedented number of death sentences passed at the previous sitting of Leeds Assizes.

Czeslaw Kowalski was a Polish refugee, who for two days every week shared a home with Doris Douglas in Leeds. When Douglas wasn't with Kowalski she lived and worked as a housekeeper to an elderly man in Leeds. Kowalski found out about this arrangement and stabbed her in the head with a scout knife. His failed defence at the trial before Mr Justice Stable was that he was too drunk at the time to have formed any intention to commit murder. Two days before he was to be executed, Kowalski had attempted to cheat the gallows. He had succeeded in scraping the skin off his penis with his fingernails, in an attempt to bleed himself to death; he spent the last hours of his life in great agony.

On 11 February, Tom Pierrepoint passed away at the home of his daughter in Bradford. He was 84 years old and severely disabled by arthritis. Albert had paid a farewell visit to him a few days after returning from Shrewsbury, where he hanged Desmond Hooper for the murder of a young girl whom he had thrown down a ventilation shaft. She had drowned in the shallow pool of stagnant water at the bottom.

In a two-week period in April, Albert carried out four executions in every country in the United Kingdom and Ireland. On 14 April he travelled down to Wandsworth for the execution of James Doohan, who had shot dead his girlfriend's stepfather. Five days later, he and Jock Stewart flew over to Ireland for the execution of Michael Manning, a carter of Limerick, convicted of the rape and murder of a nursing sister at a Limerick Hospital. Manning had dragged her into a nearby field where he assaulted her. Death was due to suffocation caused by the vicim having grass forced into her mouth to stop her screaming. Manning was the last man hanged in the Irish Republic. With a revolver in his pocket, Albert spent the afternoon following the execution driving around the country with Jock before they made their way to the airport and the evening flight home.

Three days later Albert and Jock travelled up to Scotland, where they carried out an execution at Edinburgh, and five days later, again with Jock Stewart as his assistant, Albert travelled down to Swansea, where he hanged 24-year-old Ronald Thomas Harries for the murder of his aunt and uncle. Farmer John Harries and his wife Phoebe had last been seen alive following a visit to a church service near their home on a Carmarthenshire farm on 16 October 1953. Nephew Ronnie explained away their disappearance by saying they had gone to London for a secret holiday. Detectives immediately suspected foul play and Scotland Yard were called in. A forged cheque was found made out to Ronnie Harries and officers soon deduced that he had killed his aunt and uncle after they had refused to loan him money. It was suspected that Harries had buried the bodies in fields close to his own farm and a trap was set. Cotton thread was tied over entrances leading into the fields and noises were made to make Harries think police had searched the fields. On the following day, Harries entered the fields and the trail of broken thread led police to a spot in the fields where they found the bodies battered to death in a shallow grave. Harries lost his composure completely in the death cell and had to be assisted on the short walk to the gallows. As Harries stood on the drop, Albert just had time to place the noose over his neck before he collapsed in a faint. Officers supported him until the trapdoors opened, but Harries was already unconscious before he dropped to his death.

Although the Royal Commission report had made a recommendation that two executioners be employed at a double execution, their request seemed to fall on deaf ears. When Albert was engaged at Pentonville in June, he had three assistants: two, Royston Rickard and John Broadbent, had joined the list in the previous year; the third was Harry Smith, the most experienced of the trio but with less than four years' service himself. None had sufficient experience to carry out the duties as a second executioner. Albert would therefore carry out the double execution as he had done in the past, as the only principle hangman.

George Smart worked as a porter at a Kensington Hotel. On 9 March he was found bound and gagged in the basement at the hotel; he had been battered about the head but death had been due to suffocation caused by the gag. A small amount of cash and a large quantity of cigarettes had been stolen from the hotel stores. On the following day, 24-year-old Ian Grant told a friend that he and another friend, Ken Gilbert, aged 21, had killed the porter and stashed some stolen cigarettes in a left-luggage locker at Victoria station. The friend contacted the police and both men were soon taken into custody. Their Old Bailey trial heard how Gilbert, a former employee at the hotel, had led them into the building via the coal cellar, but that they were disturbed by Smart. Both admitted striking the victim before he was tied up. There was no incident on the morning of the execution. Albert allowed Harry Smith to lead one of the men onto the drop but he placed both caps and nooses onto the men and pulled the lever. It was the last double execution carried out in Great Britain.

Albert made another trip to Edinburgh later that summer, travelling direct from Liverpool, where he had carried out an execution on the previous day. When he was next called into action in August, it was again to carry out two executions in two days.

On 11 August, he hanged 62-year-old William Sanchez de Pina Hepper at Wandsworth. Hepper had persuaded his daughter's friend's parents to let their young daughter visit him at his Brighton apartment, where he said he would paint her portrait while she recovered from a broken arm. She was later found raped and strangled. Hepper fled to his native Spain, and tried to fight extradition on the grounds of nationality. When it came to light that he had fought on the opposing side during the civil war, his deportation back to England was sealed. Following the execution at Wandsworth, Albert caught a train to Lincoln, where he hanged Harold Fowler for the murder of his wife's new lover.

The year drew to a close with Albert making his first visit to Holloway Gaol. The north-London all-female gaol hadn't witnessed an execution since his father had officiated there half a century before, when he hanged Sach and Walters, the two baby farmers.

Fifty-three-year-old grandmother Mrs Stylou Christofi had left her native Cyprus to live with her son, daughter-in-law, and three children at Hampstead in the summer of 1953. From the outset the two women did not get along and German-born Hella told her husband that his mother must leave the house. At the end of July, shortly after Mrs Christofi had been told she must leave, a neighbour saw her lighting a fire in the back yard. In the early hours of the following morning, the body of Hella was found in the yard. She had been strangled and battered about the head with a heavy, iron ash plate before paraffin was poured onto her body.

Sentenced to death by Mr Justice Devlin at the Old Bailey, Mrs Christofi claimed the death had been an accident, but her account of the incident, related through a translator, failed to convince the jury. Following the passing of the death sentence it was revealed in court that Mrs Christofi had stood trial once before, for the murder of her mother-in-law in her native Cyprus. She had been accused of murdering the woman by ramming a burning wooden torch down her throat, although on that occasion she was found not guilty. She stood less than 5 feet tall and weighed a slight 117 pounds; Albert worked out a drop of 8 feet 4 inches. Unable to speak any English, she was in tears as she was led onto the drop, where a large crucifix had been placed on the wall at her request.

Albert's final year as a hangman got off to a slow start. There was one execution at Liverpool in March 1955, but that went to Steve Wade, and it was not until mid-April that Albert and Jock travelled down to London together for an appointment at Wandsworth to hang Sidney Clarke, who had killed a prostitute on a London bombsite. In May, Albert carried out an execution at Lincoln and in June he hanged Richard Gowler, a dockworker, who committed the murder of his girlfriend's mother at Wallasey, Liverpool. Albert and Jock Stewart hanged Gowler on 21 June.

A few hours after the hangmen left Liverpool's Walton Gaol, 200 miles away at the Old Bailey a tiny piece of black cloth was draped on the wig of Mr Justice Havers as he pronounced sentence of death on a 28-year-old former model and club hostess from South Kensington. Ruth Ellis was sentenced to death for the murder of David Blakely, her former lover, whom she shot dead outside a Hampstead public house. The mother of two young children, Ellis was alleged to have been given the gun by one of her lovers. At her trial she was asked what her intentions were when she pulled the trigger. She had replied that when she shot Blakely, a Buckinghamshire racing driver, after he had tried to end their relationship, she had intended to kill him. With that statement her fate was sealed.

As prisoner 9656, Ruth Ellis spent just 23 days in the condemned cell at Holloway. Her execution date was fixed for 9.00 a.m., Wednesday, 13 July, and letters were duly sent to Albert and to assistant Royston Rickard. Public sentiment about the case ran high, and thousands had signed petitions for clemency. On the Tuesday evening, as the two executioners rested in their quarters after preparing the scaffold, the Governor of Holloway was forced to call in police reinforcements as the crowd outside the prison's gates swelled to over five hundred, some singing hymns, others shouting and protesting at the injustice of the sentence. Several broke through a police cordon and rushed the gates, but they were forced back as more police arrived.

Albert had been told that Ellis weighed 103 pounds, was 5

feet 2 inches tall, and her age was 28. He worked out a drop of 8 feet 4 inches. As they finished their supper and drank the limited supply of beer in the company of the warder assigned to keep them company in the prison, the two hangmen could hear the disturbance outside the main gates, and the noise continued long after they had both retired to bed.

The two men rose early on the morning of execution reset the trap and with the noose coiled up at head height, the chalk 'T' mark was re-done over the join of the two heavy hinged trapdoors. The cross that had been placed on the far wall of the execution chamber for Mrs Christofi stayed in place at Ellis's request.

Ellis had also woken early. She penned several letters, including one to Blakely's mother, apologising for shooting him. She was given her own clothes to wear at the execution, with the addition of a pair of canvas undergarments to wear. These had been compulsory for executed women prisoners since the 1920s. She was attended by a Catholic priest, who sat with her as the clock ticked slowly towards the fatal hour.

Five minutes before the appointed time, a telephone call was received at Holloway. Claiming to be from the Home Secretary's office, the caller said that a stay of execution had been granted and advised the authorities to await further details. Governor Dr Taylor immediately telephoned the Home Office and was told that no such action had been taken and that the call should be treated as a hoax.

This delayed the execution slightly. Receiving the signal, Albert entered Ellis's cell, pinioned her hands briskly behind her back and led her the five yards to the gallows room. She remained silent throughout. Reaching the trap, he placed the white cotton hood over her head and adjusted the noose round her neck. Rickard pinioned her legs and stepped back.

Albert removed the safety pin, pushed the lever, and turned to see the trap open with a thud. It had taken less than 15 seconds. Outside the prison a crowd of over a thousand stood in silence.

Pathologist Dr Keith Simpson performed the autopsy an hour later and found that she had died instantaneously. An inquest was held later that morning. Ellis's brother made the formal identification of her body, the deep imprint of the noose covered by a scarf. She was buried in the grounds of Holloway prison shortly after lunch. The autopsy report was later published, and Simpson noted the presence of brandy in her stomach. The official inquest report read:

POST MORTEM EXAMINATION

Name Ruth Ellis
Apparent age 28 years
At H. M. Prison Holloway Date July 13 1955

EXTERNAL EXAMINATION
Well nourished. Evidence of proper care and attention.
Height 5ft. 2ins. Weight 103 lbs.
Deep impressions around neck from noose with a suspension point about 1 inch in front of the angle of the L. lower jaw.
Vital changes locally and in the tissues beneath as a consequence of sudden constriction.
No ecchymoses in the face, or indeed, elsewhere.
No marks of restraint.

HOW LONG DEAD
1 hour.

INTERNAL EXAMINATION
Fracture-dislocation of the spine at C.2 with a 2
inch gap and transverse separation of the spinal
cord at the same level.

CAUSE OF DEATH
Injuries to the central nervous system consequent
upon judicial hanging.

REMARKS
Deceased was a healthy subject at the time of
death.
Mark of suspension normally situated and
injuries from judicial hanging – to the spinal
column and cord – such as must have caused
instant death. Injuries to the central nervous
system consequent upon judicial hanging.

When Albert arrived back at the Rose and Crown that evening, he found the car park full to bursting with cars, coaches and charabancs, as scores of curious drinkers clamoured for a peek at the hangman.

On Tuesday, 26 July, Albert travelled to Birmingham's Winson Green Gaol to hang Frederick Arthur Cross, an unemployed concrete mixer from Staffordshire. Cross's wife had left him, taking their two children with her. He was devastated and bought some rat poison, with the intention to commit suicide. Lacking the courage to take his own life, but wishing to die, he hatched a plan to commit murder so that when convicted he would be executed. His victim was chosen at random.

On 25 February, Donald Lainton, a 28-year-old insurance salesman, happened to stop in a snowstorm to ask directions.

Cross offered to show him the way if he could give him a lift. Approaching Uttoxeter, he told Lainton to pull off the road and then stabbed him to death with a pair of scissors. Cross gave himself up and after being arrested he told the police, 'I don't want legal aid and I don't want defending – I just want to hang.'

He pleaded guilty at Birmingham Assizes on 5 July and the date for execution was set for the first Tuesday after three clear Sundays had passed. He had even smiled when the judge sentenced him to death. Housed in the death cell on the following morning, fear now took over and Cross told his representatives he no longer wanted to die and announced that he wished to appeal. All appeals for a reprieve failed, and a letter written to the Queen by his wife failed to stop the execution going ahead.

Cross managed to keep calm during the days leading up to his execution, but on the morning of the execution, as Albert and assistant Harry Allen went to secure his wrists, he began to resist, kicking out and struggling as the warder took hold and restrained him. The procession to the scaffold was slow, with Cross fighting and screaming all the way until the drop silenced him forever.

Albert drove back to Much Hoole after the execution, but was home just long enough to change his shirt and meet up with Jock Stewart, before they set off together to Liverpool, where Norman Green was to be hanged on the following morning.

On Easter Monday, ten-year-old Norman Yates had left his home in Wigan to run an errand. A short time later he was found stabbed to death. It was the second murder of a young boy in the town in the last year. Witnesses had seen a blond-haired man in the area and investigations led to Norman Green, a corn grinder. He denied the accusations but later confessed to both murders, taking police to his workplace, where the murder weapon was located. It was shown at his trial that Green was epileptic and there was a history of insanity in his family. Following his arrest he told detectives he kept getting the urge to kill, and that he might kill again. He made no appeal after sentence of death was passed. Albert saw Green exercising in the prison yard and worked out a drop of 7 feet 7 inches. On the following morning the execution passed off quickly without incident and by lunchtime the two executioners were enjoying a drink in the Rose and Crown.

There were just three more executions in 1955, two in the same week at Birmingham, and the final one at Leeds on 12 August. Steve Wade officiated at them all. The furore raised by the execution of Ruth Ellis, the controversial execution of Derek Bentley, and the feeling that a miscarriage of justice had taken place following the execution of Timothy Evans, led to mounting press and public campaigns for the abolition of the death penalty. Coming as quickly as it did following the four-year Royal Commission Report, there was little chance that a total abolition would find favour with the Law Lords, but it was decided that in light of recent events, a major overhaul of the types of murder warranting the death penalty would be debated. This led to an extraordinary amount of reprieves being granted – having a detrimental financial impact on the hangman's income. For Albert, though, these fees would not make too much of a dent in his pocket. He was already in discussions with a major newspaper about a series of articles on his life and cases that would bring in a very healthy cheque – and the end of the long Pierrepoint dynasty.

CHAPTER 10:
TWILIGHT YEARS

Immediately after the execution of Ruth Ellis, the press had bombarded Albert as he hurried to catch his train, asking how it felt to hang a woman. He could have told them that Ruth Ellis was the sixteenth woman he had hanged, and that only the week before he had travelled to Holloway to hang the glamorous nightclub hostess, there had been another date in his diary to hang Leeds housewife Sarah Lloyd at Manchester's Strangeways Gaol. With just 48 hours left to live, Mrs Lloyd, who had battered to death a cantankerous elderly neighbour following a quarrel, received word that her sentence had been commuted. Albert was angered at the attitude of the press. Just because one convict an attractive club hostess while the other a plain suburban housewife, he believed that both should have been worthy of the same treatment.

Jamaican, Albert Lumelino, became another date in Albert's diary that summer. Lumelino was awaiting execution in the condemned cell at Wandsworth, having committed murder during the course of a robbery at Folkestone. His execution was scheduled for 30 August, but, like Mrs Lloyd, a reprieve was issued two days before he was to die. Later that year Annie Drinkall, housed in the death cell at Manchester, heard notice of her reprieve four days before the execution, set to take place on 6 December. She had been convicted of the murder of her one-year-old daughter in Sheffield.

There were three final engagements added to Albert's diary in early December. The first was scheduled to be a double execution at Manchester; the other, received a fortnight later, was to carry out the execution of Leslie Grinstead at Wandsworth. At Manchester, Adam Nuttall was to hang for the murder of his wife at Bury, and sharing the drop with him was Thomas Bancroft of Middleton, who had been convicted at the same assizes for the murder of a baby boy.

Grinstead was soon reprieved and the execution cancelled. Meanwhile a new date had been fixed for the double execution at Manchester to take place on Tuesday, 3 January 1956. On Saturday, 31 December, Nuttall received word that his life had been spared, but in the case of Thomas Bancroft the Home Office wrote that there were insufficient grounds for interfering with the due course of the law.

Heavy snow covered the north of England as Albert made the short car journey to Manchester on the afternoon of Monday, 2 January 1956. It was now to be a single execution, which obviously meant a smaller fee than he would have got for the double. The Rose and Crown had been doing a roaring trade over Christmas and New Year, and with Albert having to be away for the Monday night, he had employed extra staff to cover his duties.

Albert reached the prison in good time and met up with assistant Harry Allen. They viewed the prisoner in the cell, worked out a drop, tested the equipment and returned to their quarters. No sooner had they started their evening meal than word reached the prison that Bancroft had been spared. It had been a close call. With just 12 hours before he was due to die, no man had come closer to the gallows in the last century. It was the first time Albert had been in the prison in readiness for an execution when a reprieve had been granted, but unlike his father almost half a century earlier, he did not go with the governor to break the news to the condemned man. With their duties now at an end, Albert packed away the ropes and left the prison at 8.30 p.m. The weather hadn't relented and with a thick layer of snow still on the ground, Albert decided against making the potentially hazardous car journey back to Hoole. He booked into a Manchester hotel for the evening, returning home on the following morning.

What had started off as a potentially profitable day when the original date had been entered into his diary, with a full fee of £25 (approximately £400 in today's money), had now come to nothing. The ruling still held in England and Wales that hangmen were 'paid by the neck': no job meant no fee. On 25 January, after mulling over this for several days, Albert wrote to the prison commissioners:

```
Rose and Crown
Hoole
Nr Preston
Lancs
25 January 1956

Dear Sir,
I was engaged by the Under-Sheriff of Lancashire
to carry out an execution of T. Bancroft at H.M.
Prison Manchester on the 3rd of January last.
```

I reported for duty in the usual way, later in the evening I was informed by the Governor that Bancroft had been respited.

I left the prison about 8.30 p.m. and as it was a very bad evening I had to stay overnight in Manchester, also on leaving work I had to engage extra staff to look after my business during my absence.

On returning home I was only paid my out of pocket travelling expenses.

The Under-Sheriff informs me that he has no ruling in the matter of paying fees in this particular case. I feel sure after making all necessary arrangements and reporting for duty I was entitled to my full fees, which has been granted to me on other occasions.

I would be much obliged if you would give me a ruling concerning this matter.

I am,
Your Obedient Servant

A. Pierrepoint

The authorities wasted little time in reminding Albert of the rules he had agreed to many years before. They were fully aware, of course, that Albert had never been paid the full fee in the event of a last-minute reprieve in England or Wales. Scotland may have had that ruling, but that involved a different authority, with their own rules. The English commissioners wrote to Albert, outlining the terms and conditions he had agreed to in 1932. Two weeks later he penned a reply.

Rose and Crown
Hoole
Nr Preston
Lancs

23rd February 1956

Dear Sir,
I beg to acknowledge the receipt of your letter of
the 8th instant.

From the Under-Sheriff of Lancashire I have
received a cheque of a £4 which apparently was
regarded as adequate recompense for my
attendance at H.M. Prison Manchester, concerning
a contract in which a reprieve was granted.

I must inform you that I was extremely
dissatisfied with this payment, and now I regard
this kind of meaness as surprising in view of my
experience and long service.

In the circumstances I have made up my mind to
resign and this letter must be accepted as a letter
of resignation. I request the removal of my name
from the list of Executioners forthwith.

Yours faithfully
A. Pierrepoint

The press were immediately made aware of this decision and
a short paragraph appeared in most newspapers on the
following day.

26th February 1956

PIERREPOINT RESIGNS

Mr Albert Pierrepoint the executioner is
resigning. A Home Office spokesman said
yesterday: 'Pierrepoint has asked the Prison
Commissioners to remove his name from the list of
executioners which they supply to the Sheriffs.'
Mr Pierrepoint who is about 50, became chief
hangman in 1946, when his uncle, Mr Thomas
Pierrepoint retired at the age of 76. His father
was also a public executioner.

On the surface it appears that the decision to resign was a
spur-of-the-minute reaction at Albert's being denied payment
he believed – wrongly – he was entitled to. Behind the scenes,
however, he had already entered into correspondence with
the editor of the Empire News and Sunday Chronicle for a
series of articles. Under the heading 'The Hangman's Own
Story' he proposed (for a fee believed to be in today's money
the equivalent of £500,000) to reveal the last moments of
many of the notorious criminals he executed.

On 3 March, the Home Office wrote to Albert asking if he
could confirm the rumour they had heard that he had entered
into an agreement to publish his memoirs in the press. The
letter also again reminded him of the agreement he had made
when becoming an assistant executioner, and which he had
been reminded of from time to time over the years through a
variety of correspondence as he gained subsequent promotions.

On the following day the Empire News and Sunday
Chronicle led with the story that Albert Pierrepoint, who had
resigned in the previous week, was set to tell his amazing life

and experiences. They also claimed that he would throw light on the subject of capital punishment, 'one of the most hotly debated issues of the day'.

Albert replied to the Home Office's letter, confirming that he had indeed entered into an agreement with the Empire News but adding that he did not intend to reveal any details other than those that had already been published and which were already in the public domain. On 12 March the Home Office wrote back acknowledging that they noted his remarks about the series of articles but suggesting it would be best if Albert submitted the articles to them for approval before publication, in order to remove any passages to which objection could be taken.

Albert apparently ignored the request and commencing on Sunday, 18 March, under the heading 'Pierrepoint Speaks', a two-page article began with an introduction telling readers of how Albert had taken over from his uncle and that he carried out the execution of 433 men and 17 women. He also wrote of how it was a relief to him that since his retirement he was able to answer the phone or read a morning paper without the interruption of someone asking if he was available to carry out an execution.

Illustrated with photographs of Albert playing 'find the thimble' with customers, and pulling a pint from behind the bar, the two-page account recounted the tale of his father's first execution and of how Albert himself had first acquired the ambition to follow in the family 'business'. There was nothing to whet the appetite of readers hoping to discover something a little more sensational, graphic or controversial. He did, however, propose in future editions to reveal how he hanged Christie ('a coward'), the last moments of Heath, Haigh and Ruth Ellis, and how he went to Germany to hang 'The Beasts of Belsen'.

The Home Office reacted to the planned series of articles at once, and in the following week publishers Kemsley Newspapers were visited by Detective Superintendent Kennedy. He interviewed Mr Berry, the proprietor, and the editor, who had openly defied the Home Office the previous week. Albert was also interviewed and they promised to submit the following week's article for censoring.

The second instalment appeared on the following Sunday, and although proofs were sent to the Home Office, the original version with Albert's recollections and account of Christie's final moments went to press anyway. Again Whitehall were enraged and contacted the publishers. This time they threatened legal action under the Official Secrets Act.

Discussing that week's revelations, which dealt with the Christie case, they had found that the newspaper account contradicted evidence from other witnesses who had been present at the execution. When a similar overly dramatised account appeared in the following week's paper, concerning Neville Heath's execution, serious talks were held at a high level. These discussions debated whether it was worthwhile pursuing legal action against the recently retired executioner, as again, when witnesses were questioned who had been present at Pentonville, they found that in the main his version of the facts differed from their memories of the events. It was decided therefore that journalistic fiction was probably behind the majority of the 'startling revelations' and that there was no point in pressing ahead with a prosecution against Albert Pierrepoint under the Official Secrets Act. Pressure was seemingly brought to bear on the publishers, who had much to lose by getting involved in a lawsuit with the Home Office, and what had started out as a major exclusive soon became little more than a damp squib; the series of articles stopped on the following week. Albert

returned from a holiday on the French Riviera and went back
to running the Rose and Crown.

* * * * *

Shortly after he retired Albert bought a pony, which he
named Trio, possibly in reference to the family threesome
who had shared the same profession. He took the pony to a
nearby farm where it was broken in; the son of the
horseman there remembered him as a chain smoker of
'Wills Whiffs' cigars.

In 1961, Albert contributed to a television programme
entitled The Death Penalty, in which he read from a piece of
paper to camera the duties of an executioner almost word
for word as they appeared in the Royal Commission Report.
In the same year a report appeared in a Yorkshire newspaper
stating that Tom Pierrepoint's memoirs had been sold to an
antique dealer in Bradford. To date, these archives and
papers have remained hidden and have not appeared in the
public domain.

In 1965, the journalist and broadcaster Ludovic Kennedy
wrote a book on the Christie and Evans case. Entitled 10
Rillington Place, it told the 'full story of an appalling
miscarriage of justice', and lead to the case eventually being
heard in Parliament. The 'Brabin Report', as it became
known, came out the following year and found that although
it was likely that Timothy Evans had murdered his wife, he
probably did not strangle his daughter. As this had been the
offence he was convicted of, Home Secretary Roy Jenkins
granted Evans a posthumous pardon later that year. In 1971,
the book was turned into a massively successful film starring
Richard Attenborough as Reg Christie and John Hurt as
Timothy Evans. Albert offered his services to the film as a

technical advisor, though his name was kept off the credits. Many years later John Hurt told of how Albert Pierrepoint was not averse to making jokes in rather bad taste on set and that following the harrowing execution scene, a number of the female secretaries were physically sick.

Around this time Diana Dors published a biography that included a chapter entitled 'H is for Hangman'. She recalled her unhappy experiences in meeting Albert Pierrepoint, and how during filming a movie, she had been invited back to Help the Poor Struggler with other members of the cast. Her reminiscences portrayed the hangman as an attention seeker, who took great pride in his job, and boasted of the people he had hanged. She ended the chapter by saying that happily it was the only time she had been in his company.

In 1973 Albert wrote a biography entitled *Executioner Pierrepoint*, in which he retold his father's story from newspaper cuttings and from his own recollections, along with details of his training and work during the war. The book is effectively in three parts, with three different subjects: his father; Uncle Tom and Albert; and the Royal Commission Report.

Albert makes a number of contradictions during the course of the book, and includes one or two errors. The most obviously contradictory statement is his claim that he does not want to put a number to the executions he had carried out, as to do so would make it appear as if he were trying to claim some kind of world record. This conveniently overlooks the fact that 17 years earlier he was paid a large sum to boastfully announce the total number of people he had executed. Evidence that Albert certainly had a highly idiosyncratic sense of humour is not thin on the ground. Many people who knew Albert Pierrepoint, customers at both Help the Poor Struggler, and later at the Rose and

Crown have attested that at various times there were signs up over the bar stating, 'No hanging around the bar.'

Syd Dernley was shocked to find veiled references to himself in the book, when Albert told a tale about blistering a new assistant after he had made a tasteless remark following an execution, and how Albert had seen to it he never worked with him again. Syd had been guilty of making a crass comment following the execution of John Livesey at Wandsworth in 1952, but Albert had not rebuked him as he had claimed, nor had he done anything to terminate Syd's career as a hangman. Syd had a lean spell of reprieves that lasted a whole year, and his career ended in the following year in circumstances that had nothing to do with his role as a hangman.

Not long after the book appeared, Albert was interviewed for a Lancashire radio programme. Talking frankly about his life and how he took up the role of hangman, he again littered the programme with errors of fact. The programme starts with him twice repeating that he was just 22 when he was interviewed for the position, despite the autobiography clearly showing he was 26 at the time he applied. Discussing the execution of Ruth Ellis he said that she 'had wobbled a bit' as they led her to the drop, but that she had been as brave as any man: 'She was as good as bloody gold really,' he commented.

In 1974, Ruth Ellis's sister had written to Albert in an attempt to put the record straight on what Ruth had said as her final words. By now Albert had already said in print, on more than one occasion, that Ruth Ellis hadn't spoken a word on the short walk to the gallows. Albert talked about his relationship with her sister on the radio show, and had even told of how they had gone out for a picnic shortly after the execution 'before the shock had sunk in'. Albert also said, on his honour, that they had gone for a drive in a car together and were singing as they took a detour to see where Ruth was buried, in the family plot at Amersham. Many years later Ruth's sister Muriel Jakubait wrote a book entitled Ruth Ellis: My Sister's Secret Life, in which she gives a totally different take on their meeting, claiming that newspaper reporters tricked her into meeting Albert. She also said that Albert wrote her many letters, often under the alias of his wife's maiden name – Fletcher – suggesting that they meet up in a variety of locations in and around the capital. She claimed to have refused all offers of meeting up with him until she found herself set up by the press into finally meeting her sister's executioner.

By the time Albert appeared on the BBC television programme Read All About It, broadcast on 2 January 1977, he had retired from the Rose and Crown and was living in a bungalow in Preston New Road, Southport. He was questioned by host Melvyn Bragg and a panel that consisted of footballer Rodney Marsh, novelist Angela Huth and explorer Chris Bonnington. Marsh congratulated Albert on a 'wonderful book' and asked him about his reaction to hanging Christie, after having hanged Evans three years before. Albert replied that he didn't wish to comment on individual cases. Asked by Angela Huth why he had chosen to break his silence after all these years, he commented – straight-faced – that as he had refused to speak about his craft, and as so much rubbish had been written by the press about his career, the public didn't know what to believe, so he was now setting things right. Albert also revealed that although he had admitted at the end of his book that he was now on the side of abolition, the steady rise in crime, which had included a few years earlier the shooting dead of one of his friends, Police Superintendent Gerald Richardson, in Blackpool, he was now on a 'see-saw', unsure what he believed.

In 1986, Albert appeared as a guest on Robert Kilroy-Silk's Day to Day programme to take part in a discussion about the death penalty for child killers. Footage that was recorded before the programme went to air shows Kilroy-Silk explaining to the audience how the programme would work, telling them to put their hands up if they wanted to ask a question or make a point, etc. In this footage, Albert states that he wishes to make a point on the 1966 Moors Murders case, which had recently been in the headlines after the police went back onto the moors in an attempt to locate missing bodies following a statement from Myra Hindley. He is warned that he is not allowed to comment on the case, but responds by saying that he will speak if he wants to. The host warns him that any comments he makes about Brady or Hindley may be libellous and could result in the programme being taken off the air. Albert is asked for the sake of all the other guests to refrain from commenting. The programme was broadcast with the only comment from the now 81-year-old hangman being that he believed that he had never hanged anyone whom he hadn't believed was guilty and deserved to be hanged. Wearing a bizarre-looking black leather-palmed tweed glove on his left hand, covering a scar from a recent operation, and looking a little lost and uncomfortable whenever the camera picked him out during the debate, he was asked if he had ever made a mistake and hanged the wrong man. His reply was that nobody knew if anyone innocent had been hanged but that it hadn't been his decision who to hang, as he had merely been a servant of the law; Albert claimed he slept soundly at night. Also sitting in the audience that day was Ruth Ellis's sister.

Soon after the programme was aired, Albert's Southport bungalow was burgled while both he and his wife were in hospital being treated for illnesses, and shortly afterwards they moved into the Melvyn Nursing Home at Southport. Following his retirement, Albert had sold the bulk of his papers, memorabilia and diaries to a former neighbour Michael Forman, who put the items up for auction at Christie's in May 1992. Albert was seriously ill at the time and it was reported in the press that staff and relatives kept news of the auction a secret from him so as to avoid causing him upset. Albert had said in his biography that the true total of his executions was a secret he would take to the grave. Copies of his diaries, various photographs and documents were sold to collectors and the auction was covered in most national newspapers.

On the night of Friday, 10 July 1992, Albert Pierrepoint died peacefully in his sleep at the nursing home where he had lived for the last four years of his life. He was 87 years old. His death brought an end to the Pierrepoint dynasty. Over the span of 55 years, his father, uncle and Albert had hanged over eight hundred and thirty people between them, in eight countries.

* * * * *

Postscript

Following Albert's retirement, Harry Allen and close friend Robert Leslie 'Jock' Stewart were promoted to chief executioners. The intention was that there would be no longer be a 'number one' hangman and that jobs would be shared between the two. Harry Allen had been the first to gain promotion, having replaced Steve Wade, who was pensioned off in October 1955, and, as such, claimed seniority. Jock Stewart was promoted following Albert's resignation, and between them they carried out 35 executions in the period 1957-64. On 13 August 1964, both were in action, hanging two young Preston dairymen for a brutal murder during the course of a theft. Harry Allen was on duty at Manchester, while Jock Stewart officiated at Liverpool.

The dairymen were the last two men to be hanged for murder in Great Britain. Capital punishment was suspended the following year and finally abolished in 1969.

APPENDIX 1

A FORM OF SERVICE TO BE USED
AT AN EXECUTION

The priest, meeting the condemned at the door of his cell, shall walk before him to the place of execution, and shall say

I am the resurrection, and the life, saith the Lord; he that believeth in me, though he were, yet shall he live; and whosoever liveth and believeth in me shall never die.

I know that my Redeemer liveth, and though after my skin worms destroy this body, yet in my flesh shall I see God, whom I shall for myself, and mine eyes shall behold and not another.

At the place of execution he shall stand facing the condemned prisoner, and shall say

Remember not, Lord, the offences of this Thy servant, and be not angry with him for ever.

By Thine agony and bloody sweat, by Thy cross and passion, By Thy precious death and burial, by Thy glorious resurrection and ascension, good Lord, deliver Thy servant.

In the hour or pain and anguish; in the hour of darkness and death; in the day of judgement, good Lord, Deliver Thy servant.

O Lord God, let the prayer of the prisoner appointed to die come before Thee.

O Lord, Jesus Christ, Lamb of God, that takest away the sins of the world, have mercy upon him and receive his soul.

When the drop falls the Priest shall say

Into Thy hands, O Lord we commend the spirit of this Thy servant.

O Lord, we beseech Thee, mercifully hear our prayers, and spare all who confess their sins unto Thee; that they whose consciences by sin are accused, by Thy merciful pardon may be absolved; through Christ our Lord.

Amen

APPENDIX 2

List of Executed Persons: Henry Pierrepoint: 105

Name	Age	Executed	Prison	Executioner	Ass1	Ass2
FAUGERON Marcel	23	19-Nov-1901	Newgate	JsB	HP	
McKENNA Patrick	53	3-Dec-1901	Manchester	JsB	HP	
WIGLEY Richard Frederick	54	18-Mar-1902	Shrewsbury	HP	JE	
EARL Charles Robert	56	29-Apr-1902	Wandsworth	WB	HP	
BEDFORD John	41	30-Jul-1902	Derby	WB	HP	
HIBBS George	40	13-Aug-1902	Wandsworth	WB	HP	
MACDONALD John	23	30-Sep-1902	Pentonville	WB	HP	
WILLIAMS Henry	32	11-Nov-1902	Pentonville	WB	HP	
MCWIGGINS Henry	29	2-Dec-1902	Manchester	WB	HP	
BARROW Thomas Fairclough	49	9-Dec-1902	Pentonville	WB	HP	
BROWN William	42	16-Dec-1902	Wandsworth	HP	JE	
PLACE George	28	30-Dec-1902	Warwick	HP	JE	
SACHS Amelia	29	3-Feb-1903	Holloway	WB	HP	JB
WALTERS Annie	54	3-Feb-1903	Holloway	WB	HP	JB
EDWARDS Edgar	44	3-Mar-1903	Wandsworth	WB	HP	
HUDSON William George	26	13-May-1903	Manchester	WB	HP	
TUFFEN William Joseph	23	11-Aug-1903	Wandsworth	HP	JE	
PALMER Edward Richard	25	17-Nov-1903	Devizes	WB	HP	
HAYWOOD William	61	15-Dec-1903	Hereford	HP	JE	
STAR Henry Bertram	31	29-Dec-1903	Liverpool	JB	HP	
CLARKSON James Henry	19	9-Mar-1904	Leeds	JB	HP	
KIRWAN William	39	31-May-1904	Liverpool	WB	HP	
LUN Pong	43	31-May-1904	Liverpool	WB	HP	
SULLIVAN John	40	12-Jul-1904	Pentonville	WB	HP	

Name	Age	Executed	Prison	Executioner	Ass1	Ass2
ROWLEDGE Samuel	37	13-Jul-1904	Northampton	WB	HP	
KAY John Thomas	52	16-Aug-1904	Leeds	JB	HP	
DONOVAN Conrad	34	13-Dec-1904	Pentonville	JB	HP	
WADE Charles	22	13-Dec-1904	Pentonville	JB	HP	
HALL Edmund	49	20-Dec-1904	Leeds	JB	HP	
FEE Joseph	23	22-Dec-1904	Armagh	HP		
JEFFRIES Arthur	44	28-Dec-1904	Leeds	JB	HP	
HARRISON Edward	62	28-Feb-1905	Wandsworth	JB	HP	
BRIDGEMAN Albert	22	26-Apr-1905	Pentonville	JB	HP	
STRATTON Albert	20	23-May-1905	Wandsworth	JB	HP	
STRATTON Alfred	23	23-May-1905	Wandsworth	JB	HP	
BENALI Ferat Mohamed	19	1-Aug-1905	Maidstone	HP	JE	
HANCOCKS William Alfred	35	9-Aug-1905	Knutsford	JB	HP	
DEVEREUX Arthur	24	15-Aug-1905	Pentonville	HP	JE	
BUTLER George William	50	7-Nov-1905	Pentonville	HP	JE	
LIFFEY Pasha	20	14-Nov-1905	Glasgow	HP		
YARNOLD William	48	5-Dec-1905	Worcester	HP	JE	
PERKINS Henry	40	6-Dec-1905	Newcastle	HP	JE	
CURTIS Samuel	60	20-Dec-1905	Maidstone	HP	WF	
EDGE Frederick William	23	27-Dec-1905	Stafford	HP	JE	
SMITH George	48	28-Dec-1905	Leeds	HP	JE	
SILK John	31	29-Dec-1905	Derby	HP	JE	
GRIFFITHS John	19	27-Feb-1906	Manchester	HP	JE	
WALTERS Harold	38	10-Apr-1906	Wakefield	HP	TP	
GLYNN Edward	26	7-Aug-1906	Nottingham	HP	WW	
MOUNCER Thomas Acomb	25	9-Aug-1906	Wakefield	HP	TP	
REYNOLDS Frederick	23	13-Nov-1906	Wandsworth	HP	JE	
HARTIGAN Edward	58	27-Nov-1906	Knutsford	HP	WW	
BUCKHAM Richard	20	4-Dec-1906	Chelmsford	HP		
MARSH Walter	40	27-Dec-1906	Derby	HP	JE	
CONNAN Thomas	29	19-Feb-1907	Jersey	HP		
JONES Joseph	60	26-Mar-1907	Stafford	HP	WW	
SLACK Wilfred Edward	47	16-Jul-1907	Derby	HP	JE	
PATERSON Charles	37	7-Aug-1907	Liverpool	HP	TP	
JAMES Leslie	44	14-Aug-1907	Cardiff	HP	TP	
BRINKLEY Richard Clifford	53	13-Aug-1907	Wandsworth	HP	JE	
AUSTIN William George	31	5-Nov-1907	Reading	HP	TP	
DUDDLES William	47	20-Nov-1907	Lincoln	HP	TP	
STILLS George	30	13-Dec-1907	Cardiff	HP	TP	
HUME Joseph	25	24-Mar-1908	Inverness	HP		
LAWMAN William Robert	35	24-Mar-1908	Durham	HP	TP	
NOBLE Joseph William	48	24-Mar-1908	Durham	HP	TP	
RAMSBOTTOM John	34	12-May-1908	Manchester	HP	JE	
BALLINGTON Frederick	41	28-Jul-1908	Manchester	HP	WW	
SIDDLE Thomas	29	4-Aug-1908	Hull	HP	JE	
DODDS Matthew James	43	5-Aug-1908	Durham	HP	TP	

Pierrepoint: A Family of Executioners

Name	Age	Executed	Prison	Executioner	Ass1	Ass2
BERRYMAN John	55	20-Aug-1908	Londonderry	HP		
PHIPPS James	21	12-Nov-1908	Knutsford	HP	TP	
NICHOLS James	35	2-Dec-1908	Norwich	HP	TP	
ELLWOOD James William	43	3-Dec-1908	Leeds	HP	TP	
BOULDRY William	41	8-Dec-1908	Maidstone	HP	WW	
PARKER Henry Taylor	32	15-Dec-1908	Warwick	HP	JE	
COLLINS Noah Percy	24	30-Dec-1908	Cardiff	HP	JE	
MURPHY John Esmond	22	6-Jan-1909	Pentonville	HP	WW	
O'CONNOR Jeremiah	52	23-Feb-1909	Durham	HP	WW	
HUTCHINSON Ernest	24	2-Mar-1909	Wakefield	HP	TP	
MEADE Thomas	33	12-Mar-1909	Leeds	HP	JE	
LEE See	38	30-Mar-1909	Liverpool	HP	TP	
JONES Joseph Edwin	39	14-Apr-1909	Stafford	HP	TP	
FOY William Joseph	25	8-May-1909	Swansea	HP	JE	
REUBENS Mark	22	20-May-1909	Pentonville	HP	TP	WW
REUBENS Morris	23	20-May-1909	Pentonville	HP	TP	WW
EDMUNDS John	24	3-Jul-1909	Usk	HP	JE	
DAVIS Walter	37	9-Jul-1909	Wakefield	HP	TP	
HAMPTON William	23	20-Jul-1909	Bodmin	HP	TP	
SHAWCROSS Mark	24	3-Aug-1909	Manchester	HP	TP	
WAMMER Julius	42	10-Aug-1909	Wandsworth	HP	WW	
DHINGRA Madar Lal	25	17-Aug-1909	Pentonville	HP	TP	
JUSTIN Richard	31	19-Aug-1909	Belfast	HP		
ATHERTON Abel	30	8-Dec-1909	Durham	HP	WW	
ATHERLEY Samuel	39	14-Dec-1909	Nottingham	HP	TP	
FREEMAN John	46	7-Dec-1909	Hull	HP	JE	
HEFFERMAN Richard	27	4-Jan-1910	Dublin	HP	TP	
MURPHY William	49	15-Feb-1910	Carnarvon	HP	WW	
WREN John	23	22-Feb-1910	Manchester	HP	JE	
PERRY George Henry	27	1-Mar-1910	Pentonville	HP	WW	
BUTLER William	62	24-Mar-1910	Usk	HP	JE	
JESSHOPE Thomas William	32	25-May-1910	Wandsworth	HP	WW	
HANCOCK James Henry	54	14-Jun-1910	Cambridge	HP	TP	
CRAKE Thomas	24	12-Jul-1910	Durham	HP	WW	
FOREMAN Frederick	45	14-Jul-1910	Chelmsford	HP	JE	

List of Executed Persons: Thomas Pierrepoint: 294

Name	Age	Executed	Prison	Chief	Ass1	Ass2	Ass3
WALTERS Harold	38	10-Apr-1906	Wakefield	HP	TP		
MOUNCER Thomas Acomb	25	9-Aug-1906	Wakefield	HP	TP		
PATERSON Charles	37	7-Aug-1907	Walton	HP	TP		
JAMES Leslie	44	14-Aug-1907	Cardiff	HP	TP		
AUSTIN William George	31	5-Nov-1907	Reading	HP	TP		
DUDDLES William	47	20-Nov-1907	Lincoln	HP	TP		
STILLS George	30	13-Dec-1907	Cardiff	HP	TP		
LAWMAN William Robert	35	24-Mar-1908	Durham	HP	TP		
NOBLE Joseph William	48	24-Mar-1908	Durham	HP	TP		
DODDS Matthew James	43	5-Aug-1908	Durham	HP	TP		
PHIPPS James	21	12-Nov-1908	Knutsford	HP	TP		
NICHOLS James	35	2-Dec-1908	Norwich	HP	TP		
ELLWOOD James William	43	3-Dec-1908	Armley	HP	TP		
HUTCHINSON Ernest	24	2-Mar-1909	Wakefield	HP	TP		
JONES Joseph Edwin	39	14-Apr-1909	Stafford	HP	TP		
LEE See	38	30-Mar-1909	Walton	HP	TP		
REUBENS Mark	22	20-May-1909	Pentonville	HP	TP	WW	
REUBENS Morris	23	20-May-1909	Pentonville	HP	TP	WW	
DAVIS Walter	37	9-Jul-1909	Wakefield	HP	TP		
HAMPTON William	23	20-Jul-1909	Bodmin	HP	TP		
SHAWCROSS Mark	24	3-Aug-1909	Strangeways	HP	TP		
DHINGRA Madar Lal	25	17-Aug-1909	Pentonville	HP	TP		
ATHERLEY Samuel	39	14-Dec-1909	Nottingham	HP	TP		
HEFFERMAN Richard	27	4-Jan-1910	Dublin	HP	TP		
HANCOCK James Henry	54	14-Jun-1910	Cambridge	HP	TP		
Coulson John Roper	32	9-Aug-1910	Armley	TP	WWk		
WOOLFE Andrew Noah	38	21-Dec-1910	Pentonville	JE	TP		
ISON Henry	45	29-Dec-1910	Armley	TP	WW		
SEYMOUR Thomas	64	9-May-1911	Walton	JE	TP		
COLLINS Michael	36	24-May-1911	Pentonville	JE	TP		
THOMAS Frederick Henry	38	15-Nov-1911	Wandsworth	JE	TP		
LOAKE George	64	28-Dec-1911	Stafford	TP	WW		
SEDDON Frederick Henry	40	18-Apr-1912	Pentonville	JE	TP		
PHILPS Sargent	33	1-Oct-1912	Wandsworth	JE	TP		
GALLOWAY Robert	27	5-Nov-1912	Norwich	TP	GB		
SMITH Gilbert Oswald	35	26-Nov-1912	Gloucester	TP	AL		
GALBRAITH William Wallace	25	20-Dec-1912	Wakefield	TP	WW		
HOPWOOD Edward	45	29-Jan-1913	Pentonville	TP	AL		
PALMER Edward Henry	22	19-Mar-1913	Bristol	TP	GB		
SYKES Walter	24	23-Apr-1913	Wakefield	TP	AL		
BURTON William Walter	29	24-Jun-1913	Dorchester	TP	GB		
FLETCHER Thomas	28	9-Jul-1913	Worcester	JE	TP		
AMOS John Vickers	35	22-Jul-1913	Newcastle	TP	WW		
GREENING Frank	34	13-Aug-1913	Winson Green	TP	GB		

Pierrepoint: A Family of Executioners

Name	Age	Executed	Prison	Chief	Ass1	Ass2	Ass3
SEEKINGS Frederick	39	4-Nov-1913	Cambridge	TP			
LAW George Frederick	34	31-Dec-1913	Wakefield	TP	AL		
WHITE Walter James	23	16-Jun-1914	Winchester	JE	TP		
BOOKER Herbert	32	28-Jul-1914	Lewes	JE	TP		
CLIFFORD Percy Evelyn	32	11-Aug-1914	Lewes	JE	TP		
QUARTLY Henry	55	10-Nov-1914	Shepton Mallet	TP	GB		
ROSENTHAL Robert	23	15-Jul-1915	Wandsworth	TP	RB		
MARRIOTT Walter	24	10-Aug-1915	Wakefield	TP	WW		
THOMPSON Harold	55	22-Dec-1915	Wakefield	TP	ET		
McCARTNEY John William	40	29-Dec-1915	Wakefield	TP	RB		
THOMPSON John William	43	27-Mar-1917	Armley	TP	WW		
GADSBY Robert	65	18-Apr-1917	Armley	TP	RB		
CAVANAGH William James	29	18-Dec-1917	Newcastle	TP	RB		
WALSH John William	35	17-Dec-1918	Armley	TP	WW		
BENSON Benjamin Hindle	41	7-Jan-1919	Armley	TP	RB		
CARDWELL George Walter	22	8-Jan-1919	Armley	TP	RB		
BARRETT Percy George	19	8-Jan-1919	Armley	TP	RB		
MASSEY Lewis	29	6-Jan-1920	Armley	TP	WW		
WRIGHT William	39	10-Mar-1920	Lincoln	TP	WW		
McHUGH Miles	32	16-Apr-1920	Armley	TP	ET		
WILSON Thomas Hargreaves	45	6-May-1920	Armley	TP	RB		
RILEY James	51	30-Nov-1920	Durham	TP	ET		
SOWERBY Edwin	28	30-Dec-1920	Armley	TP	ET		
LEVER George Edwin	51	7-Jan-1921	Maidstone	TP	RB		
FIELD Jack Alfred	19	4-Feb-1921	Wandsworth	TP	RB	WW	
GRAY William Thomas	29	4-Feb-1921	Wandsworth	TP	RB	WW	
MAHER Patrick	32	7-Jun-1921	Dublin	TP	RB		
FOLEY William	23	7-Jun-1921	Dublin	TP	RB		
MITCHELL William		7-Jun-1921	Dublin	TP	RB		
WILLIAMSON James Hutton	37	21-Mar-1922	Durham	TP	WW		
FOWLER Frank	35	13-Dec-1922	Lincoln	TP	RB		
ROBINSON George	27	13-Dec-1922	Lincoln	TP	RB		
DOON Lee	27	5-Jan-1923	Armley	TP	TPh		
CASSIDY Daniel	60	3-Apr-1923	Durham	TP	RW		
MOHAMED Hassan	33	8-Aug-1923	Durham	TP	RW		
DELANEY Thomas	38	12-Dec-1923	Dublin	TP			
McDonagh Thomas	42	12-Dec-1924	Dublin	TP			
HYNES Peter	40	15-Dec-1925	Dublin	TP			
NUNN Matthew Frederick	24	2-Jan-1924	Durham	TP	TPh		
WARDELL William Horsely	47	18-Jun-1924	Armley	TP	WW		
GOLDENBERG Jack Abraham	22	30-Jul-1924	Winchester	TP	WW		
McMULLEN Felix	26	1-Aug-1924	Dublin	TP			
MAHON Patrick Herbert	33	3-Sep-1924	Wandsworth	TP	WW		
SMITH William George	26	9-Dec-1924	Hull	TP	RB		
SIMMS Arthur	25	17-Dec-1924	Nottingham	TP	RB		
BIGNELL William Grover	32	24-Feb-1925	Shepton Mallet	TP	RB		

Name	Age	Executed	Prison	Chief	Ass1	Ass2	Ass3
BRESSINGTON William Frances	21	31-Mar-1925	Bristol	TP	TPh		
GRAHAM Henry	42	15-Apr-1925	Durham	TP	WW	HPo	LM
SHELTON Thomas Henry	24	15-Apr-1925	Durham	TP	WW	HPo	LM
THORNE John Norman	22	22-Apr-1925	Wandsworth	TP	RW		
DALTON Hubert Ernest	39	10-Jun-1925	Hull	TP	RB		
O'LEARY Cornelius		28-Jul-1925	Dublin	TP			
TALBOT Michael	23	5-Aug-1925	Dublin	TP			
WALSH Annie	31	5-Aug-1926	Dublin	TP			
BOSTOCK Alfred David	25	3-Sep-1925	Armley	TP	RW	HPo	
FOWLER Wilfred	25	3-Sep-1925	Armley	TP	RW	HPo	
FOWLER Lawrence	23	4-Sep-1925	Armley	TP	LM		
KEEN John	22	24-Sep-1925	Glasgow	TP	WW		
LAX Lorraine	28	7-Jan-1926	Armley	TP	WW		
BURROWS Herbert	22	17-Feb-1926	Gloucester	TP	WW		
LINCOLN John Ignatius	21	2-Mar-1926	Shepton Mallet	TP	LM		
THOMPSON Henry	36	9-Mar-1926	Maidstone	TP	WW		
CALVERT Louisa	33	24-Jun-1926	Strangeways	TP	WW		
MYLES James	22	15-Jul-1926	Dublin	TP			
SMITH James	23	10-Aug-1926	Durham	TP	TPh		
FINDEN Charles Edward	22	12-Aug-1926	Winchester	TP	RB		
LEAH James	60	16-Nov-1926	Walton	TP	LM		
McHUGH James	31	24-Nov-1926	Dublin	TP			
HOUGHTON Charles	45	3-Dec-1926	Gloucester	TP	RW		
McCABE Henry	48	9-Dec-1926	Dublin	TP			
JONES William Cornelius	22	5-Jan-1927	Armley	TP	RB		
KNIGHTON William	22	27-Apr-1927	Nottingham	TP	HPo		
HARNETT Arthur	27	2-Sep-1927	Armley	TP	LM		
ROBERTSON William Maynell	32	6-Dec-1927	Walton	TP	TPh		
O'NEILL William	19	29-Dec-1927	Dublin	TP			
FIELDING Frederick	24	3-Jan-1928	Strangeways	TP	TPh		
KIRBY Bertram Horace	47	4-Jan-1928	Lincoln	TP	HPo		
DUNN John Thomas	49	6-Jan-1928	Durham	TP	TPh		
CASE Samuel	24	7-Jan-1928	Armley	TP	HPo		
POWER James Joseph	33	31-Jan-1928	Winson Green	TP	RW		
HAYWARD George Frederick	32	10-Apr-1928	Nottingham	TP	HPo		
KENNEDY William Henry	36	31-May-1928	Wandsworth	TP	RW		
BROOKS Walter	48	28-Jun-1928	Strangeways	TP	LM		
ABSALOM Albert George	28	25-Jul-1928	Walton	TP	HPo		
MAYNARD William John	36	27-Jul-1928	Exeter	TP	TPh		
SMILEY William	33	8-Aug-1928	Belfast	TP	RB		
ELLIOTT Norman	22	10-Aug-1928	Durham	TP	RW		
TOAL Gerard	20	29-Aug-1928	Dublin	TP			
MIAO Chung Yi	28	6-Dec-1928	Strangeways	TP	HPo		
CONLIN Charles William	22	4-Jan-1929	Durham	TP	FR		
CLARKE Joseph Reginald	21	12-Mar-1929	Walton	TP	HPo		
CARTLEDGE George Henry	27	4-Apr-1929	Strangeways	TP			

Pierrepoint: A Family of Executioners

Name	Age	Executed	Prison	Chief	Ass1	Ass2	Ass3
COX John	33	25-Apr-1929	Dublin	TP			
JOHNSON James	43	7-Aug-1929	Durham	TP			
RAVENEY Arthur Leslie	24	14-Aug-1929	Armley	TP	LM		
MAGUIRE John	43	26-Nov-1929	Walton	TP	TPh		
CUSHNAHAN Samuel	26	8-Apr-1930	Belfast	TP	RW		
PODMORE William Henry	30	22-Apr-1930	Winchester	TP	AA		
MARJERAM Albert Edward	23	11-Jun-1930	Wandsworth	TP	HPo		
BETTS Victor Edward	21	3-Jan-1931	Winson Green	TP	AA		
GILL Frederick	26	4-Feb-1931	Armley	TP	RW		
ROUSE Alfred Arthur	37	10-Mar-1931	Bedford	TP	TPh		
LAND Frances	40	16-Apr-1931	Strangeways	TP			
DORNAN Thomas	41	31-Jul-1931	Belfast	TP	RW		
O'SHEA David	33	4-Aug-1931	Dublin	TP			
SEYMOUR Henry Daniel	52	10-Dec-1931	Oxford	TP	AA		
STEIN Solomon	21	15-Dec-1931	Strangeways	TP			
CULLENS Edward	28	13-Jan-1932	Belfast	TP	RW		
RICE George Alfred	32	3-Feb-1932	Strangeways	TP			
POPLE George Thomas	22	9-Mar-1932	Oxford	TP	HPo		
MICHAEL George Emmanuel	49	27-Apr-1932	Hull	TP	HPo		
RILEY Thomas	36	28-Apr-1932	Armley	TP	RW	AA	TPh
ROBERTS John Henry	22	28-Apr-1932	Armley	TP	RW	AA	TPh
COWLE Charles James	18	18-May-1932	Strangeways	TP			
McDERMOTT Patrick	26	29-Dec-1932	Dublin	TP	AP		
HANBURY Jermiah	49	2-Feb-1933	Winson Green	TP	RW		
COURTNEY Harold	23	7-Apr-1933	Belfast	TP	AP		
HETHERINGTON Richard	35	20-Jun-1933	Walton	TP	AP		
MORSE Frederick	32	25-Jul-1933	Bristol	TP	TPh		
PARKER Ernest Wadge	25	6-Dec-1933	Durham	TP	AP		
BURTOFT William	48	19-Dec-1933	Strangeways	TP			
HOBDAY Stanely Eric	21	28-Dec-1933	Winson Green	TP	AP		
GREGORY Roy	28	3-Jan-1934	Hull	TP	TPh		
FLEMING John	32	5-Jan-1934	Dublin	TP	AP		
BROWN Ernest	36	6-Feb-1934	Armley	TP	RW		
HAMILTON Lewis	24	6-Apr-1934	Armley	TP	AA		
HINKS Reginald Ivor	33	3-May-1934	Bristol	TP	HPo		
PARKER Frederick William	21	4-May-1934	Wandsworth	TP	AP	SC	TPh
PROBERT Albert	26	4-May-1934	Wandsworth	TP	AP	SC	TPh
MAJOR Ethel Lillie	42	19-Dec-1934	Hull	TP	AP		
RUSHWORTH Frederick	29	1-Jan-1935	Armley	TP	SC		
BLAKE David Maskill	29	7-Feb-1935	Armley	TP	AA		
ANDERSON Percy Charles	21	16-Apr-1935	Wandsworth	TP	AA		
BAINBRIDGE Joseph Stephenson	26	9-May-1935	Durham	TP			
BRIDGE John Harris	25	30-May-1935	Strangeways	TP	AP		
FRANKLIN Arthur Henry	44	26-Jun-1935	Gloucester	TP	RW		
WORTHINGTON Walter Osmond	56	10-Jul-1935	Bedford	TP	AP		
HAGUE George	23	16-Jul-1935	Durham	TP			

Name	Age	Executed	Prison	Chief	Ass1	Ass2	Ass3
WADDINGHAM Dorothea Nancy	36	16-Apr-1936	Winson Green	TP	AP		
RUXTON Buck	37	12-May-1936	Strangeways	TP	AP		
BRYANT George Arthur	38	14-Jul-1936	Wandsworth	TP	HPo		
BRYANT Charlotte	33	15-Jul-1936	Exeter	TP	TPh		
JENDEN Wallace	57	5-Aug-1936	Wandsworth	TP	RW		
JACKSON Christopher	24	16-Dec-1936	Durham	TP	AP		
BAGLEY Andrew Anderson	62	10-Feb-1937	Armley	TP	RW		
HASLAM Max Mayer	23	4-Feb-1937	Strangeways	TP	AP		
HORNICK John	42	17-Jun-1937	Dublin	TP	AP		
DAVIS Phillip Edward	30	27-Jul-1937	Exeter	TP	TPh		
BRUNT Horace William	33	12-Aug-1937	Strangeways	TP			
STONE Leslie George	24	13-Aug-1937	Pentonville	TP	AA		
RODGERS John Thomas	22	18-Nov-1937	Pentonville	TP	HPo		
MOSS Ernest John	26	7-Dec-1937	Exeter	TP	AP		
NODDER Frederick	44	30-Dec-1937	Lincoln	TP	SC		
SMITH Walter John	34	8-Mar-1938	Norwich	TP	TPh		
CALDWELL Charles James	49	20-Apr-1938	Strangeways	TP	AP		
HOOLHOUSE Robert William	21	26-May-1938	Durham	TP	AP		
MOHAMED Jan	30	6-Jun-1938	Walton	TP	AP		
RICHARDS Alfred Ernest	37	12-Jul-1938	Wandsworth	TP	AP		
GRAVES William James	38	19-Jul-1938	Wandsworth	TP	TPh		
PARKER William	25	26-Jul-1938	Durham	TP	AR		
BRAIN George	27	1-Nov-1938	Wandsworth	TP	SC		
SMYTH Dermot	33	7-Jan-1939	Dublin	TP	AP		
DAYMOND John	19	8-Feb-1939	Durham	TP			
BUTLER William Thomas	29	29-Mar-1939	Wandsworth	TP	TPh		
SMITH Ralph	41	7-Jun-1939	Gloucester	TP	AP		
HUCKER Leonard George	30	10-Oct-1939	Wandsworth	TP	HM		
BOON Stanely Ernest	28	25-Oct-1939	Wandsworth	TP	SC		
SMITH Arthur John	26	26-Oct-1939	Wandsworth	TP	TPh		
BARNES Peter	32	7-Feb-1940	Winson Green	TP	AP	SC	TPh
RICHARDS James	29	7-Feb-1940	Winson Green	TP	AP	SC	TPh
COWELL William Charles	38	24-Apr-1940	Wandsworth	TP	SC		
OSTLER Vincent	24	11-Jul-1940	Durham	TP	AP	SC	AR
APPLEBY William	27	11-Jul-1940	Durham	TP	AP	SC	AR
ROBERTS George Edward	28	8-Aug-1940	Cardiff	TP	SC		
WRIGHT John William	41	10-Sep-1940	Durham	TP	AP		
COLE Stanley Edward	23	31-Oct-1940	Wandsworth	TP	HM		
COOPER William Henry	24	26-Nov-1940	Bedford	TP	AP		
SCOLLEN Edward	42	24-Dec-1940	Durham	TP	HC		
DOCHERTY David	29	7-Jan-1941	Dublin	TP	AP		
HOLMES Clifford	24	11-Feb-1941	Strangeways	TP	HHA		
WHITE Henry Lyndo	39	6-Mar-1941	Durham	TP	HHA		
MORGAN Samuel	28	4-Apr-1941	Walton	TP	HM		
GLEESON Henry	39	29-Apr-1941	Dublin	TP	AP		
ARMSTRONG George Johnson	39	9-Jul-1941	Wandsworth	TP	SW		

Pierrepoint: A Family of Executioners

Name	Age	Executed	Prison	Chief	Ass1	Ass2	Ass3
JENNINGS David Miller	21	24-Jul-1941	Dorchester	TP	AR		
ANDERSON Edward Walker	19	31-Jul-1941	Durham	TP			
DRUEKE Karl Theo	35	6-Aug-1941	Wandsworth	TP	AP	SC	HK
WAELTI Weiner Heindrich	25	6-Aug-1941	Wandsworth	TP	AP	SC	HK
SMITH John	32	4-Sep-1941	Strangeways	TP	HHA		
RICHARDS Eli	46	19-Sep-1941	Winson Green	TP	SC		
WATSON Lionel Rupert	31	12-Nov-1941	Pentonville	TP	HC		
KELLY Patrick	31	18-Dec-1941	Dublin	TP	AP		
THORPE Thomas William	61	23-Dec-1941	Leicester	TP	AP		
PEACH Arthur	23	30-Jan-1942	Winson Green	TP	HC		
WILLIAMS David Roger	33	25-Mar-1942	Walton	TP	HHA		
AUSTIN Frederick James	28	30-Apr-1942	Bristol	TP	HK		
JOHNSON Cyril	20	15-Apr-1942	Wandsworth	TP	HC		
HILL Harold	26	1-May-1942	Oxford	TP	AP		
EDMUNDSON Douglas	28	24-Jun-1942	Walton	TP	HM		
WILLIAMS Thomas Joseph	19	2-Sep-1942	Belfast	TP	AP		
MERRY Harold Oswald	40	10-Sep-1942	Winson Green	TP	HC		
COLLINS William Ambrose	21	28-Oct-1942	Durham	TP	AP		
BOUNDS Herbert Heram	45	6-Nov-1942	Wandsworth	TP	HC		
ROBERTS Ronald	28	10-Feb-1943	Walton	TP	HK		
COBB David		12-Mar-1943	Shepton Mallet	TP	AP		
TURNER William Henry	19	24-Mar-1943	Pentonville	TP	HC		
TRENOWETH Gordon Horace	33	6-Apr-1943	Exeter	TP	HM		
KIRWAN Bernard	35	2-Jun-1943	Dublin	TP	AP		
SMITH Harold		23-Jun-1943	Shepton Mallet	TP	AP		
RAYMOND Charles Arthur	23	10-Jul-1943	Wandsworth	TP	SW		
QUAYLE William	52	3-Aug-1943	Winson Green	TP	AR		
O'SHEA William	24	12-Aug-1943	Dublin	TP	AP		
ELVIN Trevor	21	10-Sep-1943	Armley	TP	HK		
DAVIS Lee		14-Dec-1943	Shepton Mallet	TP	AR		
KOOPMAN Charles William	22	15-Dec-1943	Pentonville	TP	SW		
DORGAN John Joseph	46	22-Dec-1943	Wandsworth	TP	HC		
JAMES Thomas	26	29-Dec-1943	Walton	TP	HM		
McEWAN Mervin Clare	35	3-Feb-1944	Armley	TP	SW		
WATERS John H	38	16-Feb-1944	Shepton Mallet	TP	AR		
DIGBY Ernest Charles	34	16-Mar-1944	Bristol	TP	SW		
de la SALLE Sydney James	39	13-Apr-1944	Durham	TP	HC		
LEATHERBERRY John C	21	16-May-1944	Shepton Mallet	TP	AP		
HARRIS Wiley	26	26-May-1944	Shepton Mallet	TP	AR		
DAVIDSON John Gordon	19	12-Jul-1944	Walton	TP	AR		
MEFFEN William Frederick	52	8-Aug-1944	Leicester	TP	AP	HK	AR
COWLE William Alfred	31	8-Aug-1944	Leicester	TP	AP	HK	AR
BRINSON Eliga	25	11-Aug-1944	Shepton Mallet	TP	AP		
SMITH Willie	21	11-Aug-1944	Shepton Mallet	TP	AP		
THOMAS Madison		12-Oct-1944	Shepton Mallet	TP	AP		
KERINS Charles	26	1-Dec-1944	Dublin	TP	AP		

Name	Age	Executed	Prison	Chief	Ass1	Ass2	Ass3
CLARK Ernest Lee		8-Jan-1945	Shepton Mallet	TP	AP		
GUERRA Augustine	20	8-Jan-1945	Shepton Mallet	TP	AP		
THOMPSON Arthur	34	31-Jan-1945	Armley	TP	HM		
HULTEN Karl Gustav	23	08-Mar-1945	Pentonville	TP	HC		
HEYS Arthur	39	13-Mar-1945	Norwich	TP	SW		
PEARSON Robert		17-Mar-1945	Shepton Mallet	TP	HM		
JONES Cubia		17-Mar-1945	Shepton Mallet	TP	HM		
HARRISON William		7-Apr-1945	Shepton Mallet	TP	HM		
SMITH George E	27	8-May-1945	Shepton Mallet	TP	HM		
MARTINEZ Ancetio		15-Jun-1945	Shepton Mallet	TP	AP		
GROSSLEY Howard Joseph	38	5-Sep-1945	Cardiff	TP	SW		
RICHARDSON Tom Eric	28	7-Sep-1945	Armley	TP	HM		
BATTY William	27	8-Jan-1946	Armley	TP	HHA		
LYON John	21	8-Feb-1946	Glasgow	TP			
PRESCOTT Charles Edward	23	5-Mar-1946	Durham	TP			
CARRAHER Patrick	39	6-Apr-1946	Glasgow	TP			
BERRY Harold	30	9-Apr-1946	Strangeways	TP			
COFFEY Martin Patrick	23	24-Apr-1946	Strangeways	TP			
HOLMES Leonard	32	28-May-1946	Lincoln	TP	SW		
CALDWELL John	20	10-Aug-1946	Glasgow	TP			

List of Persons Executed: Albert Pierrepoint: 435

Name	Age	Executed	Prison	Chief	Ass1	Ass2	Ass 3
McDERMOTT Patrick	26	29-Dec-1932	Mountjoy	TP	AP		
HANBURY Jermiah	49	2-Feb-1933	Winson Green	TP	RW	AP	
COURTNEY Harold	23	7-Apr-1933	Belfast	TP	AP		
HETHERINGTON Richard	35	20-Jun-1933	Walton	TP	AP		
HOBDAY Stanely Eric	21	28-Dec-1933	Winson Green	TP	AP		
PARKER Frederick William	21	4-May-1934	Wandsworth	TP	AP	SC	TPh
PROBERT Albert	26	4-May-1934	Wandsworth	TP	AP	SC	TPh
MAJOR Ethel Lillie	42	19-Dec-1934	Hull	TP	AP		
WORTHINGTON Walter Osmond	56	10-Jul-1935	Bedford	TP	AP		
WADDINGHAM Dorothea Nancy	36	16-Apr-1936	Winson Green	TP	AP		
JACKSON Christopher	24	16-Dec-1936	Durham	TP	AP		
HASLAM Max Mayer	23	4-Feb-1937	Strangeways	TP	AP		
HORNICK John	42	17-Jun-1937	Mountjoy	TP	AP		
MOSS Ernest John	26	7-Dec-1937	Exeter	TP	AP		
CALDWELL Charles James	49	20-Apr-1938	Strangeways	TP	AP		
MOHAMED Jan	30	6-Jun-1938	Walton	TP	AP		
RICHARDS Alfred Ernest	37	12-Jul-1938	Wandsworth	TP	AP		
SMYTH Dermot	33	7-Jan-1938	Mountjoy	TP	AP		
ARMSTRONG Harold	37	21-Mar-1939	Wandsworth	TPh	AP		
SMITH Ralph	41	7-Jun-1939	Gloucester	TP	AP		
BARNES Peter	32	7-Feb-1940	Winson Green	TP	AP	SC	TPh
RICHARDS James	29	7-Feb-1940	Winson Green	TP	AP	SC	TPh

Pierrepoint: A Family of Executioners

Name	Age	Executed	Prison	Chief	Ass1	Ass2	Ass3
OSTLER Vincent	24	11-Jul-1940	Durham	TP	AP	SC	AR
APPLEBY William	27	11-Jul-1940	Durham	TP	AP	SC	AR
SINGH Udam	37	31-Jul-1940	Pentonville	SC	AP		
WRIGHT John William	41	10-Sep-1940	Durham	TP	AP		
COOPER William Henry	24	26-Nov-1940	Bedford	TP	AP		
WALDBERG Jose	25	10-Dec-1940	Pentonville	SC	AP	HK	HM
MEIR Karl Heindrich	24	10-Dec-1940	Pentonville	SC	AP	HK	HM
DOCHERTY David	29	07-Jan-1941	Mountjoy	TP	AP		
GLEESON Henry	39	23-Apr-1941	Mountjoy	TP	AP		
DRUEKE Karl Theo	35	06-Aug-1942	Wandsworth	TP	AP	SC	HK
WAELTI Weiner Heindrich	25	06-Aug-1942	Wandsworth	TP	AP	SC	HK
MANCINI Antonio	39	31-Oct-1941	Pentonville	AP	SW		
SMITH John Ernest	21	3-Dec-1941	Wandsworth	AP	HBA		
RICHTER Karel Richard	29	10-Dec-1941	Wandsworth	AP	SW		
KELLY Patrick	31	18-Dec-1941	Mountjoy	TP	AP		
THORPE Thomas William	61	23-Dec-1941	Leicester	TP	AP		
TREVOR Harold Dorian	62	11-Mar-1942	Wandsworth	AP	HM		
HILL Harold	26	1-May-1942	Oxford	TP	AP		
CUMMINS Gordon Frederick	28	25-Jun-1942	Wandsworth	AP	HK		
KEY Jose Estella	34	7-Jul-1942	Wandsworth	AP	SW	HK	HC
TIMMERMAN Alphonse	37	7-Jul-1942	Wandsworth	AP	SW	HK	HC
ANDERSON Arthur	52	21-Jul-1942	Wandsworth	AP	HM		
WILLIAMS Thomas Joseph	19	2-Sep-1942	Belfast	TP	AP		
SILVEROSA George	23	10-Sep-1942	Pentonville	AP	SW	HK	HM
DASHWOOD Samuel	22	10-Sep-1942	Pentonville	AP	SW	HK	HM
KINGSTON Patrick William	38	6-Oct-1942	Wandsworth	AP	HM		
COLLINS William Ambrose	21	28-Oct-1942	Durham	TP	AP		
SCOTT-FORD Duncan	21	3-Nov-1942	Wandsworth	AP	HK		
DRONKERS Johannes Marius	46	31-Dec-1942	Wandsworth	AP	SW		
WINTER Franciscus Johan	39	26-Jan-1943	Wandsworth	AP	HC		
DOBKIN Harold	49	27-Jan-1943	Wandsworth	AP	HM		
COBB David		12-Mar-1943	Shepton Mallet	TP	AP		
RAYNOR George Dudley	26	31-Mar-1943	Wandsworth	AP	SW		
SANGRET August	30	29-Apr-1943	Wandsworth	AP	HC		
KIRWAN Bernard	35	2-Jun-1943	Mountjoy	TP	AP		
SMITH Harold		23-Jun-1943	Shepton Mallet	TP	AP		
ROE Gerald Elphistone	41	3-Aug-1943	Pentonville	AP	SW		
O'SHEA William	24	12-Aug-1943	Mountjoy	TP	AP		
GAUTHIER Charles Eugene	25	24-Sep-1943	Wandsworth	AP	AR		
CASEY Terence	22	19-Nov-1943	Wandsworth	AP	HC		
CORDON-CUENCA Louis	23	11-Jan-1944	Gibraltar	AP	HK		
MUNOZ Jose Martin	19	11-Jan-1944	Gibraltar	AP	HK		
GEORGHIOU Christos	38	2-Feb-1944	Pentonville	AP	HM		
JOB Oscar John	58	16-Mar-1944	Pentonville	AP	HK		
LEATHERBERRY John	21	16-May-1944	Shepton Mallet	TP	AP		
KEMP Ernest James	20	6-Jun-1944	Wandsworth	AP	HM		

Name	Age	Executed	Prison	Chief	Ass1	Ass2	Ass3
NUEKERMANS Pierre	27	23-Jun-1944	Pentonville	AP	AR		
VANHOVE Joseph	27	12-Jul-1944	Pentonville	AP	SW		
MEFFEN William Frederick	52	8-Aug-1944	Leicester	TP	AP	HK	AR
COWLE William Alfred	31	8-Aug-1944	Leicester	TP	AP	HK	AR
MADISON Thomas	23	12-Oct-1944	Shepton Mallet	TP	AP		
KERINS Charles	26	1-Dec-1944	Mountjoy	TP	AP		
CLARK Ernest Lee		8-Jan-1945	Shepton Mallet	TP	AP		
GUERRA Augustine	20	8-Jan-1945	Shepton Mallet	TP	AP		
GORDON Horace Beresford	28	9-Jan-1945	Wandsworth	AP	SW		
BROWN Andrew	26	30-Jan-1945	Wandsworth	AP	SW		
LEHMAN James	45	19-Mar-1945	Mountjoy	AP	SJ		
MARTINEZ Anceto		15-Jun-1945	Shepton Mallet	TP	AP		
KOENIG Erich	20	6-Oct-1945	Pentonville	AP	SW	HBA	
GOTLZ Joachim	20	6-Oct-1945	Pentonville	AP	SW	HBA	
MERTENS Josef	21	6-Oct-1945	Pentonville	AP	SW	HBA	
ZUEHISDORIF Kurt	20	6-Oct-1945	Pentonville	AP	SW	HBA	
BRUELING Heinz	21	6-Oct-1945	Pentonville	AP	SW	HBA	
MAURI Ronald Bertram	32	31-Oct-1945	Wandsworth	AP	HK		
KUELNE Arnim	21	16-Nov-1945	Pentonville	AP	AR		
SCMITTENDORF Emil	31	16-Nov-1945	Pentonville	AP	AR		
VOLKENRATH Elizabeth		13-Dec-1945	Hameln	AP	R O'N		
GRESE Irma	21	13-Dec-1945	Hameln	AP	R O'N		
BORMANN Juanna	42	13-Dec-1945	Hameln	AP	R O'N		
KRAMER Josef	39	13-Dec-1945	Hameln	AP	R O'N		
KLEIN Fritz	55	13-Dec-1945	Hameln	AP	R O'N		
FRANZICH Karl		13-Dec-1945	Hameln	AP	R O'N		
WEINGARTNER Peter		13-Dec-1945	Hameln	AP	R O'N		
PINEKEN Ansgar		13-Dec-1945	Hameln	AP	R O'N		
HOHSLER Franz	39	13-Dec-1945	Hameln	AP	R O'N		
STAKEL Franz		13-Dec-1945	Hameln	AP	R O'N		
DORR Wilhelm		13-Dec-1945	Hameln	AP	R O'N		
SANDROCK Otto		13-Dec-1945	Hameln	AP	R O'N		
SCHWEINSBERGER Ludwig		13-Dec-1945	Hameln	AP	R O'N		
AMERY John	23	19-Dec-1945	Wandsworth	AP	HC		
YOUNG John Riley	40	21-Dec-1945	Pentonville	AP	SW		
McNICHOL James	27	21-Dec-1945	Pentonville	AP	HM		
BLAINE Robert	24	29-Dec-1945	Wandsworth	AP	HK		
JOYCE William	40	3-Jan-1946	Wandsworth	AP	AR		
SCHURCH Theodore William	27	4-Jan-1946	Pentonville	AP	AR		
NIESCIOR Michal	29	31-Jan-1946	Wandsworth	AP	SW		
BARCHOSS Johann		8-Mar-1946	Hameln	AP	R O'N		
BUEHNING August		8-Mar-1946	Hameln	AP	R O'N		
BUETTNER Alfred		8-Mar-1946	Hameln	AP	R O'N		
FRANKE Otto		8-Mar-1946	Hameln	AP	R O'N		
HEYER Erich		8-Mar-1946	Hameln	AP	R O'N		
KOENIG Friedrich		8-Mar-1946	Hameln	AP	R O'N		

Pierrepoint: A Family of Executioners

Name	Age	Executed	Prison	Chief	Ass1	Ass2	Ass3
MACKENSON Willi		8-Mar-1946	Hameln	AP	R O'N		
RENOTH Hans		8-Mar-1946	Hameln	AP	R O'N		
CLEGG Arthur	42	19-Mar-1946	Wandsworth	AP	HM		
GRONDKOWSKI Marian	33	2-Apr-1946	Wandsworth	AP	AR		
MALINOWSKI Henry K	25	2-Apr-1946	Wandsworth	AP	HK		
AMBERGER Karl		15-May-1946	Hameln	AP	R O'N		
BOPF Otto		15-May-1946	Hameln	AP	R O'N		
BOETTCHER Bruno		15-May-1946	Hameln	AP	R O'N		
GUENTHER Emil		15-May-1946	Hameln	AP	R O'N		
HOFFMANN Erich		15-May-1946	Hameln	AP	R O'N		
KIRCHNER Franz		15-May-1946	Hameln	AP	R O'N		
LANG Ludwig		15-May-1946	Hameln	AP	R O'N		
LOMMES Hermann		15-May-1946	Hameln	AP	R O'N		
SCHARSCHMIDT Wilhelm		15-May-1946	Hameln	AP	R O'N		
UHRIG Friedrich		15-May-1946	Hameln	AP	R O'N		
BEECK Friedrich		16-May-1946	Hameln	AP	R O'N		
GERNOTH Herbert		16-May-1946	Hameln	AP	R O'N		
HADLER Wilhelm		16-May-1946	Hameln	AP	R O'N		
KNOP Erwin		16-May-1946	Hameln	AP	R O'N		
SCHOENGARTH Eberhard		16-May-1946	Hameln	AP	R O'N		
TESCH Bruno		16-May-1946	Hameln	AP	R O'N		
WEINBACHER Karl		16-May-1946	Hameln	AP	R O'N		
HENDREN Thomas	31	17-Jul-1946	Walton	AP	HM		
CLAYTON Walter	22	7-Aug-1946	Walton	AP	HBA		
WALASEK Teofil		15-Aug-1946	Hameln	AP			
SMITH Sidney John	22	6-Sep-1946	Wandsworth	AP	HC		
MASON David Baillie	39	6-Sep-1946	Wandsworth	AP	HBA		
JASKIN Michael	20	24-Sep-1946	Karlou	AP			
SOSSNOWSKY Wasyl	20	24-Sep-1946	Karlou	AP			
BANTRO Peter	22	24-Sep-1946	Karlou	AP			
LEWKOWITZ Peter	23	24-Sep-1946	Karlou	AP			
PERCAK Michael	21	24-Sep-1946	Karlou	AP			
MEISCH Wladirmin	21	24-Sep-1946	Karlou	AP			
WERHUN Michael	21	24-Sep-1946	Karlou	AP			
MELNYTSCHUK Stefan	24	24-Sep-1946	Karlou	AP			
BAHR Wilhelm	23	8-Oct-1946	Hameln	AP	R O'N		
BREMS Andreas		8-Oct-1946	Hameln	AP	R O'N		
DREIMANN Wilhelm		8-Oct-1946	Hameln	AP	R O'N		
GERECKE Heinrich		8-Oct-1946	Hameln	AP	R O'N		
GRIMM Walter		8-Oct-1946	Hameln	AP	R O'N		
HESSLINGER Georg		8-Oct-1946	Hameln	AP	R O'N		
KITT Bruno (Dr)		8-Oct-1946	Hameln	AP	R O'N		
KNORR Ludwig		8-Oct-1946	Hameln	AP	R O'N		
MUMM Karl		8-Oct-1946	Hameln	AP	R O'N		
PAULY Max		8-Oct-1946	Hameln	AP	R O'N		
REESE Johann		8-Oct-1946	Hameln	AP	R O'N		

Name	Age	Executed	Prison	Chief	Ass1	Ass2	Ass 3
RUGE Heinrich		8-Oct-1946	Hameln	AP	R O'N		
SPECK Adolf		8-Oct-1946	Hameln	AP	R O'N		
THUMANN Anton		8-Oct-1946	Hameln	AP	R O'N		
TRZEBINSKI Alfred (Dr)		8-Oct-1946	Hameln	AP	R O'N		
WARNCKE Wilhelm		8-Oct-1946	Hameln	AP	R O'N		
BERG Franz		11-Oct-1946	Hameln	AP	R O'N		
CEGIELSKI Kasimir		11-Oct-1946	Hameln	AP	R O'N		
FISCHER Friedrich		11-Oct-1946	Hameln	AP	R O'N		
FRAHM Johann		11-Oct-1946	Hameln	AP	R O'N		
HARTLEB Georg		11-Oct-1946	Hameln	AP	R O'N		
HEIDEMANN Heinz Lueder		11-Oct-1946	Hameln	AP	R O'N		
JAUCH Ewald		11-Oct-1946	Hameln	AP	R O'N		
QUACKERNACK Walter		11-Oct-1946	Hameln	AP	R O'N		
REDDEHASE Hans Heinrich		11-Oct-1946	Hameln	AP	R O'N		
ROHDE Werner (Dr)		11-Oct-1946	Hameln	AP	R O'N		
STRAUB Peter		11-Oct-1946	Hameln	AP	R O'N		
WOLFERT Adolf		11-Oct-1946	Hameln	AP	R O'N		
HEATH Neville George	28	16-Oct-1946	Pentonville	AP	HK		
BOYCE Arthur Robert	45	1-Nov-1946	Pentonville	AP	HC		
FREIYER Frank Josiah	26	13-Nov-1946	Wandsworth	AP	HK		
RUSHTON Arthur	31	19-Nov-1946	Walton	AP	HC		
MATHIESON John	23	10-Dec-1946	Pentonville	AP	HBA		
UPSON Frank J.		22-Jan-1947	Hameln	AP	R O'N	JH	
BRUNKEN Anton Jansen		23-Jan-1947	Hameln	AP	R O'N	JH	
ERNST Albert		23-Jan-1947	Hameln	AP	R O'N	JH	
ESSER Johannes		23-Jan-1947	Hameln	AP	R O'N	JH	
HOFFMANN Emil		23-Jan-1947	Hameln	AP	R O'N	JH	
HOLLBORN Friedrich		23-Jan-1947	Hameln	AP	R O'N	JH	
KNAB Hans-Christian		23-Jan-1947	Hameln	AP	R O'N	JH	
KOECHLIN Max		23-Jan-1947	Hameln	AP	R O'N	JH	
MARKWART Max		23-Jan-1947	Hameln	AP	R O'N	JH	
NIKLAUS Wilhelm		23-Jan-1947	Hameln	AP	R O'N	JH	
SCHIPPER Sebastian		23-Jan-1947	Hameln	AP	R O'N	JH	
SCHNEIDER Wilhelm		23-Jan-1947	Hameln	AP	R O'N	JH	
ROWLAND Walter Graham	35	27-Feb-1947	Strangeways	AP	HC		
KOERBEL Hans (Dr)		7-Mar-1947	Hameln	AP	R O'N		
SINCLAIR Sydney	45	18-Mar-1947	Wandsworth	AP	HC		
REYNOLDS Frederick William	39	26-Mar-1947	Pentonville	AP	HK		
McMANUS Joseph	41	31-Mar-1947	Mountjoy	AP	SJ		
WILLIAMS David John	26	15-Apr-1947	Wandsworth	AP	HK		
BINZ Dorothea		2-May-1947	Hameln	AP	R O'N		
BOESEL Grete		2-May-1947	Hameln	AP	R O'N		
EBSEN Karl		2-May-1947	Hameln	AP	R O'N		
GROSSE Arthur		2-May-1947	Hameln	AP	R O'N		
HEITZ Johann		2-May-1947	Hameln	AP	R O'N		
MARSCHALL Elisabeth		2-May-1947	Hameln	AP	R O'N		

Pierrepoint: A Family of Executioners

Name	Age	Executed	Prison	Chief	Ass1	Ass2	Ass 3
STUMPP Heinz		2-May-1947	Hameln	AP	R O'N		
TRUSCHEL Karl		2-May-1947	Hameln	AP	R O'N		
BINDER Gustav		3-May-1947	Hameln	AP	R O'N		
RAMDOHR Ludwig		3-May-1947	Hameln	AP	R O'N		
ROSENTHAL Rolf (Dr)		3-May-1947	Hameln	AP	R O'N		
SCHIEDLAUSKY Gerhard (Dr)		3-May-1947	Hameln	AP	R O'N		
SCHWARZHUBER Johan		3-May-1947	Hameln	AP	R O'N		
SALVEQUART Vera		26-Jun-1947	Hameln	AP	R O'N		
NOWAKOWSKI Longin		26-Jun-1947	Hameln	AP	R O'N		
WINIARSKI Waclaw		26-Jun-1947	Hameln	AP	R O'N		
BACHUR Kazimierz		26-Jun-1947	Hameln	AP	R O'N		
KLINGLER Josef		26-Jun-1947	Hameln	AP	R O'N		
KEUS Wilhelm		26-Jun-1947	Hameln	AP	R O'N		
LUETKEMEYER Albrecht		26-Jun-1947	Hameln	AP	R O'N		
JEPSEN Gustav Alfred		26-Jun-1947	Hameln	AP	R O'N		
KIEFFER Hans		26-Jun-1947	Hameln	AP	R O'N		
HAUG Karl		26-Jun-1947	Hameln	AP	R O'N		
SCHNUR Richard		26-Jun-1947	Hameln	AP	R O'N		
PEEK Alfred		26-Jun-1947	Hameln	AP	R O'N		
RASCHE Kurt		26-Jun-1947	Hameln	AP	R O'N		
PATRICK Charles Edward		5-Sep-1947	Hameln	AP	R O'N	ER	
CREMER Karl		5-Sep-1947	Hameln	AP	R O'N	ER	
DAMMANN Wilhelm		5-Sep-1947	Hameln	AP	R O'N	ER	
HOCHSTAETTER Friedrich		5-Sep-1947	Hameln	AP	R O'N	ER	
KNOTH Joseph		5-Sep-1947	Hameln	AP	R O'N	ER	
KUBIK Edward		5-Sep-1947	Hameln	AP	R O'N	ER	
KUN Tadeusz		5-Sep-1947	Hameln	AP	R O'N	ER	
LUETFRING Johann Wilhelm		5-Sep-1947	Hameln	AP	R O'N	ER	
ROESENER Albert		5-Sep-1947	Hameln	AP	R O'N	ER	
ROTSCHOPF Michal		5-Sep-1947	Hameln	AP	R O'N	ER	
SCHWARZ Karl		5-Sep-1947	Hameln	AP	R O'N	ER	
SMOK Francisek		5-Sep-1947	Hameln	AP	R O'N	ER	
STELLPFLUG Heinz		5-Sep-1947	Hameln	AP	R O'N	ER	
STREIT Stephan		5-Sep-1947	Hameln	AP	R O'N	ER	
GERAGHTY Christopher James	20	19-Sep-1947	Pentonville	AP	HBA	HC	
JENKINS Charles Henry	23	19-Sep-1947	Pentonville	AP	HBA	HC	
BISSET Marian		14-Nov-1947	Hameln	AP	R O'N	ER	
BOGDANOWICZ Kazimierz		14-Nov-1947	Hameln	AP	R O'N	ER	
BORKOWSKI Jan		14-Nov-1947	Hameln	AP	R O'N	ER	
BUSSEM Josef		14-Nov-1947	Hameln	AP	R O'N	ER	
DINGE Hermann Wilhelm		14-Nov-1947	Hameln	AP	R O'N	ER	
DZIEKAN Stanislaw		14-Nov-1947	Hameln	AP	R O'N	ER	
GAWLICZEK Georg		14-Nov-1947	Hameln	AP	R O'N	ER	
GAWRONSKI Wladislaw		14-Nov-1947	Hameln	AP	R O'N	ER	
KAYSER Cornelius		14-Nov-1947	Hameln	AP	R O'N	ER	
KIWIAK Wasyl		14-Nov-1947	Hameln	AP	R O'N	ER	

Name	Age	Executed	Prison	Chief	Ass1	Ass2	Ass3
SCHULZE Fritz		14-Nov-1947	Hameln	AP	R O'N	ER	
SOLTYS Franz		14-Nov-1947	Hameln	AP	R O'N	ER	
STANCZIK Josef		14-Nov-1947	Hameln	AP	R O'N	ER	
STANICKI Hubert		14-Nov-1947	Hameln	AP	R O'N	ER	
WASKIEWICZ Jan		14-Nov-1947	Hameln	AP	R O'N	ER	
BIELSKI Tadeus		14-Nov-1947	Hameln	AP	R O'N	ER	
JURKIEWICZ Eugene	34	30-Dec-1947	Bristol	AP	HHA		
FRICKE Otto		29-Jan-1948	Hameln	AP	R O'N	ER	
HENNINGS Wilhelm		29-Jan-1948	Hameln	AP	R O'N	ER	
KETTENBEIL Udo		29-Jan-1948	Hameln	AP	R O'N	ER	
SCHUETTE Carl Otto		29-Jan-1948	Hameln	AP	R O'N	ER	
TESSMANN Willi		29-Jan-1948	Hameln	AP	R O'N	ER	
BARTSCH Peter		30-Jan-1948	Hameln	AP	R O'N	ER	
KORDIC Mihajlo		30-Jan-1948	Hameln	AP	R O'N	ER	
MEHMEDOVIC Pasaka		30-Jan-1948	Hameln	AP	R O'N	ER	
MITRASINOVIC Stojadin		30-Jan-1948	Hameln	AP	R O'N	ER	
NICOLIC Manojlo		30-Jan-1948	Hameln	AP	R O'N	ER	
OSUCH Marion		30-Jan-1948	Hameln	AP	R O'N	ER	
PARUSKIEWICZ Andrzej		30-Jan-1948	Hameln	AP	R O'N	ER	
PAVCOVIC Miloslaw		30-Jan-1948	Hameln	AP	R O'N	ER	
SAFRANAUSKAS Franc		30-Jan-1948	Hameln	AP	R O'N	ER	
ZUNDE Ansins		30-Jan-1948	Hameln	AP	R O'N	ER	
EVANS Hadyn	22	3-Feb-1948	Cardiff	AP	HK		
MYSZKA Stanlislaw	23	06-Feb-1948	Perth	AP	SW		
CROSS Walter John	21	19-Feb-1948	Pentonville	AP	HBA		
GEITH Eduard		26-Feb-1948	Hameln	AP	R O'N		
GMEINER Josef		26-Feb-1948	Hameln	AP	R O'N		
HAUSER Friedrich		26-Feb-1948	Hameln	AP	R O'N		
HERBERG Walter		26-Feb-1948	Hameln	AP	R O'N		
JACOBS Walter		26-Feb-1948	Hameln	AP	R O'N		
KAEHLER Hans		26-Feb-1948	Hameln	AP	R O'N		
OPITZ Friedrich		26-Feb-1948	Hameln	AP	R O'N		
POST Johannes		26-Feb-1948	Hameln	AP	R O'N		
PREISS Otto		26-Feb-1948	Hameln	AP	R O'N		
SCHIMMEL Alfred		26-Feb-1948	Hameln	AP	R O'N		
SCHMIDT Oskar		26-Feb-1948	Hameln	AP	R O'N		
SCHNEIDER Johann		26-Feb-1948	Hameln	AP	R O'N		
SCHULZ Emil		26-Feb-1948	Hameln	AP	R O'N		
WEIL Emil		26-Feb-1948	Hameln	AP	R O'N		
ZACHARIAS Erich		26-Feb-1948	Hameln	AP	R O'N		
IWANOWITSCH Wasili		24-Mar-1948	Hameln	AP	R O'N		
LEHMANN Johannes		24-Mar-1948	Hameln	AP	R O'N		
SKIBA Wasyl		24-Mar-1948	Hameln	AP	R O'N		
STREBLINSKI Nicolay		24-Mar-1948	Hameln	AP	R O'N		
BAUMANN Otto		9-Jun-1948	Hameln	AP	R O'N		
CZERWICK Josef		9-Jun-1948	Hameln	AP	R O'N		

Name	Age	Executed	Prison	Chief	Ass1	Ass2	Ass3
DOBOSZ Jurco		9-Jun-1948	Hameln	AP	R O'N		
FINKENRATH Karl		9-Jun-1948	Hameln	AP	R O'N		
GRIESEL Georg		9-Jun-1948	Hameln	AP	R O'N		
HEEREN Heinrich Johann		9-Jun-1948	Hameln	AP	R O'N		
KLOS Peter		9-Jun-1948	Hameln	AP	R O'N		
MOHR Otto		9-Jun-1948	Hameln	AP	R O'N		
CLOSIUS Ruth		29-Jul-1948	Hameln	AP	R O'N		
TRAWINSKI Jerzy		29-Jul-1948	Hameln	AP	R O'N		
SCHMIDT Luis		29-Jul-1948	Hameln	AP	R O'N		
CONRAD Arthur Albin		17-Sep-1948	Hameln	AP	R O'N		
SONNTAG Walter (Dr)		17-Sep-1948	Hameln	AP	R O'N		
ORENDI Benno (Dr)		17-Sep-1948	Hameln	AP	R O'N		
SCHREIBER Ida Bertha	38	20-Sep-1948	Hameln	AP	R O'N		
ZIMMER Emma Anna	60	20-Sep-1948	Hameln	AP	R O'N		
DIKTY Gottlieb Friedrich		29-Oct-1948	Hameln	AP	R O'N		
CLARK Stanely Joseph	32	18-Nov-1948	Norwich	AP	HK		
GRIFFITHS Peter	22	19-Nov-1948	Walton	AP	HBA		
GAMBON William	28	24-Nov-1948	Mountjoy	AP			
RUSSELL George	45	2-Dec-1948	Oxford	AP	SW		
KUHL Guenther (Dr)		9-Dec-1948		AP	R O'N		
WODENKO Adolf		9-Dec-1948		AP	R O'N		
FIATKOWSKI Stanislaus		9-Dec-1948		AP	R O'N		
ZYLINSKI Romuold		9-Dec-1948		AP	R O'N		
ALLEN Margaret	42	12-Jan-1949	Strangeways	AP	HK		
SCHNABEL Dietrich		20-Jan-1949		AP	R O'N		
SWIDERSKI Czeslaw		20-Jan-1949		AP	R O'N		
SIEBKEN Bernhard		20-Jan-1949		AP	R O'N		
KNOECHLEIN Fritz		21-Jan-1949		AP	R O'N		
SEMINI George	24	27-Jan-1949	Walton	AP	HBA		
JAREMCZUK Theodor		17-Feb-1949		AP	R O'N		
STRICKSON Kenneth	21	22-Mar-1949	Lincoln	AP	HK		
FARRELL James	18	29-Mar-1949	Winson Green	AP	HK		
LEWIS Harold	21	21-Apr-1949	Pentonville	AP	HBA		
CIEPLAK Josef		18-May-1949	Hameln	AP	R O'N		
COOPER Bernard Alfred	49	21-Jun-1949	Pentonville	AP	HK		
SCHMIDT Caspar		26-Jul-1949	Hameln	AP	R O'N		
THEILENGERDES Friedrich		26-Jul-1949	Hameln	AP	R O'N		
CHAMBERLAIN Sydney Archibald	32	28-Jul-1949	Winchester	AP	HHA		
JONES Rex Harvey	25	4-Aug-1949	Swansea	AP	HK	GD	HM
MacKINTOSH Robert Thomas	21	4-Aug-1949	Swansea	AP	HK	GD	HM
HAIGH John George	39	10-Aug-1949	Wandsworth	AP	HK		
DAVIS William John	31	16-Aug-1949	Wandsworth	AP	HK		
ANTONOWICZ Miecyslaw		31-Aug-1949	Hameln	AP	R O'N		
KLINSKI Roman		31-Aug-1949	Hameln	AP	R O'N		
JONES William Claude	31	28-Sep-1949	Pentonville	AP	HBA		
ANNDZIAK Jerzy		6-Dec-1949	Hameln	AP	R O'N		

Name	Age	Executed	Prison	Chief	Ass1	Ass2	Ass3
COUZINS Ernest Soper	49	30-Dec-1949	Wandsworth	AP	HBA		
RAVEN Daniel Myer	23	6-Jan-1950	Pentonville	AP	HK		
RIVETT James Frank	21	8-Mar-1950	Norwich	AP	HHA		
EVANS Timothy John	25	9-Mar-1950	Pentonville	AP	SD		
KELLY George	27	28-Mar-1950	Walton	AP	HBA		
MAKISMOWSKI Piotr	33	29-Mar-1950	Winson Green	AP	SD		
JENKINS Albert Edward	38	19-Apr-1950	Swansea	AP	HK		
GOWER Zwigniew	23	7-Jul-1950	Winchester	AP	HK	HHA	SD
REDEL Roman	23	7-Jul-1950	Winchester	AP	HK	HHA	SD
BROWN George Finlay	23	11-Jul-50	Durham	AP	HK		
ATWELL Ronald Douglas	24	13-Jul-1950	Bristol	AP	SD		
PRICE Albert	32	16-Aug-1950	Wandsworth	AP	HHA		
HENSMANN Frank Edward	22	31-Aug-1950	Egypt	AP	JR	GT	
SMITH Robert Edward	23	31-Aug-1950	Egypt	AP	JR	GT	
GOLBY John Lionel	29	31-Aug-1950	Egypt	AP	JR	GT	
HARRIS Paul Christopher	28	30-Oct-1950	Barlinnie	AP	SW		
CORBITT James Henry	37	28-Nov-1950	Strangeways	AP	HHA		
WOODFIELD Edward Isaac	49	14-Dec-1950	Bristol	AP	HHA		
ROBERTSON James Ronald	33	16-Dec-1950	Barlinnie	AP	SW		
CROSBY Nicholas Persulius	22	19-Dec-1950	Strangeways	AP	SD		
GRIFFIN Frank	40	4-Jan-1951	Shrewsbury	AP	HM		
KOVACEVIC Nenad	29	26-Jan-1951	Strangeways	AP	HHA		
WATKINS William Arthur	49	3-Apr-1951	Winson Green	AP	HHA		
BROWN Joseph	30	25-Apr-1951	Wandsworth	AP	SD	HBA	HHA
SMITH Edward Charles	30	25-Apr-1951	Wandsworth	AP	SD	HBA	HHA
VIRRELS James	56	26-Apr-1951	Wandsworth	AP	SD		
INGLIS James	30	8-May-1951	Strangeways	AP	SD		
SHAUGHNESSY William Edward	48	9-May-1951	Winchester	AP	HBA		
DAND John	32	12-Jun-1951	Strangeways	AP	HHA		
WRIGHT John	30	3-Jul-1951	Strangeways	AP	HS		
MOORE Dennis Albert	22	19-Jul-1951	Norwich	AP	SD	RS	HBA
REYNOLDS Alfred George	24	19-Jul-1951	Norwich	AP	SD	RS	HBA
SMITH Robert Dobie	30	15-Sep-1951	Edinburgh	AP	SW		
O'CONNOR John	29	24-Oct-1951	Pentonville	AP	HHA		
MILLS Herbert Leonard	19	11-Dec-1951	Lincoln	AP	HHA		
CARTER Horace	30	1-Jan-1952	Winson Green	AP	SD		
BRADLEY Alfred	24	15-Jan-1952	Strangeways	AP	RS		
HARRIS Herbert Roy	23	26-Feb-1952	Strangeways	AP	RS		
SMITH James	21	12-Apr-1952	Barlinnie	AP	SW		
DEVLIN Edward Frances	22	25-Apr-1952	Walton	AP	SD	RS	HS
BURNS Alfred	22	25-Apr-1952	Walton	AP	SD	RS	HS
SINGH Ajit	27	7-May-1952	Cardiff	AP	HBA		
MANNEH Backery	26	27-May-1952	Pentonville	AP	HS		
DEVENEY Patrick	42	29-May-1952	Barlinnie	AP	SW		
HOUGHTON Thomas	23	24-Jun-1952	Egypt	AP			
HUXLEY Harold	42	8-Jul-1952	Shrewsbury	AP	HBA		

Pierrepoint: A Family of Executioners

Name	Age	Executed	Prison	Chief	Ass1	Ass2	Ass3
EAMES Thomas	31	15-Jul-1952	Bristol	AP	RS		
BURGESS Frank	21	22-Jul-1952	Wandsworth	AP	SD		
BUTLER Oliver George	24	12-Aug-1952	Oxford	AP	HS		
MATTEN Mahood Hussein	28	3-Sep-1952	Cardiff	AP	RS		
GODAR John Howard	31	5-Sep-1952	Pentonville	AP	RS		
MULDOWNEY Dennis George	41	30-Sep-1952	Pentonville	AP	RS		
CULL Raymond Jack	25	30-Sep-1952	Pentonville	AP	RS		
JOHNSON Peter Cyril	24	9-Oct-1952	Pentonville	AP	HBA		
SIMON Donald Neil	32	23-Oct-1952	Shrewsbury	AP	SD		
NORTHCLIFFE Eric	30	12-Dec-1952	Lincoln	AP	RS		
LIVESEY John Kenneth	23	17-Dec-1952	Wandsworth	AP	SD		
GREEN Leslie	29	23-Dec-1952	Winson Green	AP	SD		
ALCOTT James John	22	2-Jan-1953	Wandsworth	AP	HS		
SHAW George Francis	25	26-Jan-1953	Barlinnie	AP	SW		
BENTLEY Derek William	19	28-Jan-1953	Wandsworth	AP	HBA		
GIFFORD Miles William	26	25-Feb-1953	Bristol	AP	HS		
TODD John Lawrence	20	19-May-1953	Walton	AP	JBr		
CHRISTIE John Reginald	55	15-Jul-1953	Pentonville	AP	HS		
HENRY Phillip	25	30-Jul-1953	Armley	AP	RR		
MERRIFIELD Louisa	46	18-Sep-1953	Strangeways	AP	RS		
GREENAWAY John Owen	27	20-Oct-1953	Bristol	AP	HBA		
REYNOLDS Joseph Christopher	31	17-Nov-1953	Leicester	AP	RS		
JURAS Stanislaw	43	17-Dec-1953	Strangeways	AP	RR		
WHITEWAY Alfred Charles	22	22-Dec-1953	Wandsworth	AP	JBr		
NEWLAND George James	21	23-Dec-1953	Pentonville	AP	HBA		
KOWALEWSKI Czeslaw	32	8-Jan-1954	Strangeways	AP	JBr		
HOOPER Dennis Donald	27	26-Jan-1954	Shrewsbury	AP	RS		
DOOHAN John Reginald	24	15-Apr-1954	Wandsworth	AP	HBA		
MANNING Michael	25	20-Apr-1954	Mountjoy	AP	RS		
LYNCH John	43	23-Apr-1954	Edinburgh	AP	LS		
HARRIES Thomas Ronald	24	28-Apr-1954	Swansea	AP	RS		
GILBERT Kenneth	21	17-Jun-1954	Pentonville	AP	JBr	HS	RR
GRANT Ian Arthur	24	17-Jun-1954	Pentonville	AP	JBr	HS	RR
TAYLOR Milton	23	22-Jun-1954	Walton	AP	RS		
ROBERTSON George Alex	40	23-Jun-1954	Edinburgh	AP	HBA		
de HEPPER William Sanchez	62	11-Aug-1954	Wandsworth	AP	RR		
FOWLER Harold	21	14-Aug-1954	Lincoln	AP	HBA		
WELLS Rupert Geoffrey	53	1-Sep-1954	Wandsworth	AP	RS		
CHRISTOPHI Stylou Pantopiou	53	15-Dec-1954	Holloway	AP	HBA		
CLARKE Sydney Joseph	32	14-Apr-1955	Wandsworth	AP	RS		
ROBINSON James	27	25-May-1955	Lincoln	AP	HBA		
GOWLER Richard	43	22-Jun-1955	Walton	AP	RS		
ELLIS Ruth	28	13-Jul-1955	Holloway	AP	RR		
CROSS Frederick Arthur	33	26-Jul-1955	Winson Green	AP	HBA		
GREEN Norman William	23	27-Jul-1955	Walton	AP	RS		

Key to abbreviated names:

HP	=	Harry (Henry Albert) Pierrepoint
JsB	=	James Billington
WB	=	William Billington
JB	=	John Billington
WF	=	William Fry
TP	=	Tom Pierrepoint
WW	=	William Willis
WWk	=	William Warbrick (aka Wilkinson)
JE	=	John Ellis
GB	=	George Brown
AL	=	Albert Lumb
RW	=	Robert Wilson
WC	=	William Conduit
RB	=	Robert Orridge Baxter
HPo	=	Henry Pollard
LM	=	Lionel Mann
FR	=	Frank Rowe
AA	=	Alfred Allen
JR	=	'Joseph Robinson' – all un-named assistants in Ireland up to 1930 were known by this assumed name.
AP	=	Albert Pierrepoint
SC	=	Stanley William Cross
TPh	=	Thomas Mather Phillips
AR	=	Alex Riley
HK	=	Harry Kirk
HM	=	Herbert Morris
HC	=	Henry 'Harry' William Critchell
HBA	=	Harry Bernard Allen
ET	=	Edward 'Ted' Taylor
HHA	=	Herbert 'Harry' Allen
SW	=	Steve Wade
R'ON	=	Richard O'Neill
ER	=	Edwin Roper
JH	=	Joseph Hunter
SJ	=	Thomas Johnstone (in Albert's diary he lists him as S Johnstone)
GD	=	George Dickinson
SD	=	Syd Dernley
JR	=	James Patrick Riley
GT	=	George Jellico Train
RS/LS	=	Robert Leslie 'Jock' Stewart
JBr	=	John Broadbent
RR	=	Royston Rickard
HS	=	Harry Smith

BIBLIOGRAPHY

BOOKS

Bailey, Brian, *Hangmen of England*, London 1989

Bleackley, Horace, *Hangmen of England*, Wakefield 1976

Calvert, E Roy, *Capital Punishment in the 20th Century*, London 1927

Carey, Tim, *Mountjoy – The Story of a Prison*, Cork 2000

Dernley, Syd & Newman, David, *The Hangman's Tale*, London 1989

Duff, Charles, *A Handbook on Hanging*, London 1974

Ellis, John, *Diary of a Hangman*, London 1996

Fielding, Steve, *Cheshire Murder Casebook*, Newbury 1996

Fielding, Steve, *Lancashire Murder Casebook*, Newbury 1994

Fielding, Steve, *North Wales Murder Casebook*, Newbury 1995

Fielding, Steve, *The Hangman's Record Vol 1 1868-1899*, Kent 1994

Fielding, Steve, *The Hangman's Record Vol 2 1900-1929*, Kent 1995

Fielding, Steve, *The Hangman's Record Vol 3 1930-1964*, Kent 2005

Fielding, Steve, *Yorkshire Murder Casebook*, Newbury 1997

Gowers, Ernest, *A Life for a Life*, London 1956

Koestler, Arthur, *Reflections on Hanging*, London 1956

Koestler, Arthur & Rolph, C. H., *Hanged by the Neck*, London 1961

Laurence, John, *A History of Capital Punishment*, New York 1960

McLaughlin, Stewart, *Execution Suite*, London 2004

Pierrepoint, Albert, *Executioner Pierrepoint*, London 1974

Royal Commission Report on Capital Punishment 1949-1953, London 1987

Templewood, Viscount, *The Shadow of the Gallows*, London 1951

Van der Elst, Violet, *On the Gallows*, London 1937

NEWSPAPERS AND DOCUMENTS

Reynolds News, Autumn 1922

Thompson Weekly News, Summer 1916

Newspaper serialisations concerning: John Ellis, William Warbrick, James Billington and William Willis.

PCOM papers relating to Mr H A Pierrepoint, Mr T W Pierrepoint and Mr A Pierrepoint open to the public at The National Archives, Kew.

Prison Execution Books (LPC4) relating to executions have been examined for the majority of prisons in Great Britain. These carry all details of the hangmen and assistant, plus official recording of all weights, heights and drops.

Confidential private papers examined in detail during the research of this and previous studies on the hangmen of England include diaries and official papers relating to Henry A. Pierrepoint; Thomas W. Pierrepoint; Albert Pierrepoint; James, William and John Billington; John Ellis; Robert Baxter; William Willis; Thomas Phillips; Stephen Wade; Harry W. Critchell; Harry B. Allen; Robert L. Stewart; Sydney Dernley; Thomas Cunliffe and Harry Robinson. I am grateful to those who generously allowed me to view their collections.